The Comprehensive Guide To
Shipwrecks Of The
North East Coast

Volume One (1740-1917)

Ron Young

TEMPUS

First published 2000

PUBLISHED IN THE UNITED KINGDOM BY:

Tempus Publishing Ltd
The Mill, Brimscombe Port
Stroud, Gloucestershire GL5 2QG

PUBLISHED IN THE UNITED STATES OF AMERICA BY:

Arcadia Publishing Inc.
A division of Tempus Publishing Inc.
2 Cumberland Street
Charleston, SC 29401
(Tel: 1-888-313-2665)

Tempus books are available in France, Germany and Belgium
from the following addresses:

Tempus Publishing Group	Tempus Publishing Group	Tempus Publishing Group
21 Avenue de la République	Gustav-Adolf-Straße 3	Place de L'Alma 4/5
37300 Joué-lès-Tours	99084 Erfurt	1200 Brussels
FRANCE	GERMANY	BELGIUM

British Library Cataloguing in Publication Data.
A catalogue record for this book is available from the British Library.

ISBN 0 7524 1749 5

Typesetting and origination by Tempus Publishing.
PRINTED AND BOUND IN GREAT BRITAIN.

Contents

Acknowledgements

First of all I wish to say a big heart-felt thank-you to my wife Rose for putting-up with the piles of paper, letters and clusters of photographs and information that have lain strewn around our living room for many months. I should also like to thank her for the patience, practical help and time spent proof-reading my work, especially after finishing a hard days work in the Sunderland Eye Infirmary, without ever so much as a complaint. I should also like to thank my daughter Denise for some of the excellent drawings and maps she has produced.

Some people have provided me with a mine of information, for which I am truly indebted; one of those being my long-term penfriend Bill Butland of Lingwood, Norwich, whose help, advice and assistance I deeply appreciate. Bill and I first corresponded with each other when I was writing monthly articles for the Sub Aqua Scene and Underwater World magazines in the mid-1980s and he was involved in writing and documenting the British Sub Aqua Club's (BSAC) Wreck Register.

Bill, now a retired Chartered Civil Engineer, was a keen sport-diver in his younger days, having taken his first dip in Britanny in 1953. He became so hooked on the underwater environment, that he went out immediately and bought a mask, fins and snorkel. In 1956, he joined the BSAC and eventually went on to become the National Equipment Officer on the General Committee. In about 1964, while working in North Wales, Bill became seriously interested in shipwrecks and started recording information on a card-index system. However, when business and a family finally took up too much time, he was prevented from diving, but kept going with the wreck research. He probably now has one of the biggest collections of wreck information in the UK. Presently, he assists a number of authors, answers questions on the Internet and is building his own website on DIY shipwreck research. He has certainly been an enormous help to me, over the past two years or so.

Special thanks must also go to sport and enthusiastic wreck-diver Peter Hale, of Middlesbrough, for supplying me with so much detailed information about the many shipwreck-sites around Teesmouth and the Durham coast and the interesting discussions we had, over a few pints of bitter at Beadnell, during the summer of 1999. Peter has dived all over the world, including wrecks on the Dogger-Bank and has just recently returned from the Andaman Sea where he dived around the Burma Banks, Similin and Surin Islands on a live-aboard yacht, based at Phuket, in Thailand.

A very special thank you also goes to Don Foster of Norton, Stockton-on-Tees, for his terrific, detailed write-ups about the many wrecks he has visited over more than twenty years of sport-diving, especially in the Tees to Whitby area. Don, who is a member of Teeside 43 Branch of the British Sub Aqua Club, is an advanced diver, having been Chairman, Diving Officer and Acting Assistant Diving Officer in his club over the years. From his reports, I would be very surprised if there was anyone else around who has observed so many details at wreck-sites as Don has done and his time spent writing the information down for this book is all very much appreciated.

Another wealth of deeply appreciated information, has come from guys, all volunteers, who look after the World Ship Society's (WSS) various ship archives and records. They have been able to solve many of the puzzles and problems relating to wrecks and ships, where the details have been rather obscure, or where the records have long since disappeared. No ship enthusiast can afford not to join their excellent organization.

Many thanks goes to Bob Scullion, owner of Marsden Dive-Centre, 6, Fallow Road, Marsden, South Shields for helping with details of many of the local wreck-sites between the rivers Tyne and Wear. Bob is a B.S.A.C. Advanced Instructor, P.A.D.I. Master Instructor and I.A.N.T.D. Mixed Gas Instructor and is now exploring many of the undived wrecks in the fifty metres plus range, off the Durham and Northumberland coast.

A special mention must go to sport-diver and angling-boat skipper Keith Sharpe, of Blyth, for the information he supplied about his particular area.

I am also greatly indebted to the following sport-divers, anglers, wreck enthusiasts, diving centres and charter-boat skippers for their wealth of knowledge, which has made this book possible:

My two buddies Trevor Corner, of Chester-le-Street and Joe Fletcher, of South Hetton; Keith Lawrence of Seaham; Andy Anderson of Spennymoor; Ian Wright of Bishop Auckland; Keith Birtle of Blyth; Jeff Maine of Tyne Wear Marine at Jarrow-on-Tyne; Ian and Andrew Douglas, skippers of Sovereign Divers charter-boats at 143 Main Street, Seahouses; Selby Brown of North Sunderland; Collin Varty of Wallsend-on-Tyne; Scott and colleagues of Deep Blue Dive Centre, 69a Front Street, Tynemouth; Michael Pearson of Sunderland; Dave Cordes, skipper of the charter-boat *Merlin*; Alan Holmes of 6 Stone Cross Road, Whitby; archaeologist Raymond Selkirk B.A. (Hons) of Chester-le-Street, who originally showed me how to prepare a synopsis; John Laing of Saltburn; Ian and Chris Denny of Denny Diving, The Esplanade Redcar; Edward Bourke of Dublin; keen amateur underwater archaeologists Rolf Mitchinson and Bob Middlesmas of County Durham and the many dozens of other individual people, whose help and co-operation has made it possible to compile and complete such a detailed book about the shipwrecks off the north-east coast. Thanks must also go to the many people who, for their own reasons, requested me not to mention their names and many more who must remain anonymous. Even the smallest snippets of information were appreciated and have proved invaluable in piecing together a visual picture of wreck-sites, historic events, incidents and various tragedies that happened, often long, long ago.

I wish to acknowledge the co-operation, help or advice given to me by the courteous staff at: the Sunderland, North Shields and South Shields reference libraries, Whitby R.N.L.I. lifeboat visitors centre, Grace Darling Museum in Bamburgh, Liverpool Maritime Museum, the Royal Navy Submarine Museum, South Shields Museum & Art Gallery, the U-boat Archive Museum in Cuxhaven, Germany, South Tyneside Metropolitan Borough Council, Newcastle City

Council, Whitby Literary and Philosophical Society, Strathclyde University, Lloyds Register in London and Sea Breezes magazine.

Thanks must go to Jeff Morris, of Coventry, whose lifeboat books and information helped piece together many of the wreck rescues off the north-east coast. Jeff's books about the history of the various R.N.L.I. lifeboat stations, cost around £3 each and are available at most lifeboat stations along this coast, or from Jeff Morris, Honorary Archivist, Lifeboat Enthusiast's Society, Coventry.

A special message of appreciation goes to the Wrecks' Officer at the Hydrographic Office, Nelson McEachan and his colleagues for the exchange of information over the past couple of years or so, which has helped in the cross reference of co-ordinates of wrecks that I have researched.

A special thank you for their encouragement and help goes to Owen Harrington of Billingham and Ian White of Middlesbrough who, between them, build the very special and seaworthy Oceanic R.I.B. for divers, by divers in Middlesbrough.

On the pictorial side, I wish to gratefully acknowledge the following organizations and individuals: Captain Fred Roberts and Tom Cavanagh, curator/keeper at the Volunteer Life Brigade Watch-House at Roker, Sunderland and the Keeper at Tynemouth Watch House for assisting and allowing me to photograph some of the interesting old pictures of wrecks that their brigades have given assistance to in days gone by. The watch-houses are usually open to visitors and free on most Sunday afternoons throughout the year. Out of the 350 or so life brigades that used to operate around the country, just four of them that I know of, were manned by volunteers. These were at Tynemouth, South Shields and the two at Sunderland: Roker and Sunderland South. However, I believe only the Roker Brigade remains at Sunderland today.

Thanks to the friendly staff at the Zetland Museum in Redcar, where I was also allowed to photograph many of the pictures of shipwrecks around Teesmouth and, the stories associated with the many rescues. The museum, which stands on The Esplanade, opposite Denny's Dive Centre, holds the *Zetland*, which is claimed to be the world's oldest lifeboat. Anyone visiting the museum is guaranteed an interesting day out, looking at the vast array of equipment, models and pictures, with help from the very friendly staff.

The R.N.L.I. volunteer staff at Whitby lifeboat house and the visitor's centre helped with my questions and allowed me to photograph items in the centre and thanks must go to their colleagues throughout the country for the first class job they do; Roger and Graham Pickles, Joint Hon. Keepers of Whitby Museum and Mr. D.G. Sykes for sorting out the best pictures of local wrecks in the Whitby area and the Whitby Literary & Philosophical Society for granting permission to reproduce the photographs in this book and John Tindale of Whitby for giving me permission to publish his wreck photograph.

Many thanks must go to Selby Brown of North Sunderland for permission to copy and reproduce the photograph of him, taken by Mike Brett, standing holding the ship's wheel on the Chris Christenson in thirty-two metres, Mr J. Shaw of The Sutcliffe Gallery at Whitby, for kind permission to reproduce the photograph Flag of Distress, from the work of Frank Meadow Sutcliffe; Debbie Corner, Keeper of Photographs at the Royal Submarine Museum at Gosport, for allowing permission to reproduce a photo of the U-boat, UC-59 and, last but not least, Ron Enwright of Newbottle, Houghton-le-Spring for helping with shipwreck photographs on his computer. Ron whose hobbies include fast cars and computers, retires next year as a Senior Officer of P&O, after spending most of his life at sea, visiting most of the countries around the world.

Finally, if I have forgotten anyone, I sincerely apologize and offer my belated appreciation.

Ron Young.

Introduction

The word 'shipwreck' is a subject that often conjures up images of pirate's treasure or sunken gold. Over the years, stories of wrecks have continued to fascinate people from the poorest to the very richest, for many different reasons.

For many people, contentment is found sitting in the relative safety and comfort of an armchair just reading and dreaming about the world's second greatest profession: treasure hunting. The treasure hoards which have been discovered on Spanish galleons, Chinese junks and British East India ships are mind boggling and never fail to fascinate the imagination.

Others may enjoy reading about the brave and heroic acts of the volunteer lifeboat crews, who often have to battle against the odds in horrendous conditions and mountainous seas, or the Volunteer Rocket & Life Brigades, Coastguard and other individuals who have risked their own lives, by scrambling down cliffs, or wading into the foaming surf to rescue people from almost certain death, when ships have foundered or been driven ashore during storms. Their magnificent self-less deeds were and still are sometimes unbelievably brave.

A lifelong interest in shipwrecks can be discovered while helping someone trace information about loved ones that went down with the vessel during the First or Second World Wars. In war-time, the government placed a restrictions on news and information about ships sunk, so very often little was known about the vessel's precise location and the resting place of lost sailors. However, now with modern technology, many wrecks are gradually being discovered.

Boat-anglers have an obvious reason to be interested in shipwrecks, because fish are usually found in heavy concentrations around large wreck-sites. The seabed in general has huge vast plains of rather flat featureless submarine scenery and any large stationary object such as a wreck, provides shelter, food and protection for many various species of fish, so boat angling over a wreck, can not only provide an excellent day's angling to fill up the freezer, but it could also produce a record specimen.

On the other hand, shipwrecks attract divers for a multitude of reasons. There is a terrific thrill in exploring sunken wrecks, especially ones that have just been newly discovered and souvenir hunting for brass trinkets like portholes (an action that is illegal without the appropriate permission) is another popular pastime or hobby, as well as underwater photography.

Shipwrecks found in depths of more than sixty metres are usually well beyond the reach of most amateur sport-divers. However, they still attract a special breed of modern technical divers, who use mixed gases and special equipment to explore wrecks, which were thought to be lost forever a few years ago. These are wrecks in depths where the slightest mishap by the diver or his support team can cause serious decompression problems, which can often have fatal consequences.

A vessel ashore near Redcar being broke up for scrap. Courtesy of the Zetland Lifeboat Museum, Redcar.

However, the deadly risks seem to have a magical allure all of their own, producing an adrenaline rush, spurring the diver on to even deeper depths.

Whatever the reasons, shipwrecks will always have a magical attraction to many thousands of ordinary people.

How to Use this Book

Many thousands of vessels have come to an untimely end along this part of north-east coastline over the past few centuries. However, until the late 1800s, the vast majority were built of wood and usually disintegrated within hours of sinking. Many hundreds of iron or steel vessels have rapidly rusted away when they were left to the ravages of the elements, especially close in shore. Although their stories may be very interesting to read about, there is nothing left to look at on the rocks or seabed. Therefore, this book with a couple of exceptions, is only about those wrecks which can still be seen in various forms of preservation or decay.

Volume One is a geographical dictionary listing 165 vessels, almost every known one, which foundered or were wrecked between 1740 and 1917, from five miles north of Scarborough to the Scottish Border at Berwick and can still to be seen on the sea-bed.

Volume Two covers the same part of the coastline between 1918 and 2000, detailing 204 ships that foundered or were wrecked and can still be seen today.

For a quick reference and to help in differentiating between the various conditions of the wrecks, a star-rated system has been devised, using one star (★) to five stars (★★★★★). One star represents a wreck-site where very little of it remains,

The brig Griffin *crashed through Coatham Pier during a storm on 9 December 1874, just a year after the pier was built.* Courtesy of the Zetland Lifeboat Museum, Redcar.

except perhaps the tide and wave battered boilers and engine or a few mangled and un-recognizable pieces of rusting debris. A five star wreck is one that may be completely intact and has lots of interesting things to see on a dive. Two to four stars are wrecks are in varying states of decay or preservation, from poor to excellent.

The scenery surrounding the wreck has also been given a star-rated system. One star represents a rather boring seabed, with little to see or nothing of interest. On the other hand, five-star scenery represents an area where there might be interesting and colourful coral reefs, caves and varied marine life.

The depth shown, will be one of two things, either (1) what was actually registered by the diver or boat's echo-sounder at the time the wreck-site was visited and the information received from the person giving the report; or (2) the lowest astronomical depth, which is usually the same as that shown on the admiralty chart. This represents the minimum depth that will be encountered at the lowest spring tide. There can be up to another six metres depth or so over the wreck-site, depending on the time and date the site is visited. However, where it shows an astronomical depth, the reader will be informed of this in the text.

The reference co-ordinates (latitude & longitude) supplied for each wreck are GPS numbers, but in a few cases they are in Decca conversions, so they should be fairly accurate, as most have been supplied by individual divers, sub-aqua clubs, diving officers, charter-boat skippers/operators, survey-boat personnel and fishermen and each one has been double-checked and cross-referenced many with the Hydrographic department. However, there are a couple of issues which should be borne in mind:

The Saxon Prince, *a wooden steam paddle tug, registered at North Sheilds, owned by G.W. Todds of Jarrow-on-Tyne, built in 1874, two-cylinder compound steam engine, one boiler, open bridge-deck, manned by a crew of four. In July 1907 she was towing a lighter when she ran aground in fog and left stranded. Her hull was badly damaged and she was declared a loss.* Courtesy of the Zetland Lifeboat Museum, Redcar.

1) some areas of the sea-bed have not been reliably surveyed for many years, which means that the wreck supplied in the book may not be marked down on the Admiralty chart in the position given, because the wreck was never officially plotted.
2) GPS or/and Decca navigator units all vary slightly from one unit to another and the accuracy of the position, usually depends on a number of factors when the position was taken or plotted, how many satellites the unit picks up and in the case of Decca, weather conditions at the time. So, although the majority of positions offered in this book should be more or less spot-on, the exact position cannot be totally guaranteed and it may require a few minutes of searching the immediate vicinity with an echo sounder to finally locate the wreck.

Some wrecks may also have been given two sets of coordinates to help the reader:
1) 'Also:' below 'Reference:' at the top left hand side of the page, will mean it is part of the same named wreck, but a different section of it.
2) 'Also given:' below 'Reference:' at the top left hand side of the page, will mean that two completely different sets of coordinates have been supplied for that particular wreck and, because the author was unsure which of them is correct for the named vessel in question, both sets have been supplied; in this way, the interested reader can check them for him/herself and the result should be two wrecks for one.

The general text about the vessel and wreck-site in question is set out in an easy and uniform way for quick and ease of reference.

German U-boats

A Brief History of the U-boat up to 1918

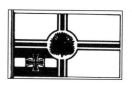

From the very earliest days in our history man has relied on the sea and wind, using their powers to travel the world and explore the planet, but when these forces of nature combine, they also provided the sailor, with his worst nightmare, the storm. The horrendous conditions created by gales and storms have wrecked many thousands of vessels and many more have foundered without trace, especially during the age of sail. There are probably hundreds of thousands of mariners who have perished around the coast of Britain alone, as a direct result of the power of the wind over past few centuries. However, during the First World War, those nightmares took on an even more sinister turn as German submarines, the dreaded 'U-boat', appeared on the scene.

In 1900 there were only about a dozen submarines throughout the world and they belonged to eight different countries, including Britain, France, Russia, Spain, Turkey, Greece, Germany and the United States.

The term U-boat derives from the German word for submarine, 'Unterseeboot', meaning undersea boat. This was quickly shortened, in military slang, to 'U-boot', hence the English U-boat. However, in the early years of the First World War most German submariners referred to their boat as the 'steamer'.

Early submarines were developed in 1882 by the Swedish industrialist and inventor, Thorsten Nordenfelt, who saw the advantages of the submarine as a weapon. So he supplied the capital and began to build a prototype submarine at Stockholm, under the guidance of a Liverpool clergyman, the Rev. George Garrett.

Most of the early designs of submarines were powered by steam, using latent heat from hot water tanks and the fires and furnaces, or smoke-boxes. However, this produced poisonous fumes and smoke, usually leaving the crew sick and drowsy, so the vessels were never looked on with much enthusiasm by governments at the time.

Then, in 1886 a young, Spanish Naval Officer, Lieutenant Isaac Peral, designed and built an electric-powered submarine, which was totally independent from the atmosphere. Other countries began to follow suit. However, Admiral Alfred von Tirpitz, creator of the modern German Navy, adamantly refused to spend money on these new and untried vessels, which were only capable of cruising in home waters.

The Sunderland Echo reported a further advance in submarine technology on 10 June 1887.

> Romanian Engineer Trajan Theodoresco by name, has invented a new description torpedo or submarine boat capable of manoeuvring under water for 12 hours at a stretch. it can act at depths of 100 feet in rivers and 800 feet in the sea. It is able through the agency of screws to rise or sink noiselessly and either suddenly or gradually by

The U-1 was the first submarine built for the German navy. Completed in 1906, she had a displacement of 237 tons, had one 45.7cm (18in) bow torpedo tube and carried three torpedoes, but it was only a partial success. However, future designs lead to one of the most devastating war machines in history

successive stages and can move or manoeuvre in any direction. The illumination of the vessel is internal and allows the Officers upon her to see at a distance of 130 feet underwater. Upon the surface of the water the vessel managed to manoeuvre as an ordinary iron clad boat.

Experiments in submarine design continued and in 1890, Nordenfelt finally persuaded the German government to buy his design. Two boats, the W-1 and W-2 were then built at Kiel and Danzig, followed by an improved type, which was built at Howald's yard at Kiel.

However, it wasn't until 1906 that the first German submarine, the 237-ton *U-1*, entered service, and only as an experimental weapon. The *U-1* was based on three earlier submarines built to a French design, by Krupps, for the Russian Navy. She handled well on the surface, but was a slow diver. Being equipped with just one torpedo tube, she was not looked on as a very efficient fighting machine either. However, after a great deal of experimenting and a number of changes, the *U-1* successfully completed a 600-mile surface cruise from Heligoland around the Danish Peninsula to Kiel in 1908, which convinced the German High Command that there was a genuine future for the submarine. (After the First World War, the *U-1* was re-acquired by her builders as a museum exhibit. After the Second World War she was restored to her original condition and is said to be still on display in the Deutsches Museum in Munich.)

Within the next twelve months Germany quickly outstripped the rest of the world in submarine technology and in 1909 they built two new submarines, capable of a 12 knot surface speed and a more respectable armament of four torpedo tubes and a large deck gun. By 1913, the very latest class of submarine, *U-19*, was equipped with a new and more efficient diesel/oil engine, capable of covering a distance of 5,000 miles at a steady eight knots. The Germans continued to experiment with their submarines, which were becoming much more of a lethal weapon of war. However, by 4 August 1914, when hostilities broke out and Britain declared war on Germany, the German Navy only had twenty-nine submarines ready for combat, with a further twenty-eight being built. Austria had another six. Britain on the other hand had a total of seventy-seven boats all ready for action, France had forty-five, Italy eighteen, Denmark seven, Holland seven, Norway four, Russia nineteen, Sweden five, Japan thirty-five and the U.S.A thirty-five boats. However, unlike Britain, who viewed the submarine as a defensive weapon, the German High Command had a different and more sinister intention for their U-boats.

The first few days of the First World War were rather quiet, as far as the submarines were concerned, except for the British placing a line of six submarines in the Heligoland Bight, but the German U-boats took no part in the surface foray that followed. However they had not been sitting idle, because on 6 August the first submarine war-patrol in history took place, when ten U-boats set out from their base at Heligoland, bound for the Orkney Islands, their mission, to attack the British Grand Fleet. Unfortunately for them, everything went desperately wrong and they failed to sink one single ship. One of the U-boats ran into a mine-field and disappeared without trace, while another, the *U-15*, fired torpedoes at three British Dreadnoughts, but missed each one, and then, soon after developing mechanical problems, she was caught on the surface by the light-cruiser *Birmingham*, was rammed and sunk. Following those incidents, U-boat strategy was changed to hunting singly or in pairs.

On 5 September 1914, one month after the First World War began, Lieutenant Otto Hersing, one of Germany's future U-boat aces, fired a single torpedo and sank the 2,940-ton British light-cruiser *Pathfinder*. The torpedo exploded her magazine, causing the vessel to go down in just four minutes and taking 259 lives with her. The *Pathfinder* was the very first casualty of submarine warfare, but much worse was to follow for the British during the next seventeen days. Just after dawn on 22 September, another future U-boat ace, Lieutenant Otto Weddigen in command of the submarine *U-9*, sank three British armoured cruisers twenty miles off the Dutch coast, the *Aboukir*, the *Cressy* and the *Hogue*, taking a combined weight of 36,000 tons down to the bottom along with 1,460 British sailors. One month later, on 20 October, the *U-17* stopped the British merchant ship *Glitra* while fourteen miles off the Norwegian coast and ordered her crew to abandon ship in their lifeboats, then she was scuttled, by opening the sea-cocks. Then on 26 October, the *U-24* caught the world's attention when she torpedoed and sunk the steamship *Admiral Ganteaume* off Cap Griz Nez, a vessel loaded with Belgian refuges. It was denounced as an atrocity. However, at the time the German captain claimed he thought she was a French Troopship and a legitimate target.

Even after all that carnage, by the end of 1914 Germany still only had a total of twenty-nine submarines and depended mainly on its surface raiders, like that of the light-cruiser *Kolberg*, from the battle cruiser squadron. She and other German warships cruised the North Sea attacking ships and shelling the coastal towns with their large guns and causing general havoc. The *Kolberg* laid at least 100 mines between Filey and Scarborough and more down to the Humber. No one will ever know how many vessels were sunk as a result of the mines she laid, but at least twenty can be accounted for. Probably the first to fall foul of one, was on

An unknown sailing vessel off Whitby showing its final seconds after being scuttled by the crew of a German U-boat during the First World War. Author's collection.

2 September 1914, when the 120-ton steam trawler *Ajax* foundered off the mouth of the Humber estuary. The following day, the 810-ton Royal Navy torpedo-boat destroyer *Speedy* detonated a mine in the same area. With an armament of two 4.7 inch (12 cm) guns, four three pounders (1.36 kg) plus three torpedo tubes, the *Speedy* would have probably been an even match for the *Kolberg*, had she not sunk. She was 70.1m long, with a beam of 8.22m and her twin bronze propellers were powered by one of the very latest steam turbine engines using four boilers.

The *Kolberg* must have been the scourge of Yorkshire. On 16 December 1914 she and two other German warships pounded Scarborough with 200 heavy shells for twenty minutes, which killed eighteen civilians, injured over 100 more and caused considerable damage to 200 homes and property. The following three months, would see a further nineteen vessels sent to the bottom, as a result of those mines, many of them innocent fishing trawlers going about their regular daily business.

My records don't indicate what eventually happened to the *Kolberg*, but as the war progressed many of the surface warships had been sunk. German High Command then realized how effective the new submarines could be as a raider of commerce and decided to put most of their naval resources into building them as a major weapon. The result brought about a revolution in warfare at sea. However, it also brought a change in attitude and policy, because during past conflicts, warships would fight it out among themselves. The victorious ship would take prisoners when a ship was captured. Its crew was either taken off the vessel before it was sunk by gunfire, or it would be taken back to port as a prize of war.

With the introduction of the submarine these rules created a major obstacle. As they were relatively very small and extremely cramped, there was hardly enough room to accommodate the U-boat's own crew, without taking on board sometimes many dozens of prisoners of war. It took a specially dedicated kind of person to volunteer for the dangerous and hazardous duties involved in manning a submarine. The boat was constantly in motion even in deep water. The roll and pitching was very noticeable close to the surface, especially in heavy seas, where the battering from large waves was often like being on a horse which was trying to throw its rider. The force would send crewmen crashing into machinery and plummeting over the top of each other. Often at sea for week after week of stormy weather, the boat would have to spend much of her time on the surface. She would slice and crash through waves, which sent cascades of freezing water down the conning tower hatch, while the men on watch had to lash themselves onto supports for fear of being swept overboard. At other times they were enclosed and shut up for days on end, breathing in each others air, dirty body sweat and the horrible stench from oily water and diesel fumes from the bilges. Also they had to endure the constant, annoying rumble and shudder from her diesel engines, so life on board was extremely unpleasant. The crew got very little sleep, as they were on constant alert, listening for the noises from enemy vessels and depth charges. It was little wonder that many a hardened crewmen cracked up under the strain.

In the early years of the First World War, many Allied ships were sunk without warning, but usually U-boat commanders would surface and order merchant crews to abandon ship before sinking them. However, Winston Churchill, First Lord of the Admiralty, had given instructions that most merchant ships and all passenger liners should be armed and, if a U-boat was seen on the surface as an immediate threat, it had to be rammed at full speed. As a result of this, U-boat commanders became too fearful of surfacing to warn a ship's crew. Then in February 1915 Germany declared an all-out U-boat war against Allied ships. The horror of this situation was brought to the world's attention on 7 May 1915, when Lieutenant Walther Schwieger, skipper of the *U-20*, torpedoed and sunk the giant 32,000-ton luxury passenger liner *Lusitania*, eleven miles south of the Old Head of Kinsale, on the south coast of Ireland.

Apart from her 2,000 passengers and crew, the ship was also carrying hundreds of tons of ammunition from America to Britain to help in the war effort. When she sank in just eighteen minutes, it was first suspected that the ammunition had exploded. However, divers investigating the wreck recently discovered that the ammunition is still intact.

It has now been more or less proved by computer-imagery that the torpedo, which detonated next to her number one boiler-room, blasting a six by three metre hole in the hull and the thousands of gallons of icy cold water that flooded in, caused her boilers to explode. The force of this double explosion not only tore the *Lusitania* to pieces, but the shock waves were even felt in the *U-20*, which was quite a considerable distance away from her.

Among the passengers on the liner were 197 Americans, several public figures, including the thirty-seven-year-old multimillionaire and amateur sportsman, Alfred G. Vanderbilt. He died, along with no less than 1,197 other people, including 785 passengers, ninety-four of them children and 128 American citizens. Even

Lieutenant Schwieger was shocked at what he had done when the ship went down so quickly. All they could do was watch, as hundreds of innocent people scrambled into the sea, with just six of the vessel's twenty-two lifeboats still afloat.

The sinking of the liner caused a huge outcry, especially in the USA. On 6 June, Germany ordered its U-boats to stop attacking large passenger vessels. Then on 18 September the Kaiser called a halt to the U-boat war on merchant ships in British waters.

For nearly a full year Britain enjoyed a respite from torpedo attacks, but the U-boats carried on laying their mines in shipping lanes and outside of British harbours. The majority of U-boats were diverted away from the Atlantic and North Sea to the Mediterranean, where they could support their allies, the Turks. Germany however, was desperate to stop the flow of supplies arriving in Britain from the United States and other countries, so the U-boat campaign in the Atlantic and North Sea began again in earnest. (Lieutenant Schwieger and his crew were killed in 1917, when his new command, the *U-88* struck a mine.)

U-boats operating off the British and Irish coasts, particularly in the English Channel and entrances to the Irish Sea were fairly small boats of around 200 tons, capable of thirteen knots and manned by three officers and thirty-one crewmen. They were an ideal size for intercepting and harassing Allied shipping in local waters. So early in 1916, an entire flotilla of these vessels, twenty-four in all, were launched at Bruges.

The British were, by this time, even fitting large deck guns to fishing trawlers. So, during the months of 1916 U-boats purged the trawlers fleets along the North Sea coast, with dozens upon dozens being sunk, sometimes by torpedo, but usually either by gun fire or with explosive scuttling charges being placed on board.

Not all of the German U-boat skippers were ruthless killers. Very often, if the Captain thought his submarine was in no immediate danger from a merchant ship, he would surface and warn the crew to abandon ship. Then the U-boat would sink the ship with its deck gun, or place explosive charges on board. Some of the better skippers would even provide provisions and directions for the merchant crews.

By 1917 the U-boats were almost winning the war on their own, as one in every four merchant ships destined for Britain was sunk. Their actions resulted in the British Isles being starved of food. It was calculated that reserves were down to just six weeks. In the month of April 1917 alone the British merchant shipping losses rose to a staggering 881,000 tons. By the time Great Britain and Germany had negotiated peace, Britain had lost no fewer than 2,000 merchant vessels and 14,000 merchant seamen.

The stretch of water between the Humber to the Tees was a particularly dangerous place for shipping, because at least forty-two U-boats operated in this area during the First World War. Between them, they sank no less than 120 ships with torpedoes, over 100 by mines and many more which could not be accounted for. At least another eighty merchant ships were also lost between the Tees and the Tyne, during that conflict.

When Armistice came in November 1918, the Imperial German Navy could boast to have sunk over 11 million tons of allied shipping and damaged a further 7.5 million tons. However, the cost was extremely high, because they also lost forty-seven percent of their submarines, 178 in all, plus a fearful toll of 515 officers and 4,849 other ranks.

1. Robin Hood's Bay to Whitby

SPRINGHILL (ex-PORTHCAWL)

Wreck ★★★★
Scenery ★
Depth 38m
Reference N 54 21 180 W 000 23 100
5 miles N of Scarborough.

The *Springhill* was a steel 1,507-ton British steamship, registered at the port of Cardiff and had dimensions of 77.16m length, by 11.12m beam and a draught of 5.3m. When she was lost she was owned by Fisher, Renwick & Company, of Newcastle-upon-Tyne and built as the *Porthcawl* in 1904 by J. Crown & Sons Ltd at Sunderland. Her single steel propeller was powered by a three-cylinder, triple expansion steam engine, that developed 166hp, using two boilers and her machinery was built by North East Marine Engineering Company Limited at Sunderland. She also had a deck, an 18.2m bridge-deck and 9.1m forecastle.

The *Springhill* foundered at 11.34 a.m. on the 24 August 1917, with the loss of five of her crew, after detonating a mine laid by the German submarine *UB-21*. She was on passage from West Hartlepool for London with a 2,200-ton cargo of coal, under the command of Captain W. Williams. Two of the men, the Chief Engineer and a fireman were in the engine room at the time and both were killed in the explosion. Then the *Springhill*, with a huge hole torn in her side, went down in just four minutes, drowning the second steward and an able-seaman; with another man dying later. The steamship *Eden* picked up most of the survivors soon after the incident and the steam drifter *White Rose* rescued another man and landed him at Scarborough.

Wreck-site
The wreck lies orientated in a N.N.W. to S.S.E. direction on a sea-bed of gravel, stones and rock in a general depth of thirty-eight metres, being the lowest astronomical depth. She is very substantial, but totally collapsed and lying on her port side, with her two boilers exposed and surrounded by mounds of twisted steel plates, a bollard, a large winch and broken machinery. Lots of flattened copper pipes and a few brass wash/scupper valves lie intermingled with the steel debris near the midships section of the wreck. Apparently, she has been identified from her boiler details, and it is believed that the vessel's bell has also been recovered. Some large crustaceans are to be seen around the boilers/engine area

and a number of cod may be found sheltering under the steel plates. She will also make a good boat angling venue when conditions permit. The wreck-site is a fair distance from the nearest launch sites and is in the main shipping lanes so a good lookout is required at all times. Tidal streams are very strong and the normal visibility is rather dismal.

SNA-11 (ex-M.E.HARPER)

Wreck ★★★★
Scenery ★
Depth 43m
Reference N 54 22 310 W 000 22 470
5 miles SE of Ravenscar, 2½ miles from nearest land.

The *SNA-11* was a steel 2,294-ton French steamship, registered at Le Havre and had dimensions of 75.28m length and a beam of 10.05m. She was owned at the time of loss by Le Societé Nationale D'Affetements and built as the *M.E. Harper* in 1911 by the Great Lakes Engineering Works, Michigan, in the USA. Her single steel propeller was powered by a three-cylinder, triple expansion steam engine that used two boilers.

On 6 June 1917, the *SNA-11* was on passage from the Tyne for Dunkirk, with a cargo of coal, when she was torpedoed and sunk by a German submarine, six miles north of Scarborough.

Wreck-site
This wreck, believed to be the *SNA-11* lies orientated in a S.S.E. to N.N.W. direction on a dirty sea-bed of fine-sand, mud, broken-shells, stone and rock in a general depth of 43m, being the lowest astronomical depth. She is still very substantial, but broken into two sections, with her stern end standing upright. about 7m high, close to the break where her centrally positioned bridge structure was located, while the bow section, which is beginning to collapse, lies on its side. Her boilers, condenser and engine block are exposed and the upper and most exposed parts of her are covered in a colourful array of soft corals. The wreck-site also has quite a number of lobster-pots entangled in it. When the light penetrates down through the eerie green murk on a sunny day, the wreck looks very bright, however reports say that the visibility is normally very poor and tidal streams are very strong. Lots of fish can be seen around the boilers area, mostly cod and pout-whiting, but the occasional ling has also been seen, so she should make a good boat angling venue, when conditions are right. A good lookout is required by the surface cover, because the wreck-site is close to the main shipping lanes.

GLOW (ex-MONKWOOD)

Wreck ★★★★
Scenery ★
Depth 43m
Reference N 54 22 510 W 000 22 620
5 miles E.-S.E. of Ravenscar, 2 3/4 miles from nearest land.

The *Glow* was a steel 1,141-ton British steamship, registered at London and had dimensions of 71.7m length, by 10.8m beam and a draught of 4.39m. She was owned by France, W. Fenwick & Company Ltd and built as the *Monkwood* in 1900 by J. Blumer & Company Ltd at Sunderland. The single propeller was powered by a three-cylinder, triple expansion steam engine that developed 179hp, using two boilers and her machinery was built by J. Dickinson & Sons Ltd at Sunderland. She had one deck, a well-deck, a 5.8m poop-deck, a 21.7m quarter-deck, a 14.6m bridge-deck and a 6.7m forecastle. The vessel was also armed with a stern mounted deck gun that fired 13lb projectiles (shells).

At 9.30 p.m. on 22 July 1917, the steamer was making a steady ten knots, on a voyage from the Tyne to London, when she was torpedoed and sunk by the German submarine, *UB-21*, five miles E.S.E. of Ravenscar. Captain T. H. Baty, the *Glow's* skipper, saw the torpedo rapidly approaching some 100m away on the starboard side, but it was too late for him to take evasive action. It detonated about three metres above her stern post, blowing off most of the vessel's stern section and killing the chief gunner instantly. The *Glow* immediately began to sink. However, the sixteen surviving crew, including the steward, who had been injured, scrambled into one of the lifeboats, which they had quickly managed to lower. The boat had just cleared the stricken vessel when she turned completely over, and in three minutes, at 9.40 p.m. she slipped down to the bottom. A patrol boat picked up the survivors after about fifty minutes and landed them at Scarborough, where the injured steward received medical attention.

Wreck-site
The wreck, believed to be that of the *Glow*, is reported to be orientated in a south to north direction, on a sea-bed of fine-sand, shell, stone, mud and rocks in a general depth of forty-three metres, being the lowest astronomical depth. She is quite substantial, standing upright and eight metres high in the midships section around her boilers and engine. However, most of the wreck has collapsed, is well broken up and decayed, with the engine and boilers now exposed and surrounded by a mountain of debris, including pieces of broken hollow mast, steel bollards and lengths of flattened copper-pipes, with brass flanges still attached. The wreck-site is very dark and requires a good torch to see anything. Tidal streams are rather strong and visibility is usually pretty grim, but the remains are certainly worth looking at, especially as the site has not been dived on very much. The best time

to dive is at low slack water during a neap tide and following a spell of dry settled weather and light westerly. She may be also worth looking as a boat angling venue because there are almost certain to be a number of large fish lurking around among the wreckage.

LADY HELEN

Wreck ★★★★
Scenery ★
Depth 34m
Reference N 54 22 903 W 000 24 645
$3\frac{1}{2}$ miles S.E. of Ravenscar, $1\frac{1}{2}$ miles from nearest land.

The *Lady Helen* was a steel 811-ton British steamship, registered at Sunderland and had dimensions of 60.96m length, by 9.14m beam and a draught of 3.68m. She was owned by the Marquis of Londonderry of Seaham and built at Sunderland by S.P. Austin & Son in 1909. Her single steel propeller was powered by a three-cylinder, triple expansion steam engine that developed 138hp, using one boiler and her machinery was built by the North East Marine Engineering Company Ltd at Sunderland. She had one deck, a well-deck and a superstructure consisting of a 6.4m poop-deck, 13.4m quarter-deck, 14.3m bridge-deck and a 6.4m forecastle.

Under the command of Captain E.J. Roberts and carrying a crew of fourteen, *Lady Helen* was on passage from Great Yarmouth for Seaham Harbour when she detonated a German-laid mine at 9 a.m. on 27 November 1917. The explosion took place just aft of the engine room, allowing thousands of gallons of water to rush in and she began to go down by the stern, almost immediately. The fourteen crew members lowered the port lifeboat and climbed into it, but before they could clear the ship, it capsized, throwing the men into the sea. Seven crew were drowned, but the second officer and six seamen clung desperately to the upturned hull of the lifeboat for thirty minutes until a patrol vessel rescued them. It also picked up the lifeless body of the captain at the same time and landed them all at Scarborough.

Wreck-site
The wreck of the *Lady Helen* lies orientated in a north to south direction on a sea-bed of fine-sand, mud and rocks, in a general depth of thirty-four metres, being the lowest astronomical depth. She is reported to be standing on an even keel, is upright and complete from her bows to the aft hold, but with a lot of damage around her port-quarter and stern section. The upper structures are reported to be collapsing down and her hull has collapsed amidships on one side. The wreck is said to be still fairly large and makes a great dive, but it is not known if her bell and interesting bridge equipment are still in place, However, she makes an

interesting wreck to explore. The vessel was identified in the 1980s by the maker's plate and boiler/engine details. Lots of fish of varying species have been seen, so she should make a good boat angling venue. Visibility is very poor, making a good torch essential, while tidal streams are fairly strong. The best time to dive the wreck would be on a neap tide at low slack water and after a spell of dry settled weather, during the summer months. Snagged trawl nets could also be a problem in the dim murky light.

NOVILO (ex-AMASIS)

Wreck ★★★★
Scenery ★
Depth 44m
Reference N 54 23 137 W 000 22 811
5 miles E.-S.E. of South Cheek, Robin Hood's Bay.

The *Novillo* was a steel 2,336-ton Argentinian steamship, registered at Buenos Aires and had dimensions of 95.25m length, by 12.19m beam and a draught of 6.62m. She was owned at the time of loss by Soc. Anon. de Nav. Sud Atlantica and built as the *Amasis* in 1895 by Hawthorn, Leslie & Company, at Newcastle-upon-Tyne. The single steel propeller was powered by a three-cylinder, triple expansion steam engine that developed 276hp, using two boilers.

On 22 October 1917, the *Novillo* was on passage from the Tyne for Blaye with a 3,500-ton cargo of coal, under the command of a Captain Fragnul, when she was torpedoed and sunk by the German submarine, *UB-57*, five miles east-south-east of Robin Hood's Bay.

Wreck-site
The wreck lies orientated in more or less a north-east to south-west direction on a sea-bed of fine-sand, mud, stones and rock in a general depth of 44m, being the lowest astronomical depth. She is totally collapsed and partially buried at her stern end, with the highest section of just over 3m being at midships, around her boilers and the debris covered remains of her engine. The wreck is now little more than a heap of broken decayed debris covered in lots of dirty sand and silt, although, there are a number of bent and flattened copper pipes and her condenser, protruding out of it all. It is not known whether the ship's bell has been recovered, which would positively prove her identity. Very little marine life inhabits the wreck and being a rather deep dive, there will be far more interesting wrecks to dive on and explore nearby. Tidal streams are very strong and the visibility is usually pretty grim.

PURITAN

Wreck ★
Scenery ★★★
Depth 5-7m
Reference N 54 24 01 w 000 28 30
Off peak Point, Blea Wyke, Ravenscar.

The *Puritan* was an iron 219-ton British steam fishing trawler that had dimensions of 36.6m in length, by 6.23m beam and a draught of 3.35m. She was trawler No.110786, built in 1899-1900 by Cook, Welton & Gemmell in Yard 254, launched on 3 February 1900 and registered at the port of Hull as trawler H497 for her new owner, George Walton of Hull, who was the owner at the time of loss. Her single iron propeller was powered by a three-cylinder, triple-expansion steam engine that developed 60hp using one boiler and her machinery was built by C.D. Holmes of Hull.

On 4 May 1903 the *Puritan* was out on a fishing voyage from her home port of Hull when she ran aground and stranded in dense fog near to the Ravenscar Hotel off Peak Point, Blea Wyke at Ravenscar and became a total loss. The crew took to the ship's boat and after six hours were picked up by the 173-ton Hull-registered H886 steam trawler *Hero* and landed safely at Scarborough later that day.

On 3 May 1915 the *Hero* was on a fishing voyage 150 miles off Hornsea, Yorkshire, when she was captured by a German U-boat and sunk by time-bombs.

Wreck-site
The wreck of the *Puritan* is now totally collapsed, decayed and well dispersed among the dense kelp beds and rocks in a general depth of 5-7m. A few iron plates, broken pieces of machinery, an anchor and half a propeller are all that remains of her, but the surrounding reefs, rocks and battered iron plates provide shelter for numerous diferent crustaceans like lobsters, edible crabs, Green-Shore crabs, squat-lobsters and swimming crabs. In the summer months shoals of coley and pollack are common in this area. Tidal streams are very moderate, but the strength increases considerably on a spring tide. Visibility is usually poor on average, but it improves on a neap tide and after a spell of dry, settled weather and westerly winds.

GIMLE

Wreck ★★★★
Scenery ★
Depth 42m
Reference N 54 24 550 W 000 24 587
3 ½ miles E. of South Cheek, Robin Hood's Bay.

A Dutch cargo vessel (name unknown), registered in Groningen, ashore below the cliffs at Whitby, probably in the 1920s or 1930s. Note the salvage crew checking the condition of her propeller. Courtesy of John Tindale of Whitby.

The *Gimle* was a steel 1,131-ton Norwegian steamship, registered at Bergen and had dimensions of 69.64m length, by 11.04m beam and a draught of 4.8m. She was owned at the time of loss by A/S D/S Gimle and was built in 1904 by Laxevaags Msk. & Jrnskb at Bergen. The single steel screw propeller was powered by a three-cylinder, triple-expansion steam engine that developed 132hp, using one boiler.

On 4 November 1917 the *Gimle* was on passage from Blyth to Caen with a cargo of coal, under the command of Captain B.C. Pedersen, when she was torpedoed and sunk by the German submarine *UB-35* 3½ miles east of South Cheek, at Robin Hood's Bay.

Wreck-site
The wreck lies orientated in nearly an east to west direction on a sea-bed of shell, sand and mud in a general depth of 42m, being the lowest astronomical depth. In 1986 the wreck was reported as being very substantial, almost intact and complete from her bows to the after hold, but her stern-end is badly damaged where the torpedo exploded. She is now beginning to break up somewhat, but is still very large, standing some 6m high around amidships which makes a first class dive-site. The wreck has been positively identified from the boss on the ship's wheel, however, it is not known whether the ship's bell has been discovered yet. Interesting items are still being found on this wreck-site, but it is very dark and a good torch is essential to see anything at all. One or two good cod have been seen amongst the wreckage, so this wreck should make an interesting boat angling venue, when conditions are right. Tidal streams are very strong and visibility usually poor to dismal, so it is a wreck-site for experienced divers only.

The 148 ton steamer Mandalay as H77 *in 1899, under-way to the fishing grounds.* Courtesy of the Kingston -upon-Hull Museum & Art Gallery.

MANDALAY

Wreck ★
Scenery ★★★
Depth 5-7m
Reference N 54 24 63 W 00 29 20
South Cheek, Ravenscar.

The *Mandalay* was an iron 148-ton British steam fishing trawler that had dimensions of 31.4m length and 6.1m beam. She was built as trawler No 95845 at Hull by Cook, Welton & Gemmell in Yard 53 in 1890 and registered on 27 August 1890 at the port of Hull as H105 for her new owners, George Beeching & Thomas Kelsall of Hull. Her single iron propeller was powered by a two-cylinder, compound steam engine that developed 50hp using one boiler, giving the vessel a registered speed of ten knots. The machinery was built by C.D. Holmes at Hull. On 8 January 1897 she was transferred to Fleetwood as FD146, then returned to Hull and registered as H77 by Kelsall Bros & Beeching on 1 January 1904.

On 22 October 1904 the *Mandalay* was fishing over the Dogger-Bank with other vessels of the trawler fleet from Hull when they were attacked by the Russian Navy Baltic Fleet, which was *en-route* to the Pacific. It was said that the Russians, who were at war with Japan, had mistaken the trawlers for Japanese torpedo boats and opened fire on them, damaging many, including the *Mandalay*. Luckily, she survived the attack.

However, on 14 February 1908 the *Mandalay* was not so fortunate. On a fishing voyage from her home port of Hull she ran aground in thick fog and became a total wreck. Fortunately, all her crew was rescued.

Wreck-site

The wreck is now totally collapsed, decayed and smashed to pieces, lying among the dense kelp, reefs and boulders in a general depth between 5-7m. All that remains of the wreck are the remnants of a few bent iron plates, a section of her boiler, the propeller, anchor and a length of rusting chain, which leads away from the anchor and disappears under long strands of bladder-wrack and kelp. The surrounding reefs and boulders, however, make an excellent forage dive for crustaceans early during the summer months when visibility improves and lots of coley can be seen. Tidal streams are reasonable, but can be fairly strong on a spring tide.

OAKWELL

Wreck ★★★★
Scenery ★
Depth 45m
Reference N 54 25 278 W 000 25 170
3 miles E.N.E. of South Cheek, Robin Hood's Bay.

The *Oakwell* was a small iron 248-ton British steamship, registered at Stockton and had dimensions of 38.1m length, by 6.73m beam and a draught of 3.14m. She was owned by United Glass Bottle Manufacturers Ltd and built by Craig, Taylor & Company Ltd at Stockton-on-Tees in 1887. Her single iron-propeller was powered by a two-cylinder, compound steam engine that developed 50hp, using one boiler and her aft positioned machinery was built by Westgarth, English & Company, at Middlesbrough. She had one deck, a well-deck and a superstructure consisting of a 12.8m quarter-deck, 2.4m bridge-deck and a poop-deck of 5.4m.

Under the command of Captain W. Chilvers, this little merchant vessel was on passage from Seaham for London, with a cargo of empty bottles and a crew of nine when at 11.40 a.m., on 28 March 1917, she detonated a German-laid mine nearly three miles east-north-east of the North Cheek at Robin Hood's Bay. The vessel foundered almost immediately, taking four crew members down with her, while the others, including her captain, clung to floating wreckage, until they were picked up sometime later by a Royal Navy destroyer and taken to North Shields.

Wreck-site

The wreck is reported as orientated in an east-north-east to west-south-west direction on a hard sea-bed of dirty sand, mud and black shells, in a general depth of 45m, being the lowest astronomical depth. She is said to be totally collapsed, decayed and broken up, with her boiler and engine visibly exposed and the condenser burst open. The highest point is around her boiler and engine, which stands about $3\frac{1}{2}$ m high at the stern end, while the rest of the wreck is just a mound of broken machinery, bent pipes and flattened iron plates, standing no more than a metre high. Occasionally, part of her cargo of empty bottles can be found among the pile of debris, but otherwise there are not too many interesting things to be seen, although there are portholes still being discovered. She has been dived on a number of times and her bell has been recovered by local divers, along with some other artefacts. However, she is reported to be a reasonable dive-site and still worth a visit. Fair numbers of cod have been seen on and around the wreck and large lobsters are not an uncommon sight. Usually, this is a fairly dark dive with very poor visibility, which requires a good torch. Tidal streams are strong and the best time to dive her would be on a neap tide after a spell of settled, dry weather and light south-westerly winds. The dive also requires a little pre-planning.

SUNTRAP (ex-SHERWOOD)

Wreck ★★★★
Scenery ★
Depth 44m
Reference N 54 25 311 W 000 25 686
2 ½ miles E.N.E. of South Cheek, Robin Hood's Bay.

The *Suntrap* was a steel 1,353-ton British steamship, registered at London and had dimensions of 70.1m length, by 10.99m beam and a draught of 4.57m. She was owned at the time of loss by France, W. Fenwick & Company Ltd and built as the *Sherwood* in 1904 by Sunderland Ship Building Company Ltd, Sunderland. Her single steel propeller was powered by a three-cylinder, triple expansion steam engine that developed 159hp, using one boiler and her machinery was built by North East Marine Engineering Company Ltd at Sunderland. She had one deck, a well-deck and a superstructure consisting of a 6.7m poop-deck, 20.5m quarter-deck, 15.2m bridge-deck and 6.7m forecastle. This vessel was also armed with a large stern mounted deck gun that fired 18lb shells.

On 7 November 1917, she was steaming south, under the command of Captain W. Clayburn, on passage from Newcastle for London with a cargo of coal, when she was torpedoed at 4.30 p.m. by the German submarine *UB-22*. Some of her nineteen crew saw the wake of the torpedo heading towards the ship, but before anyone could take evasive action it detonated against her port-quarter, about 11m from the stern-end. Her crew abandoned ship in the two lifeboats, without any serious casualties and were picked up by patrol vessels, then transferred to fishing drifters and later landed at Scarborough.

Wreck-site
The wreck, believed to be that of the steamer *Suntrap*, lies orientated in a north-north-east to south-south-west direction on a hard sea-bed of dirty sand, mud and black shells in a general depth of 44m, being the lowest astronomical depth. She

lies on her starboard side and has collapsed onto the sea-bed, with the highest section of 5m being around amidships where her exposed boiler, engine and condenser are located. The wreck is in one piece, but very broken up and decayed, covering an area of about 75 by 12m. She is still quite a large wreck and is sure to take more than one dive to explore properly. Lots of non-ferrous metal can be seen, along with recognisable pieces of her derricks, gunnels and hollow masts and it is quite possible that her main bridge equipment is still around somewhere. However, it is understood that the ship's bell has been recovered in recent years. There have been no reports of the amount marine life that lives on and around the *Suntrap*, but it would be most unusual if there were not a variety of fish and crustaceans in and on her, especially cod, conger, ling and lobsters. As a fairly large wreck she may be worth noting as a boat angling venue, when conditions allow. Tidal streams are very strong and visibility is not very spectacular, in fact it is usually grim, so a good torch is essential.

FERRUCCIO (ex-CICERONE)

Wreck ★★★★
Scenery ★
Depth 47m
Reference N 54 26 145 W 000 25 370
3 ½ miles E.N.E. of South Cheek, Robin Hood's Bay.

The *Ferruccio* was a steel 2,192-ton Italian steamship, with dimensions of 88.4m length, by 11.3m beam and a draught of 7.6m. She was built as the *Cicerone* in 1881 by Schlesinger, Davis & Co. and her single steel screw propeller was powered by a two-cylinder, compound steam engine, that used two boilers.

On 6 February 1917, the *Ferruccio* was on passage from Sunderland for Savona, with a cargo of coal, when she was torpedoed and sunk by a German submarine.

Wreck-site
The wreck, believed to be that of the Italian steamship *Ferruccio* lies orientated in a south-south-east to north-north-west direction on a hard sea-bed of sand, mud, stone and black shells in a general depth of 47m, being the lowest astronomical depth. The wreck is in one piece but totally collapsed, well broken up and rather decayed, with the highest 4½m section being around her two boilers, condenser and engine at midships. Most of the site is a mound of steel debris, decayed and broken machinery, intermingled with copper-pipes, brass valves and flanges. A number of complete, loose portholes could be seen, but no one seems to know if her bell has been recovered, which would provide definite proof of her identity. Very little marine life, in the form of fish or crustaceans, have been observed on or around the wreck, but this does not mean they are not around, because quite a number of Dead Man's Fingers (Alcyonium Digitatum) have attached themselves to the boilers.

The wreck-site is very dark and gloomy and requires a good torch to see anything, even in the best of conditions. Tidal streams are fairly strong and this is a wreck-site only for very experienced divers.

HIGHGATE

Wreck ★★★★
Scenery ★
Depth 47m
Reference N 54 26 345 W 000 26 586
2¾ miles E. of South Creek, Robin Hood's Bay

The *Highgate* was a steel 1,780-ton British steamship, registered at London and had dimensions of 81.73m length, by 11.45m beam and a draught of 5.18m. She was owned by Cory Colliers Ltd and built in 1899 by S.P. Austin & Son at Sunderland. The single steel propeller was powered by a three-cylinder, triple expansion steam engine that developed 195hp, using two boilers and her machinery was built by George Clark Ltd at Sunderland. She had one deck, a well-deck and a superstructure, consisting of an 8.2m poop-deck, 22.6m quarter-deck, 15.2m bridge-deck and an 8.8m forecastle. This vessel was also armed with a stern mounted deck gun that fired 3lb shells.

The *Highgate* was carrying a 2,400-ton cargo of coal and a crew of twenty on a voyage from the Tyne to London, when, at 3.15 p.m. on 7 December 1917, she was torpedoed and sunk by the submerged German submarine, *UB-75*. Under the command of Captain A. Wanless, the *Highgate* was steaming at a steady eight knots when the torpedo detonated just in front of the bridge. However, the crew, three of whom were injured in the blast, managed to get away in one of the ship's lifeboats and, just three minutes later, at 3.18 p.m., they watched as their ship went down. Two motor launches picked up her crew almost at once and landed them at Whitby.

Wreck-site
The *Highgate* lies very close to the wreck of the steamship *Amulet*. She is reported to be orientated in a north-north-east to south-south-west direction, on a sea-bed of sand, mud and broken shell, in a general depth of 47m, being the lowest astronomical depth.

The wreck is standing upright, with the stern to bridge section complete and reasonably intact and 8m high, while the two forward holds and bows are collapsed onto the sea-bed. Her large stern mounted gun is still in position and brass shell casings litter the poop-deck area. Brass valves, bent and flattened copper-pipes and even the odd porthole can still be seen on this wreck, while myriads of soft corals bloom like spring flowers on the highest and most exposed sections.

The wreck has been dived on a number of times and is reckoned to be a first class dive-site where shoals of pout-whiting and large pollack can be seen at certain times of the year. It is said that she was identified by such items as the crockery, bearing the Cory house flag insignia, along with her engine details and date on the wheel pedestal. However, it is not known whether the ship's bell has been recovered. This is a very dark dive and a powerful torch is required at all times. Sediment usually lies in a cloud all the way down until the last few metres near the sea-bed and then it seems to clear, but this keeps the light from penetrating down to the bottom. Tidal streams are very strong and this is not a dive for the inexperienced.

FLORENCE

Wreck ★★★
Scenery ★
Depth 52m
Reference N 54 26 585 W 000 15 525
13 miles N-E of Scarborough.

The *Florence* was an iron 149-ton British steam fishing trawler that had dimensions of 31.24m length with a 6.22m beam and a 3.35m draught. She was built as trawler No.102969 in Yard 128 at Hull by Cook, Welton & Gemmell, launched as the *Florence* in 1894 and registered at the port of Hull as H265 for her new owners, Samuel T. White & Company of Hull. Her single iron propeller was powered by a two-cylinder compound-steam engine that developed 45hp using one boiler that gave the vessel a registered speed of ten knots and her machinery was built by C.D. Holmes & Company Ltd of Hull.

On 13 July 1916, under the command of skipper D. Crawford, she was in ballast on the way to the fishing grounds from her home port of Scarborough when she was intercepted by a German U-boat, her crew being forced to abandon ship, after which the vessel was sunk by the Germans with explosive scuttling charges.

Wreck-site
The wreck, possibly that of the *Florence* lies orientated in a north-east to south-west direction on a seabed of mud, fine sand, stone and broken shells in a depth of 52m, the lowest astronomical depth, some thirteen miles north-east of Scarborough. She stands no more than 2m high at the highest point, around the boiler area, has totally collapsed, is partially buried and well broken up with her boiler and engine exposed and surrounded by a mound of broken machinery, bent iron plates, winches and sections of mast.

The wreck is ensnared in netting. Soft corals are well established on the wreckage and most of it is covered in hard, white, marine worm casings, otherwise there is little else of interest that can be seen. Tidal streams are very strong and on average the underwater visibility is very poor to dismal. This wreck is a fair way from land and in the main shipping lanes, so a good lookout will be required at all times when diving or fishing over the remains.

AIGBURTH

Wreck ★★★★
Scenery ★
Depth 46m
Reference N 54 26 708 W 000 27 919
2 miles N.E. of South Cheek, Robin Hood's Bay.

The *Aigburth* was a steel 824-ton British-registered steamship and had dimensions of 59.43m length, by 9.44m beam and a draught of 3.65m. She was built by John Fullerton & Company, at Paisley, in 1917 and she had a single, steel propeller, powered by a three-cylinder, triple expansion steam engine that used one boiler and her machinery was built at Glasgow by Ross & Duncan. She was also armed with one stern mounted H.A. gun that fired 6lb shells.

On 5 December 1917, the *Aigburth* was on passage from the Tyne for Treport, with an unspecified cargo of coal, when she was torpedoed at 3.15 p.m. by the German submarine *UB-55*, two miles north-east of South Cheek, at Robin Hood's Bay. The torpedo detonated amidships, killing the captain and ten of her crew of fourteen. The second engineer and second mate found themselves in the sea, clinging to floating wreckage and were picked up by a patrol vessel, while the ship's only other survivor, a shipgunner, managed to swim to the patrol boat, that landed them at North Shields later that day.

Wreck-site
The wreck lies on a dirty sea-bed of sand, mud and shell in a general depth of 46m, being the lowest astronomical depth. She lies in two sections, with the part to the north orientated in a nearly north to south direction, which is some 35m long and nearly 6m high and the highest part where her aft positioned engine and boiler are located, while the other and longest part, which is well broken up, is 45m in length and lies facing south-east to north-west.

The wreck should be an interesting one to explore, because of the number of lobsters which have been reported around the wreck-site. She was positively identified when the ship's bell was recovered. This wreck may be worth marking down as a boat angling venue, because there is a fair amount of fish to be seen around it. Tidal streams are fairly strong and the visibility is not very good, in fact it will be rather grim, but the wreck-site will be well worth a visit. Best time to dive is on a neap tide, at slack low water and after a spell of settled dry weather during the summer months.

HARROW

Wreck ★★★★
Scenery ★
Depth 42m
Reference N 54 28 128 W 000 30 469
2 miles N.E. of North Cheek, Robin Hood's Bay

The *Harrow* was a steel 1,777-ton British steamship, registered at London and had dimensions of 81.78m length, by 11.45m beam and a draught of 5.18m. She was owned by Cory Colliers Ltd and built in 1900 by S.P. Austin & Son at Sunderland. Her single steel propeller was powered by a three-cylinder, triple expansion steam engine that developed 194hp using two boilers and her machinery was built at Sunderland by W. Allan & Company Ltd. She had one deck, a well-deck and a superstructure, consisting of a 8.2m poop-deck, 22.6m quarter-deck, 15.2m bridge-deck and an 8.8m forecastle. She was also armed with a large stern mounted deck gun that fired 13lb shells.

On 8 September 1917, the *Harrow* was part of a convoy on a voyage from Granton to London, with a cargo of coal, when she was torpedoed by the German submarine, *UB-41*. The torpedo exploded on the ship's port-quarter at 6.45 p.m., instantly killing the chief-officer and one gunner, leaving another gunner seriously injured, while Captain B.R. Davison was injured after the force of the blast threw him out of his cabin. The ship's stern end was shattered and her propeller and rudder were blown completely off the ship. The surviving crew abandoned ship at 7 p.m. and were picked up by an escort vessel and taken to Whitby, about the same time as the *Harrow* went down to the bottom.

Wreck-site
The wreck, which is thought to be the *Harrow*, is lying on a dirty sea-bed of mud, sand, gravel and pebbles in a general depth of 42m, being the lowest astronomical depth. She is reported to be very substantial, standing intact and upright from the stern to the bridge. Her bows, that are partly broken off from the main wreck, stand 7m proud of the sea-bed and are covered in an array of soft corals. The highest section is amidships, where her engine, boiler and machinery are located and these are also covered in soft corals. Her large stern mounted gun is said to be still in place in the poop-deck area. There is no scour around the wreck, but a large wave of sand comes up the hull side and covers part of the vessel's forward hold, however, her overall shape can still be made out. It will take a number of dives to explore this wreck and to observe all of the most interesting areas where they have collapsed inwards.

The wreck-site is reported to be a very dark and eerie dive, requiring the use of a powerful torch and visibility is very seldom more than a few metres or so.

However, it significantly improves during the middle summer months on neap tides and after a spell of settled dry weather. On ascending to the wreck-site, shoals of large pollack and pout-whiting are to be seen, hovering over the highest sections, while cod have been observed under the wreckage, making it a good boat angling venue. Tidal streams are strong, making this a low slack water dive.

This wreck was always believed to be that of the steamship *Harrow*, but she used two boilers. However, it has been reported that there is only one boiler on this wreck. So, it appears that there has been no positive identification.

QUAGGY (ex-GLENPARK)

Wreck ★★★★
Scenery ★
Depth 50m
Reference N 54 28 194 W 000 26 020
3 miles E. of North Cheek, Robin Hood's Bay.

The *Quaggy* was a steel 993-ton British steamship, registered at the port of London and had dimensions of 67.66 length, by 9.6m beam and a draught of 3.75m. She was owned at the time of loss by South Metropolitan Gas Company Ltd and built as the *Glenpark* by G. Brown & Co. at Greenock in 1904. Her single steel propeller was powered by a three-cylinder, triple expansion steam engine that developed 99hp, using one boiler. Her centrally positioned machinery was built by Ross & Duncan at Glasgow. She had one deck, a well-deck and a superstructure consisting of a 46.9m quarter-deck and a forecastle measuring 9.1m. She was also armed with a stern mounted deck gun that fired 6-lb shells.

The *Quaggy* was on passage from London for the Tyne, under the command of Captain MacFarlane when, at 11.15 a.m. on 11 April 1917, she was rocked by a massive explosion between the bridge and fore-mast. Two of the crew, who were up on the forepart of the deck, died instantly, while the rest of the crew, seventeen in all, including the captain, abandoned ship and took to the ship's boats. The *Quaggy* went down in just seven minutes, taking all of the vessel's confidential papers with her. The survivors were taken on board a trawler and later transferred to a Royal Navy torpedo boat destroyer, which landed them at Hartlepool later that day.

Wreck-site
The wreck is reported as orientated in a north-east to south-west direction, on a dirty sand, mud, pebble and gravel sea-bed, in a general depth of 50m, being the lowest astronomical depth, three miles east of the North Cheek at Robin Hood's Bay. Her remains are said to be still fairly substantial, lying in two

sections about 10m apart. The largest section to the south-west is about 65m in length and nearly 8m high in the area where she broke in two parts. The smaller section is around 30m long. The superstructure has now collapsed, but her propeller is still in place at the stern end. The highest parts of the wreck have Dead Man's Fingers adorning them and large cod and a number of ling can be seen, sheltering beneath the overhanging debris. It is very likely the ship's bell has now gone, but she is said to be an excellent wreck dive and should make an interesting boat-angling venue. Tidal streams are strong and the underwater visibility is usually poor to grim, making a powerful torch essential. Visibility improves significantly during the summer months. The best time to dive on her would be during a neap tide, after a spell of settled dry weather and westerly winds.

BALLATER

Wreck ★★★★
Scenery ★
Depth 50 metres
Reference N 54 28 444 W 000 27 320
5 $\frac{1}{4}$ miles N.N.E. of North Cheek, Robin Hood's Bay.

The *Ballater* was an iron 741-ton British steamship, registered at Aberdeen and had dimensions of 61.2m length, by 8.3m beam and a draught of 4.7m. She was built by G. Hall, Russell Co. in 1876 for J.A. Davidson of Aberdeen, who sold her to the Adams Brothers in Newcastle-upon-Tyne in 1885, who were the owners at the time of loss. Her single screw propeller was powered by a two-cylinder compound steam engine that used one boiler.

On 20 August 1886, the *Ballater* was on passage from the Tyne for Malta when she foundered 4 $\frac{1}{2}$ miles northeast of Whitby High Light, following a collision with the London registered steamship *Ceto*. The *Ballater*, which was under the command of Captain A. Wood, was carrying a cargo of coal and a crew of fifteen when the incident occurred. With a very light, variable wind blowing at the time, weather conditions were calm, however, all of the Yorkshire coast was blanketed in a dense fog. The crew, none of whom were injured or lost, are believed to have taken to the ship's boat, while the *Ceto*, which was in ballast, carried on with her voyage. The *Ceto* foundered just a few hours later, following a collision with the London-registered steamship *Lebanon*. There is also a possible chance that this wreck could be that of the wooden schooner *Kathleen Lily*.

KATHLEEN LILY (ex-EIDSVAAG, ex-ALBAN, ex-ADELAER, ex-BJORN, ex-JEMTLAND, ex-BRAGE.)

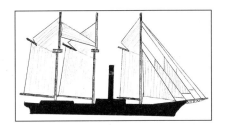

The *Kathleen Lily* was a wooden 521-ton British-registered schooner that had dimensions of 49.68m length and a beam of 8.22m. She was owned, at the time of loss, by F. A. Hobbs, although another report says Hobbs, Linsley & Co. of Grimsby (Bargate S.S. Co. Ltd). She was built as the *Brage* in 1872 by W. Haggesund at Sundswall and was equipped with schooner rigged sails and an iron propeller, powered by a three-cylinder, triple expansion steam engine, that used one boiler.

On 29 March 1917, the vessel was under the command of a Captain Woods on passage from the Tyne to Boulogne with a cargo of coke and a crew of fourteen, when she was rocked by a violent explosion at 2.45 p.m. The chief officer, who was below decks at the time rushed up to find the ship's boats being cleared away by the captain and crew. However, the davits and boats just fell away overboard tied together, the bolts and sockets holding them, having been loosened by the force of the blast. The ship was sinking rapidly. Within a matter of minutes she was submerged to the mainmast and her crew had to abandon ship by going into the sea, Captain Wood being the last to leave. Just ten minutes after the explosion, the *Kathleen Lily* went down to the bottom. Very soon, a number of mine-sweepers were at the scene and picked up her crew. Unfortunately, Captain Wood and four other crew members had drowned, but the chief officer and five men were picked up, along with the dead and landed at Whitby, while another four were taken to Scarborough.

Wreck-site
The wreck, believed to be that of the steamer *Ballater* or possibly the *Kathleen Lily*, lies orientated in an east-north-east to west-south-west direction, on a sea-bed of sand, mud and broken shells, in a general depth of 50m, being the lowest astronomical depth. The wreck, which is said to be completely collapsed, decayed, well broken up and possibly partially buried, covers an area of sea-bed of about 40m x 12m. The highest section, just under 4m, is most likely where her engine and boiler are located, at the western end of the wreck. Tidal streams are very strong, making this a low slack water dive and the visibility in this region is usually very poor to dismal. So, apart from the normal problems of diving wrecks in deep water, extra care is needed in case there are nets entangled with the wreckage.

As this is a small wreck-site and not very substantial, there will be very few fish around, so she will be little of value to boat anglers.

SAINT NINIAN

Wreck ★★★★
Scenery ★
Depth 49m
Reference N 54 28 461 W 000 28 103
3 miles N.E. of North Cheek, Robin Hood's Bay

Saint Ninian was a steel 3,026-ton British steamship, registered at Glasgow and had dimensions of 97.53m length, by 12.8m beam and a draught of 7.16m. She was managed by A. Mackay & Company of Glasgow, owned by the Saint Ninian Steam Ship Co. Ltd and D. & W. Henderson & Company built her at Glasgow in 1894. The single steel propeller was powered by a three-cylinder, triple expansion steam engine that developed 258hp, using two boilers. She had two decks and a superstructure consisting of a 13.7m poop-deck, 19.4m bridge-deck and a forecastle measuring 9.7m. *The Saint Ninian* was also armed with a large stern mounted deck gun that weighed 12cwt and fired 12lb shells.

The *Saint Ninian,* under the command of Captain J. Muckart, was on a voyage from Port Kelah to the Tees, with a cargo of pyrites, one passenger (a pilot) and a crew of twenty-seven, when she came upon the torpedoed steamship *Corsican Prince*, which was gradually sinking, three miles north-east of Robin Hood's Bay. The 2,776-ton vessel had been abandoned after having been attacked by the German submarine *UB-34*. The *Saint Ninian* stopped close alongside and one of her lifeboats was sent over to rescue survivors from the freezing sea. Unfortunately, unknown to Captain Muckart, the *UB-34* had not gone away, but was just lying submerged, close-by. The men in the lifeboat suddenly observed the U-boat's periscope, which was turning towards their ship, so they waved and yelled frantically to try and warn Captain Muckart of the imminent danger, but it was too late. At 10.15 a.m. in the morning of 7 February 1917, a torpedo fired at point blank range detonated on the *Saint Ninian* between the number three hold and the engine-room. A huge explosion followed and the she sank in just five minutes, taking fifteen people down with her, fourteen crew, including Captain Muckart and the pilot. The survivors managed to swim to an upturned lifeboat and clung to its keel until they were rescued by a minesweeper that landed at Whitby, later that day.

Wreck-site
The wreck lies orientated in a north to south direction on a dirty seabed of sand, mud, shell and gravel, in a general depth of 49m, being the lowest astronomical depth. She is said to be a huge wreck, with her bows towards the south and level on the sea-bed, but her midships and stern section to the north are still reasonably intact, standing 11m high and listing to the port side. Lots of brass shell cases are strewn around at the stern end with a mass of other broken, decaying debris. The

wreck has been positively identified by the ship's bell. However, it is not known how many divers have visited the wreck or whether the ship's bridge equipment and navigational instruments are still around. She is reported as being an excellent dive-site and will take a number of dives to explore the whole wreck.

Soft corals adorn the top structures and it is very possible that trawl nets may be entangled with it too. The wreck will be a notable boat angling venue, as large cod and ling of from 10-15kgs and a number of large lobsters have been seen on and around the site. Tidal streams are very strong and the visibility is nearly always very poor to grim, so a powerful torch is required at all times. The best time to dive the wreck-site is at low, slack water on a neap tide and after a spell of settled dry weather and westerly winds. The site is for very experienced divers only.

CORSICAN PRINCE (ex-BRIARDALE)

Wreck ★★★★
Scenery ★
Depth 46m
Reference N 54 28 478 W 000 28 619
3 ½ miles N.N.E. of North Cheek, Robin Hood's Bay.

The *Corsican Prince* was a steel 2,776-ton British steamship, registered at Newcastle and had dimensions of 96.31m length, by 12.85m beam and a draught of 5.18m. She was owned, at the time of loss, by the Prince Line Ltd and built as the *Briardale* by Short Brothers at Sunderland in 1900. The single steel propeller was powered by a three-cylinder, triple expansion steam engine that developed 265hp using two boilers. Her machinery was built by North East Marine Engineering Company Ltd at Sunderland. She had one deck, a 9.4m poop-deck, 24.9m bridge-deck and a 9.4m forecastle.

Captain J.R. Gray was in command of the *Corsican Prince*, which was on passage from Dundee for Dunkirk with an unspecified cargo of wood, when at 10 a.m. on the morning of 7 February 1917 she was torpedoed by the submerged German submarine, *UB-34*.

The crew of thirty and a pilot abandoned ship, some going into the water, where a fireman drowned. Most of them, however, got safely away in the ship's lifeboats. The U-boat surfaced shortly afterwards and then it submerged again, just prior the arrival of the steamship *Saint Ninian*. One of the *Saint Ninian's* boats was sent over to pick up survivors, but her captain did not see the U-boat's periscope or the crewmen in the ship's boat who were waving and yelling to warn him of the danger below. At 10.15 a.m. she too was sent to the bottom, along with fourteen of her crew and the pilot. Most of the *Corsican Prince's* confidential papers went down with the ship, while the survivors from both vessels were picked up by a minesweeper and landed at Whitby later that day.

39

Wreck-site

The wreck, believed to be that of the *Corsican Prince*, lies facing almost north to south on a sea-bed of dirty sand, mud, shells and gravel, in a general depth of 46m, being the lowest astronomical depth. She is quite substantial, standing around 6m from the sea-bed, but upside down and well broken up, with sections of double bottom lying over her engine and boilers. Her bows and stern-end are totally collapsed and badly broken up, with lots of scattered debris strewn around, including what appears to be the lifeboat davits and steel bollards. It is not known if the ship's bell has been recovered, but access beneath her hull will be very difficult and dangerous. It is also not known how many divers have visited the wreck, but she is reported as still being an excellent dive. Soft corals encrust most of the exposed upper parts and the hull is coated in hard, white, marine worm casings. Cod and some very large ling have been seen around the wreck, which has a number of fishing lures and monofiliment fishing lines tangled up in the top of it, so this wreck must be well known to local boatman. Tidal streams are very strong and underwater visibility is usually grim much of the time, making a good torch essential. The best time to dive the wreck is at low, slack water on a neap tide, after a spell of settled weather.

GARTHWAITE

Wreck ★★★★
Scenery ★
Depth 47m
Reference N 54 28 561 W 000 29 269
3¼ miles N.E. of North Cheek, Robin Hood's Bay.

The *Garthwaite* was a steel 5,690-ton British steamship, registered at London and had dimensions of 121.92m length, by 15.84m beam and a draught of 10.05m. She was owned by Sir William Bart. Garthwaite of Glasgow when she went down and was built in 1917 by W. Dobson & Company at Newcastle-upon-Tyne. Her single steel propeller was powered by a three-cylinder triple expansion steam engine that used three boilers. The ship was also armed with three guns; one 4.7 Q.F. and two 17 ½ inch howitzers.

At 9.50 a.m. on 13 December 1917, the *Garthwaite* was on passage from the Tyne for New York with a crew of forty-three, when she was torpedoed and sunk by the German submarine, *UB-22*, three miles north-east of Whitby. The torpedo detonated between the number three and four holds, which caused so much damage that she went down in just four minutes, however the ship's gunner still managed to fire a round from one of the howitzers at the position he thought the submerged submarine was in. Fourteen crew lost their lives, but the survivors who got away in the lifeboats were picked up by patrol vessels and landed at Whitby.

The Duc D'Aumale *was a wooden French lugger on a fishing voyage when she stranded in shallow water near Whitby on 23 July 1910. She became a total wreck and broke up soon after.* Courtesy of the Zetland Lifeboat Museum, Redcar.

Wreck-site

The wreck, believed to be that of the large steamer *Garthwaite*, lies orientated in a south-south-east to north-north-west direction, on a sea-bed of dirty sand, mud, shell and gravel, in a general depth of 47m, being the lowest astronomical depth.

The wreck is extremely large and stands 6 $\frac{1}{2}$ m high around the midships section where her engine, condenser and boilers are located. However, she has mostly collapsed, is very decayed and well broken up. Her boilers are visibly exposed through the mountain of collapsed steel plates, ribs, bollards, broken machinery, flattened copper-pipes, brass valves, wheels and cogs, with Dead Man's Fingers adorning much of the upper structures. The large howitzer guns are still on the wreck and it was from these and her boiler and engine details were eventually identified. There are reported to be masses of fish over this wreck, so she will be worth marking down as a boat angling venue. The surrounding seabed is also reported to be carpeted with thousands of brittle-starfish. Tidal streams are very strong and the visibility, like the rest of this area, is extremely poor. Only very experienced divers should attempt to dive on wrecks at these sorts of depths.

GRANIT

Wreck ★★★
Scenery ★
Depth 50m
Reference N 54 28 694 W 000 26 286
$4\frac{1}{2}$ miles N.E. of North Cheek, Robin Hood's Bay.

The *Granit* was an iron 927-ton Swedish registered steamship, built in 1877. Her single iron propeller was powered by a three-cylinder, triple expansion steam engine that used one boiler.

On 14 July 1912, the *Granit* was in ballast on passage from Rotterdam for Warkworth, when she foundered and was lost, following a collision with the Newcastle-upon-Tyne registered steamship *Saxon Prince*, five miles east-north-east of North Cheek at Robin Hood's Bay.

Wreck-site
The wreck, possibly that of the steamship *Granit* lies orientated in an almost north-east. to south-west direction on a seabed of sand, broken shell, mud and gravel in a general depth of 50m, being the lowest astronomical depth. She is well broken up, decayed and totally collapsed, with the highest point at 4m being where her boiler, donkey-engine condenser and engine are located and all visibly exposed. Most of the wreck is a mound of iron debris, broken machinery, bits of hollow mast and iron bollards, intermingled with bent and flattened copper pipes and various iron or brass cogs and wheels, brass flanges and valves. All of the wreck remains are coated in white marine worm casings and soft corals, while the sea-bed has masses of brittle-starfish slithering about. Tidal streams are very strong and with the very poor visibility, a good torch is really essential.

EAGLESCLIFFE

Wreck ★★★
Scenery ★
Depth 49m
Reference N 54 29 011 W 000 27 803
$3\frac{1}{2}$ N.E. of North Cheek, Robin Hood's Bay.

The *Eaglescliffe* was an iron 164-ton British steamship registered at Middlesbrough. She was built at Stockton in 1870 and her single iron propeller was powered by a two-cylinder, compound steam engine (as she was a very early steamship, it is possible that she may have been built with masts and auxiliary sails).

On 6 January 1873 the vessel was on passage from Middlesbrough to Dunkirk when she disappeared somewhere off Scarborough. She was carrying a crew of ten and a dead-weight cargo of 240 tons of cast pig-iron ingots.

Wreck-site
The *Eaglescliffe* was last reported somewhere off Scarborough and then she was never seen or heard of again. However, there is just the possibility that this may be her wreck-site. The wreck is iron-hulled, orientated in a west-north-west to east-south-east direction, on a seabed of sand, shell, mud and gravel, in a general depth of 49m, being the lowest astronomical depth. The wreck is totally collapsed, badly decayed and broken up, with her boiler and compound engine being the highest point at 5m, both of which are now visibly exposed and surrounded by iron debris and flattened, twisted lengths of copper-piping. Her propeller stands upright, just forward of the boiler and held in place by her own shaft on the starboard side. The aft and foreword holds, which have collapsed, are filled with large piles of cast pig-iron ingots. The wreck-site is very dark and coated in thick sediment. However, little else is known about her, or whether the ship's bell has been recovered to proclaim officially if she is the long lost *Eaglescliffe*.

MODEMI

Wreck ★★★★
Scenery ★
Depth 50m
Reference N 54 29 244 W 000 28 636
3½ miles N.E. of North Cheek, Robin Hood's Bay.

The *Modemi* was a steel 1,481-ton Norwegian steamship, registered at Christiania and had dimensions of 74.06m length, by 11.58m beam and a draught of 4.77m. She was owned at the time of loss by I. A. Christensen and built in 1912 by the Antwerp Engineering Co., Antwerp. Her single steel propeller was powered by a three-cylinder, triple expansion steam engine that used one boiler and her centrally positioned machinery was built by MacColl & Pollock Ltd at Sunderland. She only had one deck.

On 17 November 1917, the *Modemi* was in ballast on passage from Rouen for the Tyne, under the command of Captain L.M. Jensen when she was torpedoed and sunk by the German submarine *UC-48*.

Wreck-site
The wreck, believed to be that of the steamer *Modemi*, lies orientated almost north to south on a seabed of dirty sand, shell, mud and gravel, in a general depth of 50m, being the lowest astronomical depth. The wreck is said to be partially buried, with the highest 6m section being situated amidships where her collapsed

The steamship Lemberg *ran ashore during the night in the blackout on 16 December 1914. She was later refloated.* Courtesy of the Zetland Lifeboat Museum, Redcar.

bridge structure once stood. She is now well broken up and decayed, with her boiler, condenser and engine exposed. There is reported to be broken machinery, twisted, flattened and bent copper pipes and steel plates all jumbled together around the engine area where part of a derrick or lifeboat-davit stands out of the pile. Very few fish have been observed around the wreck-site, but she may have a few large congers or ling hiding amongst the pipes.

The wreck-site is very dark and gloomy and a good torch is essential. Tidal streams are very strong and visibility pretty grim and it is a site for experienced divers only.

ROHILLA

Wreck ★★★
Scenery ★★★
Depth 5-12m
Reference N 54 29 514 W 000 35 442
The Scar, Saltwick Nab at Whitby

Built for the British India Steam Navigation Co. Ltd by Harland & Wolff at Belfast in 1906, the *Rohilla* was a steel 7,409-ton luxury passenger cruise ship. She was registered at Glasgow and had dimensions of 140.28m length, by 17.14m beam and a draught of 9.29m. Her single screw propeller was powered by an eight-cylinder, quadruple steam engine, that developed 1,484hp, using six boilers and one smoke stack, giving a top speed of 17 knots. She was built with three decks, eight watertight bulkheads, a 108.8m bridge-deck, 18.8m forecastle and had the very latest and recently invented wireless telegraphy. Her smoke stack, hull and lifeboats were originally painted black, but the smoke stack had the insignia of the British India Steam Navigation Co. on it: two white rings around it, about one third of the way down. The vessel was named after a ruling tribe of Afghan Panthans in Rohilhand, India (the British Army helped some neighbouring tribal chiefs to depose them in 1773-1774.)

Almost from the day she was built, the *Rohilla* was used as a troopship, ferrying troops between Southampton and Karachi, part of India at the time. Her captain, David Landles Neilson, who was fifty years old, had spent the whole of his forty years at sea with the same company. He took command of the *Rohilla* on the day she was launched. When war broke out Captain Neilson, a naval reservist, and his officers remained at their posts, but under the command of the war-office. In the summer of 1914, the *Rohilla* was converted from a luxury passenger liner into Hospital Ship No.2 at Southhampton. Her passenger accommodation was turned into wards, operating theatres and medical staff quarters. Then she was sent to the naval base at Scapa Flow to join Admiral Jellicoe's Grand Fleet. At one time during August 1914, Prince Albert, then nineteen years old and later to become King George VI, spent some time as a patient with appendicitis on board the *Rohilla* at Scapa Flow. The ship stayed at Scapa Flow for a few weeks, but there was very little demand for her services, or the 239 hospital beds, so she was transferred to Captain Neilson's home town port of Leith, near Edinburgh, along with a Royal Navy gunner who had broken his thigh and was too ill to be taken elsewhere.

At 1 p.m on 29 October 1914, *Rohilla* left Leith Docks bound for Dunkirk, where she was to evacuate some of the troops who had been wounded on the Western Front and them bring back to England. She left carrying 229 people, including 127 crew, 100 medical staff, a Roman Catholic priest, the Royal Navy gunner, who was still on board and the ship's cat. After some two hours of steaming, Captain Neilson ordered a routine boat drill for everyone on board ship, properly testing all of the lifeboats, davits and ropes. The ship rounded Bass Rock in the Firth of Forth and steamed south-east at 12 $\frac{1}{2}$ knots, passing St Abbs Head. However, by the time she reached the Outer Farne Islands, a full blown east-south-east storm was raging. Luckily, as she was such a large ship, *Rohilla* ploughed on through the night into the teeth of the storm.

At about 3.30 a.m on 30 October, a local coastguard officer at Whitby, Mr Albert Jefferies on watch duty, saw the ship travelling at full speed, directly towards the shallow reefs. He signalled her with a morse lamp and then switched on the foghorn, keeping it blowing for thirty minutes to warn the crew of the danger, but the *Rohilla*, seven miles off her course, still ploughed on. The second officer on the ship, Archibald Winstanley had seen the flashing morse lamp, but, although he realized it was a signal lamp, could not read it or understand why a lamp was flashing at them so far out to sea. He reported his observations to the Captain, who told him to have one of the naval signallers translate it.

The Rohilla *in her glory days as a modern, luxury cruise ship.* Courtesy of J.G. Pickles and the Whitby Literary and Philosophical Society.

Minutes later, at 4.10 a.m. there was a tremendous shudder as the ship's hull impacted with something in the sea, sending people crashing and reeling about on the ship. As it was war-time, all of the bells on buoys had been silenced, lighthouses displayed no warning beams and ships sailed without navigation lights. In the darkness with a terrible storm raging, Captain Neilson believed they were some seven miles north-east. of Whitby and his first thought was that the *Rohilla* had struck a German mine. He ordered the engines 'full astern' to bring her to a stop, but then decided that she might be damaged below the water-line and probably the best course was to take her inshore. However, he changed the order to 'full ahead and helm', hard-a-port. However, the Captain's early career had been spent in sailing ships and in a moment of panic, he had given the wrong instructions. The order should have been 'helm, hard-a-starboard' to turn the ship to the right, but the helmsman had realized this and turned to starboard. The *Rohilla* carried on with her engines running at full speed. In a few minutes she crashed halfway over and on top of the jagged edge of The Scar, a high submerged reef some 550 metres out from the towering cliffs of Whitby. The impact of hitting and grinding over the reef caused tremendous structural damage to the ship's hull, cracking it in two places. She was left with about a third of her stern-end hanging over a submerged cliff face and the front bow-quarter sloping up out of the water. Conditions were horrendous and mountainous seas were breaking over the top of her. Coastguard officers set off the maroon rockets to alert the lifeboat crews and Rocket Brigade.

Thomas Langlands, the coxwain of Whitby's No.1 lifeboat, *Robert and Mary Ellis*, a native of Seahouses in Northumberland, knew that their little boat would be dashed to pieces before it could be launched in the terrible sea conditions. It would not have been practical to try and row the No.2 boat, *John Fielden,* out through the harbour mouth in such a storm, as both boats were rowing lifeboats manned by fourteen crew members. All they could do was to wait until daylight and hope the storm had abated.

The Rocket Brigades were quickly on the scene and tried again and again to reach the ship to set up a Bosun's Chair, but the ship was too far off-shore for their rocket lines. At around 7 a.m., the ship broke into three sections and many people were swept to their deaths as the stern-end slipped away and went down

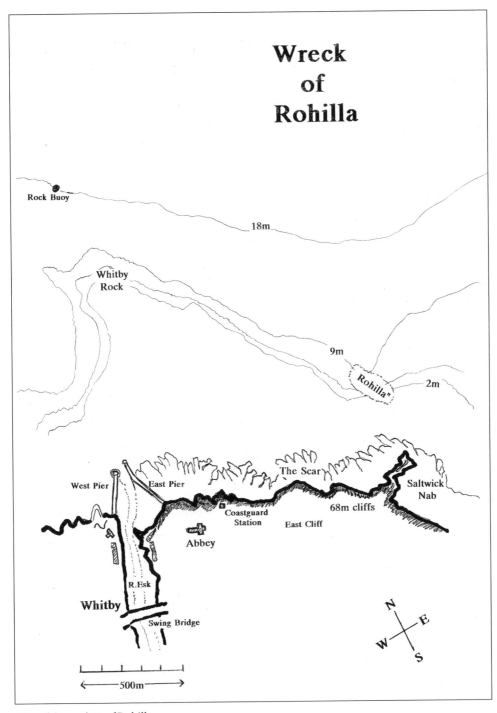

Map of the wrecksite of Rohilla.

The Rohilla *the morning she came ashore, with people still on board and awaiting rescue. Note her smoke stack still in place, as this came off shortly after.* Courtesy of the Whitby Literary and Phlosophical Society.

into deeper water. Most of it had been washed away or smashed up and nearly all the ship's lifeboats had gone the same way.

The morning brought no improvement in the weather, so the lifeboat crews, helped by local people, lifted the 36ft lifeboat *John Fielden* over the stone breakwater and dragged and carried it over the rocks, taking two hours to reach The Scar, almost a mile away. The boat was holed in two places, but the cork filling helped to keep her afloat and allow the fourteen-man crew to row her out to the *Rohilla* two times, taking seventeen and then eighteen people off the stricken ship. By this time many people had been swept away, or had drowned while attempting to swim ashore through the treacherous currents and huge waves that battered what was left of this once proud ship. After the second trip to the wreck, the *John Fielden* was too badly damaged and full of water to make any further journeys, so she was dragged up the beach and left to the elements.

Meanwhile, telephone calls had been made to the lifeboat stations at Scarborough and Teesmouth to ask for assistance. The steam trawler *Morning Star* towed Scarborough's lifeboat *Queensbury* out at 3.30 p.m. that afternoon. After battling with mountainous seas, they arrived off Saltwick Nab at 6 p.m.. By then it was pitch dark and they were unable to get close to the *Rohilla*, because of the swirling white water. However, the lifeboat and trawler both stood by all night, just in case they might be able to get alongside the stricken vessel. They made repeated attempts the following day, Saturday, but were beaten back each time and with their boat full of water and the lifeboatmen suffering badly from the appalling conditions, both vessels were forced to return to Scarborough.

The motorized 12.8m self-righting lifeboat *Bradford VI*, powered by a 35hp Tyler petrol engine, stationed twenty-two miles away at South Gare, Teesmouth, made an attempt to reach her. However, as she crossed the Tees Bar, the pounding from the huge seas caused a serious leak which stopped her engine after she filled

The remains of the hospital ship two days after stranding on The Scar at Saltwick Nab, Whitby, on 30 October 1914. Within a few days nothing was visible above the surface. Courtesy of the Whitby Literary and Phlosophical Society.

up with water and she had to be towed back to Middlesbrough by a steam-tug.

At 7 a.m. on the Saturday morning, the *Robert and Mary Ellis* was launched in Whitby harbour and Coxswain Langlands took her out to sea to await the arrival of the steam-tug *Mayfly* which had come from Hartlepool to help. She got there at 8 a.m. and took the lifeboat in tow. Unfortunately, they were unable to get any closer to the *Rohilla* than half a mile. Coxswain Langlands discussed the situation with James Hastings, coxswain of Hartlepool's No.2 lifeboat, who was on board the *Mayfly*. Reluctantly, the men decided to return to Whitby.

The crew of Upgang lifeboat *William Riley* knew that it was not practical to reach the wreck from their launch site some two miles up the coast. They decided that they could get closer, if they could haul her overland for three miles, then lower the 11m boat down the 200ft cliff to The Scar, where she could be launched. It was a terrific feat that took about 100 people and six horses $2\frac{1}{2}$ hours to complete. However, despite such a tremendous effort and repeated attempts to reach the wreck, in the end, exhausted, they were forced to give up and returned to shore.

In desperation, at 4.15 p.m., an urgent telephone message was made to Tynemouth, requesting more help. In fifteen minutes the 12.2m self-righting motorized lifeboat *Henry Vernon* was launched. She was built in 1911 and, although powered by a 40hp Tyler petrol engine, she was also equipped with oars and an auxiliary sail. She took all night to travel the hazardous forty-four miles south, in horrendous weather, reaching Whitby harbour at 1 a.m. on the Sunday, where she took on barrels of oil to lessen the effects of the heavy seas around the *Rohilla*.

The Upgang lifeboat, William Riley, *preparing to launch to aid the hospital ship, on 31 October 1914, the day after she came ashore.* Courtesy of the Whitby Literary and Phlosophical Society.

At 6.30 a.m. the *Henry Vernon* headed out of the harbour, with her Tynemouth crew, Lieut. Basil Hall RN, the District Inspector of Lifeboats and Whitby Second Coxswain, Richard Eglon, who was to at act as pilot (it was now three days since the *Rohilla* had ran aground). Gradually, the lifeboat made her way out to the wreck. When they were about 200 metres to the seaward side of her, the crew poured gallons of oil on the water's surface. This had the dramatic effect on the foaming white water, of turning it into a heavy swell. This enabled Coxswain Smith, with great courage and determination, to manoeuvre the *Henry Morgan* alongside what was left of *Rohilla's* bridge, despite the little boat being almost swamped by the massive seas. Quickly, the survivors lowered ropes and forty men slid down into the lifeboat, but just then two enormous waves washed over the *Rohilla* and crashed down into the rescue boat.

The crew managed to clear much of the water and take off the remaining ten men, all within fifteen minutes. Then just as she was clearing the stern end of the *Rohilla,* another enormous wave struck the lifeboat broadside-on. She rolled right over on her beam-ends, but within seconds righted herself and carried on back out to sea where Coxswain Smith took the *Henry Morgan* back into Whitby harbour, to be greeted by cheering crowds.

Many local people risked their own lives by wading chest deep into the raging water to pull out half dead survivors and the lifeboat crews performed some very heroic feats in horrendous conditions. Altogether, some 139 people were rescued from the 7,409-ton hospital ship, with at least eighty-five of them saved by the brave R.N.L.I. lifeboat crews. Unfortunately, eighty-four people lost their lives, including sixty-two of the

The Henry Vernon *and crew. The Tynemouth lifeboat men who braved mountainous seas for forty-five miles to aid the* Rohilla *in October 1914.* Courtesy of the Whitby Literary and Phlosophical Society.

ship's crew, on that terrible day in 1914. Captain Neilson of the *Rohilla* and the ship's (lucky) cat were the last two to be rescued from the sinking ship.

At the inquest, Captain Neilson and his four senior officers gave evidence, but the seven mile miscalculation was never satisfactorily explained. However, they were all of the same opinion that the vessel had first struck a German mine. Many local people firmly believe that the ship's course took her over the eastern end of the submerged Whitby Rock and it was that which she first struck.

One other possible explanation was: that on the day the *Rohilla* was wrecked, the 159-ton wooden brigantine *Laura* (built at Newquay in 1861), would have been in the same vicinity as the Rohilla at 4 a.m. on that Friday morning. She was on a voyage from London to Newcastle with a cargo of burnt ore. She was never seen or heard of again. However, her name-plate was washed up at Sandsend and the wreckage of a fairly large wooden vessel was found amongst that of the *Rohilla*. That may explain the sudden and tremendous shudder that went through the *Rohilla*, sending people reeling and knocking them off their feet.

For their bravery Coxwain Thomas Langlands, Coxwain Robert Smith and Captain H.E. Burton R.E. were awarded the R.N.L.I.'s gold medal for conspicuous gallantry. Silver medals were awarded to Second Coxwain Richard Eglon, Second Coxwain James Brownlee, Lieutenant Basil Hall R.N. The silver medal was also awarded to George Peart who bravely went into the violent surf repeatedly to help people who had attempted to swim ashore from the *Rohilla*. The R.N.L.I.'s Thanks on Vellum were awarded to Coxswain Pounder Robinson and to Second Coxswain T. Kelly of the Upgang lifeboat, while the crews of the

Two days after striking the rocks, the superstructure of the hospital ship Rohilla, *torn off the vessel by the huge seas, lies smashed up on the beach 500m away, while behind it the lifeboat* John Fielden *also lies smashed, almost into matchsticks.* Courtesy of the Whitby Literary and Phlosophical Society.

lifeboats involved were given money. Captain Neilson was even honoured with the Bronze Medal of the Royal Society for the Prevention of Cruelty to Animals for saving the ship's cat. The rescue of people from the wreck of the *Rohilla* still remains one of the R.N.L.I's greatest achievements.

Wreck-site

The wreck of the *Rohilla* is quite substantial, but it is broken up over a wide area of the The Scar some 500m off shore. The inshore part of the wreck lies in about 6m, however bits of her can even be found amongst the rocks at low water, while the seaward end sits in around 15m. There are lots of battered and bent steel framework, ribs, plates and pipes strewn around her very large boilers and the remains of her steam engine. Although she is well salvaged and broken up, the wreck still makes an interesting rummage dive where anything could turn up.

The bows of the *Rohilla* are mixed up with the scattered remains of the steamship *Charles*. Currents are reasonable, but the visibility is usually poor and depends a great deal on how much fresh water has come down the river Esk. Marine life, especially crustaceans, can be seen around the wreck.

2. Whitby to the Tees

SKANE (ex-DAUNTLESS)

Wreck ★★★
Scenery ★
Depth 14m
Reference N 54 29 730 W 00 37 130
½ mile N. of Whitby breakwater

The *Skane* was a steel 1,667-ton Swedish steamship, registered at Helsingborg and had dimensions of 78.63m length, by 10.87m beam and a draught of 5.79m. She was built as the *Dauntless* by W. Gray & Co., at West Hartlepool, in 1884 and was owned at the time of loss by Rederiaktiebol of Helsingborg. Her single screw propeller was powered by a two-cylinder, compound steam engine that developed 173hp, using two boilers. She had one deck, four watertight bulkheads and a superstructure consisting of an 8.8m poop-deck, a 20.6m quarter-deck, 20.3m bridge-deck and 10.7m forecastle.

The *Skane* left Stockton in November 1915, under the command of Captain A. Hanson, on a voyage to Calais, with a general cargo of timber, eighteen crew and two female passengers. During the evening of 30 November and in fine weather, she ground to a halt on the Whitby Rock. A local fisherman made an attempt to re-float her, but the grounding had ripped a hole in the vessel's hull and the engine room was heavily flooded. Next morning a tug floated her off on the incoming tide, but the deluge of water was more than her pumps could cope with and they were forced to beach at Whitby. Later that afternoon the wind turned strong south-east.

The Whitby lifeboat was launched and took off the passengers and crew, but eight salvage men stayed on board in an attempt to save the vessel. However they had to be rescued as well as the wind turned into a howling gale. Flares were set off and the lifeboat was launched once again to rescue them from the stricken ship. In another incident in December, a further seven salvage men had to be rescued from the *Skane* when they were forced off the wreck in heavy seas, leaving the *Skane* to break up where she lay.

Wreck-site
The wreck is now broken up into three parts, with lots of plate and double sections. The stern-end stands approximately 4m high on a flat sandy seabed,

surrounded by small clusters of rock, while her intact prop shaft gives a good link up to the middle section of the wreck. There is quite a good assortment of marine life about her, including; crabs, lobster, butterfish, blennies, lumpsuckers, a fine array of Dead Man's Fingers and Cup-corals.

After diving on *UC-70* or *UB-30*, the *Skane* makes a good second dive in reasonably shallow water and is excellently situated for trainees, as it is diveable at all states of the tide. The wreck-site is a good rummage dive and only some ten minutes from Whitby harbour.

LANTHORN (ex-MAGNUS MAIL)

Wreck ★★★★
Scenery ★
Depth 50m
Reference N 54 30 094 W 000 29 020
5 miles E. of Whitby

The *Lanthorn* was a steel 2,299-ton British steamship, registered at Sunderland and had dimensions of 88.52m length, by 11.91m beam and a draught of 6.55m. She was owned at the time of loss by J. Westoll and built as the *Magnus Mail* by Short Brothers, at Sunderland, in 1889. Her single steel propeller was powered by a three-cylinder, triple-expansion steam engine that developed 202hp using one boiler and her machinery was built at Hartlepool by T. Richardson & Sons Ltd. She had one deck and a superstructure consisting of a 9.7m poop-deck, a 23.8m bridge-deck and a 10.3m forecastle.

On 22 May 1917, the *Lanthorn* was in ballast steaming north, under the command of Captain W. Shewan, on passage from London for the Tyne when a German submarine, which was some 1½ miles astern, shelled her with its deck gun. Captain Shewan altered course and increased speed to bring his vessel inshore, but the submarine kept on firing for over an hour, scoring at least five direct hits on the *Lanthorn*. To save the lives of his men, the Captain stopped the engines and abandoned ship at 9 a.m. The eighteen crew left in the lifeboats, to be picked up shortly after by some motor fishing boats, which landed them at Whitby. The steamer was boarded by the crew of the submarine, *UB-41*, who placed explosive scuttling charges below her decks at 11.20 a.m., causing her to sink.

Wreck-site
The wreck, believed to be that of the *Lanthorn,* lies on a seabed of hard sand and broken shells in a general depth of 50m, being the lowest astronomical depth, approximately five miles east of Whitby piers. The wreck is very substantial and reasonably intact, with her broken superstructure standing between 6-7m up from the seabed. Part of her hull in the midship's section has now inverted in on herself, exposing many non-ferrous objects. At the stern end, the huge half-buried

propeller is still attached and above it, floats a mass of trawl net, supported by dozens of little bobble floats, causing it to sway as the tide begins to run. I have been informed that the wreck is not very often visited by divers so, most, if not all of her interesting equipment and navigational gear will probably be still around, which should make a gem of a picture. Soft corals coat the upper and most exposed parts of the wreck, which is a sure sign of the very strong tidal streams that sweep over her. Visibility is very poor to grim and the site is very dark, so a good torch is a real necessity. The *Lanthorn* should be well worth a visit by the boat-angling fraternity, as she will be home to a fair number of large cod.

POLRUAN (ex-POLLACSEK, ex-POLNAY)

Wreck ★★★
Scenery ★
Depth 27-30m
Reference N 54 30 271 W 00 36 126
E. of Whitby Bell-Buoy.

The *Polruan* was a steel 3,692-ton British steamship, registered at Cardiff, with dimensions of 100.89m length, by 14.7m beam and a draught of 6.7m. She was built as the *Pollacsek* in 1907 by W. Gray & Co. Ltd at West Hartlepool and owned at the time of loss by Hall Brothers, Cairns, Noble & Co. Her single steel propeller was powered by a three-cylinder, triple-expansion steam engine that developed 292hp, using two boilers. Her machinery was built by Central Marine Engineering Works Ltd at West Hartlepool. She had one deck, five watertight bulkheads and a superstructure consisting of a 7.3m poop-deck, a 37.7m bridge-deck and an 8.8m forecastle.

The *Polruan* was requisitioned by the Admiralty as a collier and operated under the management of its own company. On 25 October 1916, the vessel was on passage from Tyne Dock for Dunkirk with an unspecified cargo of coal and a crew of twenty-six, when she was reported to have struck a German laid mine three-quarters of a mile east of Whitby. However a Board of Trade inquiry later suggested that it was more likely that she had struck the Whitby Rock and her skipper, Captain Jeffrey, was censured and ordered to pay £50 towards the costs.

Wreck-site
The wreck of the *Polruan*, like that of the *Rohilla*, is owned by local Whitby divers. It is totally collapsed, but still quite substantial and covers a large area of seabed. The boilers are standing upright and are close to the triple-expansion steam engine, surrounded by lots of pipes, framework and broken machinery and much of it is unrecognisable. There have been no reports of any fish or marine life around the wreck, butmaybe there were not seen because of the very poor visibility (although, during the summer months, visibility is said to be six to eight

metres deep after a dry spell of settled weather and neap tides). The best time to visit the wreck-site is at low, slack water because tidal streams are fairly strong. The wreck lies just to the east of the Whitby Bell Buoy and is fairly easy to locate using an echo sounder. It only takes seven to eight minutes to reach by RIB (ridged-hulled inflatable boat) from Whitby Harbour.

POLANNA (ex-ANTONINA 1, ex-ANNA WOERMANN, 1898)

Wreck ★★★★
Scenery ★★
Depth 45m
Reference N 54 30 520 W 000 32 385
3 miles N.E. of Whitby.

The *Polanna* was a steel 2,345-ton British steamship, registered in Glasgow and had dimensions of 85.95m length and a 11.58m beam. She was owned at the time of loss by the Clyde Steam Ship Co. in Glasgow and built as the *Antonina I* in 1893. Her single steel-screw propeller was powered by a three-cylinder, triple-expansion steam engine that used two boilers and she was armed with a large stern mounted deck gun that fired 15-lb shells.

The *Polanna* was torpedoed by a German submarine, off the Cameroon River, in September 1914, but survived the attack. However, on 6 August 1917, she was on passage from the Tyne for Dunkirk with a 3,000-ton cargo of coal and a crew of twenty-six when she was torpedoed and sunk by the German submarine, *UC-40*. The vessel was proceeding at eight knots and taking a zig-zag course at the time, until one of the crew saw the track of an approaching torpedo about fifty yards away on the starboard quarter. The helm was thrown hard to port, but they were too late, as the torpedo struck and detonated on the port side in the number two hold at 3.30 p.m.

The ship went down in one and a half minutes, but not before the crew scrambled to launch one of the boats with fifteen men in it. The other men went into the sea where, unfortunately, two of them drowned. However the other nine were rescued. The survivors in the boat made their way to shore and landed two miles south of Whitby.

Wreck-site
The wreck lies on a seabed of dirty sand, mud and shells in a general depth of 45m, being the lowest astronomical depth. She is very substantial, with her midships section standing upright about 7m high. Most of the rest of the ship is reported to have collapsed down in a jumble of twisted metal, but her outline and shape can still be made out. The two boilers, condenser and engine have been reported to be exposed and the upper, highest parts have Dead Man's Fingers adorning them.

Lots of fish, of varying species, can be seen, so the wreck should make a good boat-angling venue when conditions and tides are right. It is understood that her bell has been recovered in recent years. Tidal streams are strong and the visibility is extremely poor, so a good torch is essential. This site is only for very experienced divers and a good lookout is required by the boat crew, because the wreck-site is in the shipping lanes.

CETO

Wreck ★★★
Scenery ★
Depth 51m
Reference N 54 30 673 W 000 28 227
6 miles E.N.E. of Whitby

The *Ceto* was an iron 970-ton British steamship, registered at the Port of London, with dimensions of 65.7m length, by 8.8m beam and a draught of 4.9m. She was built in 1878 by M. Pearse, at Stockton-on-Tees, for Henry Clarke of Cardiff, who sold her to W.F. Conner of London in 1886, who were the owners at the time of loss. Her single iron propeller was powered by a centrally positioned, two-cylinder, compound-steam engine that used one boiler.

On 20 August 1886, under the command of Captain J. Gibson, the *Ceto* was in ballast, on passage from Rouen for North Shields, when she was in collision with the Aberdeen registered steamship *Ballater*, six miles east-north-east of Whitby. The *Ballater* foundered and was lost, but her crew, none of whom were seriously injured, are believed to have taken to the ship's boats. The *Ceto* carried on with her voyage. However, within a couple of hours of that incident, she was in a collision with the 923-ton London-registered *Lebanon*, another steamship, but the *Ceto* was so badly damaged below the waterline that she too foundered. No one was injured or lost in either incident and the *Ceto's* crew are believed to have been taken on board the *Lebanon*, which was owned by W. J. Pope of London.

Wreck-site
The wreck, believed to be that of the *Ceto*, lies on a dirty seabed of sand, broken shells and mud in a general depth of 51m, being the lowest depth. She has now totally collapsed, is badly decayed, broken up and partly buried, standing no more than about 3m, with the remains of her boiler and engine at midships visibly exposed through the mound of twisted rusting plates and broken machinery. It is also possible her most interesting features, like the bell and telegraph, are still somewhere in the pile of decayed debris which is now beginning to concrete together.

Tidal streams are very strong and this wreck site is very dark with visibility usually less than half a metre. It is a wreck-site only for the most experienced technical divers. Little more information has come to light about the wreck-site and only time will tell if she is really worth a visit.

H.M. TRAWLER LORD RIDLEY

Wreck ★★★
Scenery ★
Depth 51m
Reference N 54 30 678 W 000 28 227
6 miles E.N.E. of Whitby.

The *Lord Ridley* was a steel 215-ton British steam fishing trawler, originally owned by the Consolidated Steam Fishing & Ice Co., but requisitioned by the Admiralty in February 1915 and converted to a mine-sweeper. She was built in 1911 by Smith's Dock Co. Ltd at Middlesbrough and had dimensions of 35.76m length, by 6.7m beam and a draught of 3.53m. Her single-steel propeller, possibly bronze, was powered by a three-cylinder, triple-expansion steam engine that developed 75hp, using one boiler and her machinery was built by W.V.V. Lidgerwood at Glasgow. She had one deck, a 21m quarter-deck and 6.4m forecastle.

On 10 May 1917, the H.M. trawler *Lord Ridley* was on mine sweeping duties off Whitby when she detonated a German mine and foundered six miles east-north-east of Whitby.

Wreck-site
The wreck, which is believed to be that of the H.M. steam trawler *Lord Ridley*, lies on a dirty seabed of sand, shell and mud, in a general depth of 51m, being the lowest astronomical depth. She has now collapsed onto the sea-bed, is badly decayed, well broken up and partly buried, with her boiler and engine visible through the mound of rusting steel debris. Very little marine life has been seen around the wreck. Tidal streams are very strong and the visibility is usually rather grim most of the time. The wreck-site is close to the main shipping lanes, so a sharp lookout is required by the surface cover.

NIL DESPERANDUM

Wreck ★★★
Scenery ★
Depth 56m
Reference N 54 30 698 W 000 07 785
20 miles E. of Whitby.

The *Nil Desperandum* was an iron 140-ton British fishing trawler, registered at the port of Scarborough and had dimensions of 30.6m length by 6.32m beam and a draught of 3.25m. She was No.95785, built in 1889 by Cook, Welton & Gemmell in Yard 33 at Hull, launched on 16 March and registered at the port of Hull as H66 by her new owners, the Humber Steam Trawling Co. Ltd at Hull. Her single iron propeller was powered by a two-cylinder, compound-steam engine that developed 45hp using one boiler, which gave the vessel a recorded speed of ten knots. She had one deck and her machinery was built by Bailey & Leetham at Hull. On 22 November 1894 her tonnage was adjusted to 148 tons, then on 5 September 1913 she was sold to the Progress Steam Trawling Company Ltd at Scarborough and registered at the port as SH186.

The trawler was on a fishing voyage on 25 September 1916, under the command of skipper H. Cammish when she was stopped by a German submarine, twenty miles north-east of Scarborough and twenty miles east of Whitby. The crew were taken on board the U-boat and the *Nil Desperandum* was then sunk by gun-fire. She was just one of thirteen trawlers to be captured by the submarine while fishing over the Whitby Fine Ground during the hours of darkness, between 24 and 25 September 1916, but the German commander must have been one of the old school, because he later stopped a Norwegian cargo ship and arranged for the 126 captured fishermen to be landed at a British port. Before they were taken to South Shields the fishing crews must have been really cramping his U-boat.

As well as the crew from the *Nil Desperandum*, there were men on the U-boat from the following eleven vessels: the 151-ton steam trawler *Game-Cock*, the 125-ton *Fisher Prince*, the iron 162-ton *Harrier*, the 133-ton *Quebec*, the iron 123-ton *Otter*, the iron 155-ton *Tarantula*, the iron 151-ton *Marguerite*, all registered at Scarborough; the 150-ton *Otterhound* and the iron 147-ton *Trinidad*, both registered at Hull; the 176-ton Hartlepool-registered steam trawler *Loch Ness* and the iron 94-ton *St Hilda*. However, a further five steam trawlers and a steamship were sunk, probably by the same U-boat, a little further to the south on that same night, possibly the *U-57*, which torpedoed the 809-ton Norwegian steamship *Laila*, ten miles north-east of Flamborough Head.

Wreck-site
This wreck has not been positively identified, but she is most likely to be that of either the *Nil Desperandum*, or one of the twelve other trawlers that were lost in the immediate vicinity during that night. She lies on a seabed of mud, sand, broken shell and stone in a general depth of 56m, the lowest astronomical depth. She is said to be orientated in a north to south direction and is reasonably intact, but partially buried, with the highest section around midships, standing almost 4m high. The bridge structures, smoke stack and masts have collapsed and are broken up and at least two trawl nets are caught up and floating above her bow section, but the wreck-site is covered in an array of soft corals. It is not known how much marine life is on or around the wreck, but tidal streams are exceptionally strong and the underwater visiblity is very poor to dismal most of the time, however, it is said to improve marginally during the summer months. The wreck is a long way from shore, so anyone deciding to visit the site should ensure that the sea conditions and weather forecast are very good and a sharp lookout will be required at all times.

SPERO

Wreck ★★★★
Scenery ★
Depth 32m
Reference N 54 30 772 W 00 37 158
1 mile N.N.E. of Whitby piers.

The *Spero*, known locally as the *Sparrow*, was an iron 827-ton British steamship, with dimensions of 64.61m length, by 8.89m beam and a draught of 4.97m. She was registered at Newcastle-upon-Tyne and owned by R. S. Gardiner & J. Reay and built by C. Mitchell & Co. at Newcastle in 1878. Her single propeller was powered by a two-cylinder, compound-steam engine that developed 98hp, using two boilers. The machinery was built by North East Marine Engineering Co. Ltd at Sunderland. She had one deck, four watertight bulkheads and a superstructure consisting of a 7.3m poop-deck and a 12.2m bridge-deck.

On 11 August 1899, under the command of Captain W. Rickinson, carrying seven passengers and a crew of twenty, the *Spero* was on a return voyage from London to Newcastle-upon-Tyne when she foundered and was lost following a collision with Glasgow-registered steamship, *Maggie*. The Runswick Bay and Whitby lifeboats were launched and both took part in the rescue.

Wreck-site
The wreck of the *Spero*, or *Sparrow*, is also often referred to as the 'Steeple-in-Street' wreck, because of the easy transit marks, which include a steeple. It can be seen half a mile north-west by north. of Whitby Bell-Buoy, bearing south, with the bell-buoy in line with Saltwick Nab, with the north cheek of Robin Hood's Bay just closing a beam line looking down the street on West Cliff, Whitby. The steeple of the church is in the same street.

The remains, although collapsed in, are still very substantial, standing some four to five metres high in places. Visibility is usually very poor to grim and the wreck, which requires a good torch to see anything, always appears dark and gloomy. It also has a number of old trawl nets draped over and around it, making diving rather precarious in the darkness. Large cod often hide among the wreckage and shoals of pout-whiting are a common sight, while the occasional large crustacean, although not always easy to reach, can be a real bonus. The best time to dive the *Spero* is at low slack water, during a neap tide and after a spell of dry settled weather and westerly winds.

VIOLA

Wreck ★★
Scenery ★★★
Depth 8m
Reference N 54 32 00 W 00 42 30
½ mile south of Kettelness Point

The *Viola* was an iron 1,900-ton British steamship registered at the port of North Shields and had dimensions of 85.34m length, by 10.66m beam and a draught of 7.49m. She was built by the Tyne Iron Shipbuilding Company at Newcastle in 1879 and owned by the Montauk Steam Ship Company Limted also in Newcastle-upon-Tyne. Her single iron-screw propeller was powered by a two-cylinder compound-steam engine that developed 185hp, using two boilers and her machinery was built by North East Marine Engineering Company Ltd at Sunderland. She had two decks, six watertight bulkheads and a centrally positioned superstructure that consisted of a 12.2m quarter-deck and a 7.9m bridge-deck.

Early in the afternoon of 19 September 1903, the *Viola* was on passage from Cartagena in Spain for Middlesborough with a cargo of iron-ore and a crew of twenty, when she ran ashore in thick fog, half a mile south of Kettleness Point. The *Viola* passed Flamborough Head at 8 a.m. and due to poor visibility, Captain McGovern altered course to give Whitby a wide berth. However, during the journey, neither he nor his crew bothered to use the sounding lead to test for depth.

Runswick Bay's lifeboat, *Cape of Good Hope* was launched at 2.30 p.m. and Coxswain Calvert took the lifeboat alongside the stricken vessel and rescued seventeen of her crew, but the Captain and two Mates refused to leave. Unfortunately, however, the wind developed into a strong east-north-east gale. With huge waves breaking all around the stranded ship and worsening weather conditions, the lifeboat had to return to the scene to take off the remaining three men. Within two weeks of her stranding, the *Viola* broke her back and became a total wreck.

Wreck-site
The wreck is lying in a general depth of about 8m, but is surrounded by high reefs making her difficult to locate with an echo sounder. She is totally collapsed, very broken up, decayed and scattered about the reef, lying under a thick forest of kelp. The wreck-site, however is a pleasant dive, especially for the novice diver or as a second dive. Bits of non-ferrous metal can still be found for those who look hard enough and lobsters are not uncommon in the surrounding reefs. Visibility is reasonable during the summer months, after a dry spell of weather and light westerly winds. The site is best dived on a flood tide, but can be safely dived at most states of the tide.

WOLF HOUND

Wreck ★
Scenery ★★★
Depth 5m
Reference; N 54 32 023 W 000 42 420
Off Kettleness Point

The *Wolf Hound* was an iron 151-ton British steam fishing trawler that had dimensions of 30.6m length, by 6.2m beam and a draught of 3.35m. She was trawler No 98738, built by Cook, Welton & Gemmell in Yard 67 at Hull in 1891, launched on 25 April and registered at the port of Hull, as H141 on 14 June for her new owners the Humber Steam Trawling C. Ltd. Her single iron propeller was powered by a two-cylinder, compound-steam engine that developed 45hp, using one boiler, giving the vessel a registered speed of ten knots. Her machinery was built by Bailey & Leetham at Hull.

On 4 December 1896 the *Wolf Hound* was on a fishing trip from her home port when, during heavy fog, she ran aground at Kettleness Point and became a total loss.

Wreck-site
The wreck, or what remains of it, is totally collapsed and well dispersed among the rocks, boulders and kelp, in a general depth of around 5m. Only a few battered iron plates and unrecognisable pieces of broken machinery are left. However, the surrounding reefs and boulders provide excellent cover for the various crustaceans that can be fond in this area.

Tidal streams are very reasonable, but the underwater visibility is very hit and miss. During the summer months it significantly improves following a spell of dry, settled weather and south-westerly winds.

BRENTWOOD

Wreck ★★★★
Scenery ★
Depth 45m
Reference N 54 32 022 W 000 35 671
2½ miles N.-N.E. of Whitby

The *Brentwood* was a steel 1,192-ton British steamship, registered at London and had dimensions of 68.5m length, by 11.04m beam and a draught of 4.36m. She was owned by Cory Colliers Ltd and built by S.P. Austin & Son in 1904 at Sunderland. Her single steel propeller was powered by a three-cylinder, triple-expansion steam engine that developed 180hp using one boiler and her machinery was built by G. Clark Ltd at Sunderland. She had one deck, a well-deck and a superstructure consisting of a 6.7m poop-deck, 17m quarter-deck, 14.6m bridge-deck and a 7.6m forecastle.

At 1.55 a.m. in the morning of 12 January 1917, the *Brentwood* was in ballast on passage from London for North Shields when she detonated a mine laid by the German submarine *UC-43*. The explosion took place at the fore part of the vessel, instantly killing the Second Mate and a fireman, both of whom were on watch duty at the time. With her bows almost blown off she filled up rapidly and went down in just four minutes, taking confidential papers with her, but her skipper, Captain R. Hunter and the thirteen surviving crew managed to get away safely in the ship's boat. Fortunately, they were rescued just over an hour and twenty minutes later by the steamship *Togston* and landed at Sunderland.

Wreck-site
The wreck lies on a seabed of sand, mud and shell in a general depth of 43-44m, being the lowest astronomical depth. She is very substantial, but has collapsed down in the midships section where the bridge was located, exposing her engine, boiler, donkey-engine, condenser and some ancillary machinery, while the bows and stern-end are reported to be covered in an array of soft corals. Pout-whiting, with their perch-like stripes, shoal in vast numbers around the stern-end and although none were actually seen, there is sure to be some large cod, ling and possibly conger within the wreck itself, so it should make an excellent boat-angling venue. Her propeller is still in place and it is very likely that some of her navigational gear and bridge equipment may still be around, however it is possible that the bell may have already been recovered. Old trawl nets, covered in soft corals, drape over this wreck, making the dive-site rather eerie and forbidding.

This is a very gloomy dive, making a good torch essential, and with tidal streams being very strong. The best time to dive her is at low slack water on a neap tide. The depth of this wreck, like most of the others in over 40m, should only be undertaken by very experienced divers who know exactly what they are doing.

ONSLOW

Wreck ★★
Scenery ★★★
Depth 9m
Reference N 54 32 10 W 000 43 30
Kettleness Point

The *Onslow* was a steel 2,722-ton British steamship, registered at London and had dimensions of 95.09m length, by 13.89m beam and a draught of 6.19m. She was owned by the Leander Steam Ship Co. Ltd and built at Whiteinch by Barclay,

Curle in 1899. Her single iron propeller was powered by a three-cylinder, triple-expansion steam engine that developed 224hp using two boilers.

On 12 August 1911 the *Onslow*, with a crew of twenty on board, was on passage from Sunderland for Piraeus with a cargo of coal, when she ran aground on the rocks at Kettleness Point in dense fog and heavy weather. The new 10.7m self-righting Runswick Bay lifeboat *Hester Rothchild* was launched and stood by the stranded ship, but then returned to station when the weather moderated. Much of the *Onslow's* cargo was thrown overboard as desperate efforts were made to save the vessel, but she was abandoned four days later, when she broke in two and became a total wreck.

Wreck-site
The wreck was identified by a diver, on 10 November 1970, from information supplied about her location by a local fisherman. The remains of the *Onslow* are scattered about under the kelp, amongst the rocks and boulders, in a general depth of 8-9m. Her boilers and the remnants of her engine are still there, along with some broken and battered machinery which are gradually concreting into the surrounding rocks.

The wreck site is nothing spectacular, but still makes a nice rummage dive, where non-ferrous metal and the odd trinket can be found with a little bit of patient searching. The best part of the wreck-site is the number of crustaceans that can be found, especially during the early summer months. It is possible to dive the area at all states of the tide, with the best time being after a spell of dry settled weather and light westerly winds, when visibility is at its best.

VANLAND

Wreck ★★
Scenery ★★★
Depth 5m
Reference N 54 32 185 W 00 43 372
Kettleness Point

The *Vanland* was a steel 1,285-ton Swedish steamship, registered at Gothenburg and had dimensions of 69.19m length, by 9.93m beam and a draught of 4.95m. She was owned at the time of loss by Angf. Aktieb. Suithied Weifdling and built by Campbeltown Shipbuilding Company at Campbeltown in 1893. Her single iron propeller was powered by a three-cylinder, triple-expansion steam engine that developed 112hp, using one boiler. Her machinery was built by Kincaid & Co. Ltd at Greenock. She also had one deck and a quarter-deck measuring 24.9m.

Late in the afternoon of 23 July 1917, the *Vanland* was on a voyage from Gothenburg to London with a general cargo, which included grease-proof paper, boxwood and undipped matchsticks. She was just off Runswick Bay, under the command of Captain C.A. Wallin, when the German submarine *UB-21* began shelling her. Desperately, Captain Wallin made an attempt to evade further attacks by the U-boat, but his vessel struck Kettleness Point at the same instant as a torpedo tore into her. The explosion killed six of her crew and caused serious damage to the vessel, then a major fire developed on board The surviving crew took to the ship's boat. Runswick lifeboat *Hester Rothschild* was launched at 8.30 p.m. and arrived at the scene just as the enemy submarine surfaced outside Runswick Bay. However, the U-boat captain made no further attacks and just watched as the remaining eighteen survivors were picked up by the lifeboat and taken back to Runswick. The ship burned for a whole week before she eventually settled on the bottom in the shallow water and became a total loss.

Wreck-site
The scattered remains of the ship are now well dispersed under a thick kelp bed, lying among the rocks just inside Kettleness Point. Very little remains, except lumps of jagged twisted steel and the occasional glimpse of non-ferrous metal. However, the wreck-site is very scenic with quite a variety of interesting marine life. It is diveable at any state of the tide and is a good novice dive, with very few currents to contend with. Visibility is reasonable during the summer months, after a spell of dry settled weather and westerly winds. The bell of the *Vanland* was recovered from the wreck and returned to her grateful owners.

MONARCH (ex-DANISH MONARCH)

Wreck ★★★★
Scenery ★
Depth 53m
Reference N 54 32 374 W 000 31 233
5 miles N.E. of Whitby.

The *Monarch* was an iron 1,318-ton Norwegian steamship, registered Christiania and had dimensions of 76.4m length, by 10.1m beam and a draught of 5.61m. She was owned, at the time of loss, by A/S D/S Monarch and built as *Danish Monarch* in 1878 by Wigham, Richardson & Co., at Newcastle-upon-Tyne. Her single iron propeller was powered by a two-cylinder compound-steam engine that developed 143hp, using one boiler.

On 23 May 1917, the *Monarch* was under the command of Captain N.O. Nielsen on a voyage from the Tees to St Nazaire, with a cargo of pitch, when she was torpedoed and sunk by the German submarine, *UB-41*, five miles north-east of Whitby.

Wreck-site

The wreck lies orientated in a north-west to south-east direction on a well swept seabed of sand, shells and pebbles, in a general depth of 53m, being the lowest astronomical depth. She is very substantial, standing upright some 6m high, although she is now collapsed, with her boiler, condenser and engine now visibly exposed through the pile of iron plates, box-sections, cogs, wheels, pipes and broken machinery. Lots of bent and flattened copper pipes and a few loose portholes can be seen amongst the jumble of iron debris that is dispersed over a fairly wide area of the seabed. Myriads of soft corals adorn the highest and most exposed structures and shoals of cod and pout-whiting hover over the boiler and engine area, while a number of very big crustaceans can usually be seen, but not easily caught.

Tidal streams are very strong and with poor to grim visibility. Therefore, this is a wreck-site for experienced technical divers only. A good lookout is also required because she is well into the main shipping lanes. The wreck should also be of interest to boat-anglers, when conditions are right.

LAMPADA (ex-SNILESWORTH)

Wreck ★★★★
Scenery ★
Depth 50m
Reference N 54 33 070 W 000 33 030
5 miles N.N.E. of Whitby

The *Lampada* was a steel 2,220-ton British steamship, registered at London and had dimensions of 85.64m length, by 12.19m beam and a draught of 5.99m. She was owned at the time of loss by the Gas Light & Coke Co. and built as the *Snilesworth* in 1889 by Short Brothers at Sunderland. Her single steel propeller was powered by a three-cylinder, triple-expansion steam engine that developed 209hp, using two boilers, her machinery was built by J. Dickinson, also at Sunderland. She had one deck, four watertight bulkheads and a superstructure consisting of a 9.7m poop-deck, 23.1m bridge-deck and a 9.7m forecastle. She was also armed with a stern mounted gun that fired 6lbs.

At 3.15 p.m. on the afternoon of 8 December 1917, the steamship was on passage from the Tyne for London with an unspecified cargo of coal, under the command of a Captain Wigam, with a crew of twenty-two, when she was torpedoed and sunk in heavy seas, by the German submarine *UB-75*. The crew all got away safely in the ship's two boats, but suddenly a huge wave swamped and capsized the boat which the captain was in, drowning two of the men. Three others were picked up dead or dying. A steamship rescued all the remaining survivors and later transferred them to a motor boat, which landed them at Whitby harbour. Altogether, five of the *Lampada's* crew died that day.

Wreck-site

This is a very large wreck, which, for her age, remains fairly substantial, standing more than 5m from the seabed in the midships section, with her stern gun still in place, but lying flat at the stern-end. She lies on a seabed of sand, gravel and broken shells in a general depth of 50m, being the lowest astronomical depth. Her boilers, condenser and engine are now visibly exposed and the propeller is still attached to the huge steel shaft at the stern-end, although the whole vessel has now totally collapsed. The wreck makes a very picturesque sight when a light is shone on the upper structures that are covered in an array of soft corals. She is dived very little, so most of her interesting equipment and navigational gear should be there too.

Often, shoals of pout-whiting and large cod are present during the summer months, so the site should make a good boat-angling venue, when conditions are right, especially on a neap tide. There is a 1m scour around the wreck-site, a sure sign of the very strong tidal streams that sweep over and round her. The site is a very dark one, with usually poor and rather gloomy visibility, so extra care should be taken, as there is always the chance of trawl nets becoming entangled on the wreck.

ELLIDA

Wreck ★★★★
Scenery ★
Depth 40m
Reference N 54 33 110 W 000 38 049
4 ½ miles N. of Whitby.

The *Ellida* was a steel 1,124-ton Norwegian steamship, registered in Bergen and had dimensions of 69.62m length, by 10.76m beam and a draught of 4.8m. She was owned by A. Halvorsen in Bergen and built in 1901 by Bergens M.V., at Bergen. Her single steel propeller was powered by a three-cylinder, triple-expansion steam engine that developed 101hp, using one boiler. She had one deck.

On the 19 April 1917, the *Ellida*, under the command of Captain S. Zahl, was in ballast on a voyage from Caen to the Tyne when she foundered and was lost after being torpedoed by the German submarine *UB-41*, some four and a half miles north of Whitby.

Wreck-site

The wreck lies on a dirty seabed of mud, sand, gravel and broken shells in a general depth of 40 metres, being the lowest astronomical depth, right next to the wreck of the *Afrique*. She is still fairly substantial, but has collapsed in on herself with her boiler, condenser and engine visible through the pile of twisted plates and box sections. Her bows and stern sections are now crumbling down, while the propeller still attached to the shaft, is standing upright and half buried in the seabed. There are lots of massive copper pipes and machinery protruding through the battered plates and remains of the collapsed bridge section. The wreck stands around four metres high and is covered in soft corals in the most exposed parts of her.

A large wolf-fish and a number of huge cod were lit up by the torch, which were sheltering among the steel wreckage, so the wreck should make an interesting boat angling venue, when conditions are right. However, there could be a few problems with the hooks and weights getting entangled in trawl nets, that hang like a shroud over the top structures, also great care is required when descending to the wreck during a dive. The best time to fish her will be during a neap tide, when things are fairly quiet. Tidal streams are very strong and visibility seriously grim, making it impossible to see anything without a good torch or lamp. This is a low, slack water dive-site and the best time to dive would be during a neap tide, after a spell of light westerly winds.

HERCULES

Wreck ★★★★
Scenery ★
Depth 39m
Reference N 54 33 655 W 000 39 948
4 miles N.E. of Runswick village.

The *Hercules* was a steel 1,295-ton Norwegian steamship, registered in Bergen, but requisitioned by the Admiralty and placed under the management of the shipping controller to use as a collier. She was built in 1909 by Bergenske Dampskibsaelskeb at Bergen and had dimensions of 71.67m length, by 10.41m beam and a draught of 4.39m. Her single steel propeller was powered by a three cylinder, triple expansion steam engine that developed 144hp using one boiler and her ancillary machinery was built by Bergens Mek Vaerks at Bergen. She had one deck and a 25.2m quarter-deck.

The vessel was also armed with one 610kg (12cwt) stern mounted deck gun that fired 5.45kg (12lb) shells.

At 3.50 p.m. on the afternoon of 30 December 1917, the *Hercules* was on passage from the Tyne for Newhaven, with a crew of twenty and an unspecified cargo of coal, under the command of Captain T. G. Schadberg, when she was torpedoed by the German submarine *UB-21*. The torpedo detonated amidships on the port side. Panic broke out among the crew as they tried to abandon ship. The captain and nine men drowned when their lifeboat capsized and the second officer had to take charge. He ordered the dinghy to be carefully lowered into the sea and the remaining ten crew clambered into it. Unfortunately, the weather was bad and, in the freezing conditions, two of the men died from exposure before they were picked up by a fishing vessel and landed at Whitby.

Wreck-site

The wreck lies on a dirty seabed of mud, sand, gravel and broken shells, in a general depth of 39m, the lowest astronomical depth. She is very substantial, but broken up and standing about 5m high, with her boiler and engine exposed and a donkey engine lying close-by, surrounded by collapsed hull plates and broken machinery. The bows and stern section are covered in soft corals and her iron propeller is still in place. However, at least one trawl net hangs over the bow section like a curtain. There are lots of large copper pipes, massive brass valves and a large pump to be seen around the midships section, which is the highest part of the wreck. Most of the vessel's interesting equipment should still be around, although it is doubtful if her bell is still in place.

This is quite a gloomy wreck-site, with very strong tidal streams and usually extremely poor visibility, which improves significantly during the summer months, although you still need a very powerful torch to see anything. Lots of big fish have also been seen, including cod and ling of at least ten kilos, so she will make an excellent boat-angling venue, with the best time being during a neap tide. The wreck is best dived at low, slack water on a neap tide, after a dry spell of weather.

MERRY ISLINGTON

Wreck ★★★
Scenery ★
Depth 48m
Reference N 54 34 002 W 000 32 120
6 miles N.E. of Whitby

The *Merry Islington* was an iron 147-ton British steam fishing trawler that had dimensions of 30.58m length, by 6.27m beam and a draught of 3.35m. She was built as trawler No.99551 in yard 81 at hull by Cook, Welton & Gemmell, launched on 21 November 1891 and registered at the port of Hull as H192 on 17 December 1891 for her new owners, the Humber Steam Trawling Co. Ltd, who were the owners at the time of loss. Her single iron propeller was powered by a two-cylinder, compound-steam engine that developed 45hp, with one boiler. Her machinery was built by Bailey & Leetham of Hull. She had one deck, three watertight bulkheads and a 6.1m quarter-deck.

On 6 May 1915, the vessel was out on a fishing trip from her home port of Hull and was some six miles east of Whitby when she was captured by a German submarine. The crew was forced to abandon ship and the *Merry Islington* was sunk by explosive scuttling charges that were placed below deck.

Wreck-site
The wreck of what is believed to be that of *Merry Islington* is said to be lying orientated in a north-north-west to south-south-east direction on a seabed of

The steam trawler Merry Islington *leaving port for the fishing ground in 1914.* Courtesy of Kingston-upon-Hull Museum & Art Galleries.

dirty sand, shell, pebbles and gravel in a general depth of 48m, the lowest astronomical depth. She is totally collapsed, well decayed, broken up and rather dispersed, with her boiler and engine exposed. The boiler is reported to be burst open and lying on its side, surrounded by a small mound of iron debris and a few pieces of non ferrous metal.

This is a dark, rather dismal wreck-site, with brittle starfish covering the seabed, but little else in the way of marine life. Tidal streams are very strong and the underwater visibility is said to be normally rather grim.

HURSTWOOD

Wreck ★★★★
Scenery ★
Depth 54m
Reference N 54 34 401 W 000 28 582
8 miles N-E of Whitby.

The *Hurstwood* was a steel 1,229-ton British merchant steamship, registered at London, with dimensions of 68.58m length, by 11.04m beam and a draught of 4.34m. She was owned by Cory Colliers Ltd and built in 1906 by S.P. Austin & Son at Sunderland. Her single propeller was powered by a three-cylinder, triple-expansion steam engine that developed 179hp, using one boiler Her machinery was built by George Clark Ltd at Sunderland. She had one deck, a 6.7m poop-deck, 17m quarter-deck, 14.3m bridge-deck and 7.6m forecastle.

On 5 February 1917, the *Hurstwood* was in ballast and carrying a crew of fifteen on a voyage from London to pick up a cargo of coal at Newcastle-upon-Tyne. She was under the command of Captain A. Carlson, making nine knots, when the periscope of a German submarine, (later identified as the *UB-3*) was seen about 140m off her port beam.

At 11.50 a.m. and almost at the same instant, a torpedo detonated on her port side, abreast of the engine room. Captain Carlson ordered the engine stopped and the crew to take to the boat. Unfortunately, three of them had been injured in the massive explosion and the master had to attend to their wounds, before helping them into the boat. After a roll-call it was discovered that a fireman, the chief and second engineer, who had all been in the engine room when she was hit, were missing. There was no response to the crew's shouts. The vessel was going down fast and the engine room was half full of oil and water, so the captain ordered the crew to abandon ship. An armed trawler picked up the survivors almost immediately and took them to Whitby, where the injured received further treatment for their wounds, However, a donkeyman, one of the three injured, had already died in the boat. The *Hurstwood* remained afloat for one hour and twenty five minutes after being torpedoed and went down to the bottom at 1.15 p.m.

Wreck-site
The wreck of the *Hurstwood* is said to be lying orientated in a north-west to south-east direction on a seabed of sand, shell, gravel, pebbles and mud in a general depth of 54m, the lowest astronomical depth. She has now totally collapsed in a large jumbled heap. The highest section is around the boiler and engine, at $4\frac{1}{2}$ m high, both of which are now exposed and visible, surrounded by a number of steel cogs, pipes, broken machinery and steel debris. The majority of the vessel's most interesting equipment and navigational gear will probably still be somewhere amongst the jumbled pile of steel debris and it will take some finding in such depths (another report has this wreck lying upside down, but totally collapsed and well broken up.).

The wreck seems to attract quite a variety of large fish and should make an excellent boat angling venue, when conditions are right. The best time to visit and fish her would be on a neap tide, when the current is not so strong. Tidal streams are usually very strong and with rather grim visibility. A good torch is an essential piece of equipment.

ENTERPRIZE

Wreck ★★
Scenery ★★★
Depth 8m
Reference N 54 34 74 W 000 47 02
Also given: N 54 33 49 W 000 47 09
Crowbar Steel, Staithes.

The *Enterprize* was a steel 2,002-ton British steamship, registered at Whitby, however other records have her down as being registered at the port of Cardiff. She was owned by F. H. Kirkhouse & Company and had dimensions of 86.56m length, by 11.6m beam and a draught of 5.53m. The vessel was built in 1888 by J.L. Thompson & Sons, at Sunderland and her machinery was built by T. Richardson & Sons, at Hartlepool. Her single steel propeller was powered by a three-cylinder, triple-expansion steam engine that developed 202hp, using two boilers. She had one deck, a well-deck, six watertight bulkheads and a superstructure consisting of a 8.8m poop-deck, a 22.6m quarter-deck and an 11m forecastle.

The *Enterprize*, under the command of Captain J. Rutherford, was on passage from Wallsend for Rotterdam in thick fog, carrying two passengers a crew of sixteen and a cargo of coal when she drove ashore on Cowbar Steel at 11 p.m. on the 15 June 1907. Several local fishing cobles put out to assist her, but the weather began to deteriorate, so they embarked the captain's wife and young daughter and returned to shore. Staithe's new 10.7m self-righting lifeboat *James Gowland* was launched on its very first call-out at 1.30 p.m. and rescued fifteen members of the steamer's crew, but the Captain, who was convinced he could save his vessel, refused to leave. The rescued men were brought ashore and the lifeboat returned to stand by the steamer. By the following morning, it was found that her double bottoms were badly damaged and with over 2m of water in the engine room, there was little hope of saving the ship so Captain Rutherford was taken aboard the lifeboat and landed back at Staithes.

The vessel's deck-machinery was recovered by a well-known local salvor, Captain Round and was landed the following week at Scotch Head, at Whitby. Then, apart from a small amount of salvage, the *Enterprize* was abandoned to the sea.

Wreck-site
Don Foster of Stockton, reckons the wreck of the *Enterprize* is the best of three wrecks which lie near to each other on the edge of Crowbar Steel and is quite easy to find, being accessible from the shore. She lies in an average depth of 8m, the lowest astronomical depth and is now totally collapsed, well broken up, with her two boilers still on site, surrounded by lots of steel plates, beams, twisted framework and ribs, some sections actually stand 2m high. Bottom plating and the propeller shaft can be found about 25m from the end of the sewer out-fall. The wreck makes a nice novice and rummage dive, where crustaceans can be found

The steamer Enterprize *drove ashore on Crow Bar Steel, near Staithes, during thick fog on 15 June 1907 and became a total wreck.*

and the odd 'goody' sometimes turns up amongst the pile of debris. The best time to dive the wreck is in calm weather and light winds at low tide.

Access to the site from the shore is via the tiny village of Crowbar, built right under the massively high cliffs. To reach the site, you can drive down the very steep, winding road, where first gear is strongly advised. Drop the diving gear off at the bottom and take the vehicle back up the hill and park near to a small row of cottages, which look as though they are going to slip into the sea. The sea here is slowly eroding the cliffs away and the approach road on the top of the cliffs is said to have been moved further inland at least three times and three cottages have disappeared.

The dive-site is on the seaward side of Crowbar Nab. It is necessary to walk along the concrete pier until you reach the old sewer pipe. The pipe is said to have a flat edge and this is your mark. At low water you can walk part of the way along its line. When you arrive at the edge of the first underwater ledge; continue on this line for about another 25m and you will come to the wreck-site.

DEPTFORD

Wreck ★★★★
Scenery ★
Depth 29m
Reference N 54 34 800 W 000 47 509
1½ miles N. of Crowbar Nab, near Staithes.

The *Deptford* was an early British iron steamship that was registered at Shields. She had a single iron propeller, which was powered by a two-cylinder, compound-steam engine that used two boilers.

On 13 March 1862, the old vessel ran aground on the Whitby Rock during a dense fog. Both of Whitby's lifeboats were launched. It was the first time in service for the *Lucy*. However, the faster and lighter of the two boats, the private lifeboat, *Fisherman's Friend*, reached the stricken steamer first. The crew shared with the steam tugs in the salvage award for saving the ship. The *Deptford* was successfully re-floated on the high tide and taken in tow, but her hull was very badly damaged. Even though frantic efforts were made to stem the flood of water rushing into her engine-room, she foundered and was lost some two and a quarter miles off Boulby, near Staithes.

Wreck-site
Local fishermen and anglers refer to this wreck as the 'Navigator', while local divers have christened her the 'Toilet Wreck', because a bronze toilet was discovered in her. The remains of the *Deptford* lie on a dirty sand-mud seabed, in a general depth of 29m, the lowest astronomical depth. She is surprisingly large for such an old wreck, although totally collapsed, except for her bow section, which is report to be still intact. The two boilers and large engine are surrounded by a mass of twisted iron plates, copper pipes, a donkey engine with a hole through it and broken machinery, although sections of her stand almost 4m high around midships. At the stern end are two propellers, one is attached to a shaft and the other is probably a spare, while the ribs and plates making up the outline of the ship, can be plainly seen. Occasionally a few small shoals of fish, mainly pout-whiting, can be seen hovering over the wreck, but she is hardly worth spending much time boat angling over.

The best time to see the *Deptford* is at low, slack water, on a neap tide. Visibility is never very remarkable, because the site is very near to the outfall from the Boulby Potash Mine. Also, tidal streams are fairly strong, so great care should be taken, especially as nets could get caught up on the wreck.

SCHALDIS (ex-WILFRID)

Wreck ★★★
Scenery ★
Depth 42m
Reference N 54 35 202 W 000 40 882
4½ miles N.-E. of Runswick village.

The *Schaldis* was an iron 1,241-ton Belgian steamship, registered in Antwerp and had dimensions of 72.56m length, by 9.75m beam and a draught of 5.48m. She was owned at the time of loss by Soc. Anon. Belge de Nav. a Vap. Sch. and built as the *Wilfred* in 1878 by T. Turnbull & Son at Whitby. Her single iron propeller was powered by a two-cylinder, compound steam engine that developed 135hp, using one boiler and her machinery was built by Blair & Co. Ltd at Stockton-on-Tees. She had one deck, a 24.7m quarter-deck, 17.6m bridge-deck and a 10.4m forecastle.

On 29 March 1917, the *Schaldis* was on a voyage from the Tyne to Calais with a cargo of coke, under the command of a Captain Hermann, when she was torpedoed and sunk by a German submarine, possibly the *UB-21*, four and a half miles north-east of Runswick Village.

Wreck-site
The wreck, believed to be the *Schaldis*, lies orientated in a north-west to south-east direction on a sea-bed of sand, shell, gravel and pebbles, in a general depth of 42m, the lowest astronomical depth. Now the wreck has completely collapsed and is well broken up, standing around 3m high amidships, where her boiler and engine are exposed and surrounded by masses of broken machinery and decayed iron plates. Lots of bent and flattened copper pipes, pieces of broken hollow mast, brass flanges and valves can be seen, intermingled with the rest of the iron debris, which is all covered in sediment. A few large fish were observed, but not very many, however this is a fair sized wreck, so there may be lots more around the wreck's perimeters or in amongst the wreckage itself.

Visibility is very poor and tidal streams are fairly strong, so this is no place for the inexperienced diver. The best time to visit her for diving or angling would be at low, slack water, during neap tides.

MIRANDA

Wreck ★★★
Scenery ★
Depth 43m
Reference N 54 36 847 W 000 42 390
3 ½ miles N.-E. of Staithes.

The *Miranda* was an iron 954-ton British steamship, registered in London and had dimensions of 71.93m length, by 8.55m beam and a draught of 4.74m. She was owned at the time of loss by the Miranda Steam Ship Co. Ltd at Sunderland and built by Palmers Company Ltd at Newcastle-upon-Tyne in 1865. The single iron propeller was powered by a two-cylinder compound steam engine that developed 105hp, using one boiler. She had one deck, a well-deck, a 20.7m quarter-deck and 10.4m bridge-deck.

On 14 March 1899, the *Miranda* was on passage from Hartlepool for London when she foundered and was lost three and a half miles north-east of Staithes. She was under the command of Captain F. Stothard and carrying a cargo of coal, sixteen crewmen and two passengers, both of whom were stowaways. It is not known why she sank or if anyone was lost, as the wind at the time was a moderate westerly force four and weather conditions were very reasonable.

Wreck-site

The wreck lies orientated in an east-north-east to west-south-west direction, on a sea-bed of dirty sand, shell, gravel and pebbles, in a general depth of 43 metres, the lowest astronomical depth. She has totally collapsed, is badly decayed and well broken up. Her highest point was around the boiler and engine area, standing three to four metres in the central midships section. Lots of flattened and bent copper-pipes, cogs, an iron wheel, broken iron and brass machinery are protruding out of the pile of iron plates, ribs and girders. A number of lobsters and several big cod and a large angler-fish have been observed in the wreck debris, so the site may be worth investigating as a boat-angling venue. It is also very likely that many, if not all, of the vessel's most interesting instruments are still somewhere in the mound of debris. This is a very dark and gloomy wreck-site, so a powerful torch is recommended. Being so deep, only experienced divers should attempt to visit her.

Tidal streams are very strong and visibility is pretty grim. The best time to dive her is on a low, neap tide, after a spell of dry settled weather, preferably during the summer months. The wreck-site is a long way from land and close to the main shipping lanes, so a good lookout is required on the boat.

COMMERCIAL

Wreck ★★★
Scenery ★
Depth 51m
Reference N 54 37 022 W 000 29 683
10 miles N-N-E of Whitby.

The *Commercial* was a steel 496-ton British steamship, registered in London and had dimensions of 50.36m length, by 8.75m beam and a draught of 4.03m. She was owned by the Commercial Gas Co. of London and built by J. Fullerton & Co. at Paisley in 1902. Her single steel propeller was powered by a two-cylinder, compound steam engine that developed 75hp, using one boiler. Her machinery was built by McKie & Baxter Ltd, at Glasgow. She had one deck, four watertight bulkheads, a 5.8m poop-deck and 5.8m forecastle.

On 16 of January 1904, during wind conditions west-north-west blowing a force five, the *Commercial* foundered ten miles north-north-east of Whitby, without the loss of any of her fourteen crewmen. She was under the command of Captain G. Skelton on passage from Tyne Dock for London carrying a cargo of coal. Unfortunately, the reason she sank is unclear.

Wreck-site
Her wreck lies orientated in a west-north-west to east-south-east direction, on a sea-bed of sand, shell and pebbles, in a general depth of 51m, the lowest astronomical

depth. She has totally collapsed, is broken up and well decayed scattered over an area of about 50 by 15m. Her boiler is on its side and the condenser has split open, while the remains of her engine appear rather flattened and are surrounded by a mound of broken machinery and steel plates. This site has a star rating of three, because it is almost certain that most of the *Commercial's* interesting bridge equipment will still be somewhere around the wreck-site, including her bell.

Very little marine life has been observed on or around the wreck-site, although a few fish were picked up with the echo-sounder. Tidal streams are very strong and a lot of pre-planning will be needed, because she is a long way off shore. This is a wreck dive for very experienced only. There are no reports of marine life around, so she will hardly be worth fishing over.

STEPHANOTIS

Wreck ★★★★
Scenery ★
Depth 47m
Reference N 54 37 402 W 000 44 255
6 miles N.-N.E. of Staithes.

The *Stephanotis* was an iron 1,045-ton British steamship, registered at North Shields and had dimensions of 67.18m length, by 9.29m beam and a draught of 5.84m. She was owned at the time of loss by Robson, Brown & Sons at Sunderland and built in 1871 by Lliff Mounsey & Co. at Sunderland. Her single iron propeller was powered by a two-cylinder, compound steam engine that developed 98hp, using one boiler and her machinery was built by R.&W. Hawthorn at Newcastle-upon-Tyne. She had one deck, four watertight bulkheads and a centrally positioned 13.7m quarter-deck.

The *Stephanotis* foundered and was lost on 30 April 1901, following a collision with the Newcastle registered steamship *Guyers*, six miles north-east of Staithes. She was on a voyage from Bilbao to Middlesbrough, carrying a cargo of iron ore and a crew of sixteen, under the command of Captain R. Thompson. Why the two vessels collided is not known, because sea and wind conditions, being south-south-east force two, were quite good at the time, although it may have been foggy or at night.

The *Guyers* sank within minutes, as she was the most seriously damaged and the smaller of the two vessels. Her crew took to the boats, while the *Stephanotis* attempted to reach shallow water, but her pumps could not cope with the deluge of water flooding through her damaged hull and she too foundered, soon after the collision. There are no records of any losses as a result of the incident or at what time the two vessels sank.

Wreck-site

The wreck, believed to be that of the *Stephanotis*, lies on a dirty sea-bed of sand, mud, gravel and shells, in a general depth of 46m, the lowest astronomical depth. She is reported as orientated in a south-south-east to north-north-west direction and has totally collapsed, is well broken up and badly decayed, with her boiler, condenser and engine visibly exposed and a large broken mast lying across the wreckage.

There are three main high points, with the highest point, part of her stern, standing some 5.2m at the southern end, while the remains of the wreck covers an area of about 70 by 20m. There appears to be very little marine life about, but extra caution is required when descending, because a large trawl net floats like a shroud above the wreck, kept up by what appears to be dozens of little plastic floats. Tidal streams are very strong and the visibility is usually pretty grim, making a good torch essential. As this wreck is so deep, this is a site only for very experienced divers.

GUYERS

Wreck ★★★
Scenery ★
Depth 47m
Reference 54 37 813 W 000 42 827
6 miles N.N.E. of Staithes

The *Guyers* was an iron 522-ton British steamship, registered at the port of Newcastle-upon-Tyne and had dimensions of 54.99m length, by 7.18m beam and a draught of 3.96m. She was owned at the time of loss by P.S. Haggie of Newcastle and was built in 1864 by Coulson, Cook & Co. Ltd at Newcastle-upon-Tyne. Her single iron propeller was powered by a two-cylinder, compound steam engine that developed 60hp, using one boiler. Her machinery was built by the Ouseburn Engineering Works, at Newcastle. She had one deck, a well-deck, four watertight bulkheads, a 27.1m quarter-deck and 6.1m forecastle.

The steamship *Guyers* foundered on 30 April 1901, following a collision with the North Shields-registered steamship *Stephanotis*, six miles off Staithes. She was under the command of a Captain Peacock, on passage from Seaham for Fecamp, with a cargo of coal and a crew of thirteen. Both vessels sank soon after the collision. However, it is not known if anyone died in the incident.

Wreck-site

This wreck, believed to be that of the steamship *Guyers*, lies on a dirty sea-bed of sand, shell, gravel, pebbles and mud, in a general depth of 47m, the lowest astronomical depth. The wreck has totally collapsed, is well broken up, badly decayed and stands only 3m high around her midships section, where a donkey-engine, a condenser, her boiler, and an engine are lying.

A number of brass wash/scupper-plates, port-holes and interesting, though flattened, brass lamps were also visible in the collapsed pile of debris. At least one trawl net is entangled with the remains and the site is a very dark and gloomy one, which requires a good torch. Extremely poor visibility and very strong tidal streams make this a wreck for only very experienced divers. Very little marine life could be seen on or around the wreck-site, but most wrecks collect a few resident fish.

LEMNOS

Wreck ★★
Scenery ★★
Depth 6m
Reference N 54 38 280 W 001 07 130
Also: N 54 38 310 W 001 07 100

The *Lemnos* was an iron 1,530-ton British steamship, registered at Dundee and had dimensions of 82.37m length, by 10.36m beam and a draught of 5.66m. She was built in 1880 by Short Brothers at Sunderland and owned by the Lawside Shipping Co. Ltd. Her single iron propeller was powered by a two-cylinder, compound steam engine that developed 174hp, using two boilers. Her machinery was built by G. Clark in Sunderland. She had one deck, four watertight bulkheads and a superstructure that consisted of a 9.7m poop-deck, 21.9m quarter-deck, 16.4m bridge-deck and a 8.2m forecastle.

The *Lemnos* was under the command of Captain G. Hadden, on a voyage from Leith to Rouen with an unspecified cargo of coal and a crew of nineteen, when she stranded in shallow water on 16 December 1915, very close to the position where the wreck of the *Guildford* now lies. The vessel is thought to have broken her back and became a total wreck. She was substantially salvaged and then sold to a Mr Riddle of Middlesbrough on 16 August 1960.

Wreck-site
The wreck was originally marked by a buoy, but it is uncertain whether the buoy still remains in place. It is well broken up and dispersed over a wide area of the slag-covered seabed. Nothing of this 1,530-ton wreck is recognisable today and there is very little of interest remaining. However, the scattered bits and pieces of iron plate and angle iron provide good shelter for numerous crustaceans. There is no need to worry about tidal streams. It is possible to dive the site at any state of the tide, but the underwater visibility is at the mercy of the river Tees. The wreck is best dived after a spell of dry, settled weather.

HARVEST

Wreck ★★★
Scenery ★★
Depth 10m
Reference N 54 38 950 W 001 07 780
Also: N 54 38 934 W 001 07 944
½ mile E. of South Gare Light.

The *Harvest* was a steel 1,380-ton British steamship, registered at Hartlepool and had dimensions of 74.67m length, by 10.08m beam and a draught of 4.87m. She was built by Irvine & Co. at Hartlepool, in 1881, for H. Smurthwaite of Middlesbrough, but at the time of her loss, she was owned by Messrs English & Co. of Middlesbrough. Her single steel propeller was powered by a three-cylinder, triple-expansion engine that developed 130hp, using one boiler. Her machinery was built by T. Richardson & Sons of Hartlepool. She had one deck, four watertight bulkheads, and her superstructure consisted of a 9.4m forecastle and a reinforced quarter-deck measuring 62.8.m.

On 30 November 1885, the *Harvest* was at the entrance to the river Tees in wind conditions west-north-west force four when she was in a collision with the Whitby-registered steamship *Stainsacre*, which foundered and was lost. The *Stainsacre* was on passage from the Tyne for Copenhagen with a cargo of coal and a crew of seventeen. It is thought that the crew were taken off the vessel before she sank.

For years later the *Harvest* left Middlesbrough on 12 September 1889, under the command of Captain G. Moorsom, on passage for Stettin, with a 1,750-ton cargo of cast iron and pig iron ingots, when she was in another collision at the Tees entrance, with the Middlesborough-registered steamship *Regent*. The *Harvest* was badly damaged and foundered soon after and fortunately her crew managed to evacuate the stricken ship without loss. At the time of the collision there was a very light force one northerly wind blowing.

The following was a report that appeared in the *North Eastern Daily Gazette* on Friday 13 September 1889:

> 'A Middlesbrough vessel sunk in the Tees: The Crew saved.'

> Early yesterday morning a serious collision occurred at the mouth of the Tees. The screw steamer *Harvest* owned by Messrs English & Co. of Middlesbrough, commanded by Captain Moorson, having loaded a cargo of 1,750 tons of pig-iron, sailed from Middlesbrough to Stettin on the morning tide, the crew of 18 hands, all told, when just at the mouth of the river, she was struck on her port side just behind her foremast, by the screw steamer *Regent*, and sank. The weather was fine and clear. The *Regent* is a vessel of 1,000 tons burthen and owned by Messrs Edward Harris & Co. of Middlesbrough. Her Master was Captain Britton and she

was making for the Tees Light from Portland, with a crew of 14 hands.

The *Harvest* was so considerably damaged that she sank almost directly after the catastrophe. The crew were picked up by the steam-tug *Ryhope* and conveyed back to Middlesbrough.

Serious damage was also done to the *Regent* about the bows, but she was able to proceed to Middlesbrough, where she was laid up by the shipyard of Messrs Raylton Dixon & Co. Ltd. Attempts are being made to raise the sunken vessel, and with the present favourable weather, the efforts will probably be successful.

Wreck-site

This wreck is used by many local sub-aqua clubs to train novice divers and as an introductory dive-site. She lies on a flat sea-bed of sand and gravel and lots of small rocks, in a general depth of 10-12m. Although well broken up, she is quite substantial and covers a large area of seabed, where some quite large sections of double bottom plates, steel deck beams and twisted balustrades can be found. The stern steering quadrant can be traced and the main stern post stands about 3m high. It is completely covered in Dead Man's Fingers, which makes it looks very ghostly as you fin towards it. By following the post down to the seabed, the stub-end remains of the propeller can be seen. Moving from this point, you come to the prop-shaft casing, which is holed in places, exposing the prop-shaft. In the middle section, you arrive at the engine block, with lots of brass valves and short lengths of copper pipes attached, polished by every passing diver. Don Foster, who gave this report, believes this to be part of another wreck, which is said to lie close by, possibly that of the steamship *Stirling*. The main feature of the *Harvest* is the remains of her cargo of pig iron and cast iron ingots, which can be seen piled up in a 4m mound at the stern-end and criss-crossed with many nooks and crannies where crustaceans are often found. Adjacent to the ingot piles are large sections of hull standing on a bed of clay. Over the past ten years or so the wreck has been steadily uncovering and many portholes have come to light, along with some pewter bowls and a wonderful old sextant. However, the ship's boiler cannot be seen, as it was salvaged not long after she sank.

Visibility can be poor on the wreck-site following north or north-easterly winds and at times the dredgers can spoil it as the dirt is washed down from the dumping grounds. However, from May to the end of October it is usually good, often averaging 4-5m. Spring tides cause some strong drift, but the site is still fairly easily dived. Shoals of pout whiting and coley frequent the wreck and the occasional crustacean can be found, sheltering under the debris, while in late August and September the area is often alive with big shoals of sandeels and mackerel.

Boats can be launched (a launch fee is payable by non-members) at the nearby South Gare Marine Club, which also has a small cafe on site. Boats can be also launched free from the lifeboat slipway at Redcar.

Air is available from B.S.A.C. 43 Branch, whose clubhouse is only 200m away, or from Chris Denny on the esplanade at Redcar, approximately two miles away.

IDA DUNCAN (ex-STURGEON)

Wreck ★★
Scenery ★★
Depth 10m
Reference N 54 39 003 W 01 07 898
½ mile off South Gare Breakwater, Teesmouth

The *Ida Duncan* was an iron steam tug of 139 tons, registered at Middlesbrough, and had dimensions of 28.95m length, by 6.17m beam and a draught of 3.17m. She was owned at the time of loss by C. Duncan & Sons Ltd and built as the *Sturgeon* in 1891 by J.P. Rennoldson & Sons at South Shields. Her single iron propeller was powered by a two-cylinder, compound steam engine that developed 40hp, using one boiler.

The vessel operated under the command of Captain I.J. Baker and she carried a crew of six, working in and around the mouth of the Tees. On 31 January 1917, she was *en-route* from Middlesbrough to Tees Bay when she struck a German mine, half a mile from the mouth of the Tees, near to the South Gare lighthouse. The explosion killed all of her crew and actually lifted the boat out of the water. Her stern-end went straight under the water, however the vessel's bows remained bobbing on the surface for a further fifteen minutes before she finally went down to the bottom. As she was very close to the shipping lane and in such shallow water, the wreck was later dispersed, using explosives.

Wreck-site
The wreck is totally collapsed and very broken up. As it is so small and dispersed the remains are really only suitable as a novice or rummage dive these days. Her boiler is collapsed, but the bow section is very clear. However, the shape of her hull can still be made out, along with a few lumps of battered machinery and iron framework, but there is not very much left of her to stir the imagination. Don Foster of Teeside informed me that some years ago two of his friends found a lovely telegraph, about one metre long, protruding from the sand, very close to the wreck-site. Later, on the same dive, they found a beautiful brass steam-whistle not far away. One week later it was cleaned up, connected to an air-line and it sounded as good as new.

There are reports that there is a broken paddle wheel on one side of the hull. However, records indicate that the *Ida Duncan* was in fact a small iron screw-driven vessel, so it may have come from the 'Tees Tug' or one of the many paddlers that operated around the Tees area. Very little marine life can be found at the wreck-site, but it may attract the occasional crustacean. Tidal streams are fairly moderate, but the underwater visibility is usually very poor and is greatly influenced by the river Tees.

Steam Paddle Tug

The wreck of the *Ida Duncan* is said to be very close to what is referred to as the 'Tee's Tug', which has similar dimensions and lies about twenty metres away to the east. Just off this site is a paddle-wheel measuring about 3.5m in diameter by 1m deep, with the spokes running from the central hub, but there is no trace of the paddles. In the centre of the wreckage is a heap of copper boiler tubes. However, I have no records to indicate what this vessel was called or why she sank.

Wooden Decked Wreck

It is worth visiting an unknown wreck of about 35m length, by 6-7m beam is also said to lie approximately 50m north-west of the *Ida Duncan* in 12-14m of water. The intact outline of her hull can clearly be made out, which stands about 1-1$\frac{1}{2}$m above the sandy seabed. There is a large section of timber decking still in position, but it has collapsed and there is a large grapple type anchor standing upright in the middle of the wreckage, while the stern-end, with rudder details, can also be seen. Three or four years ago, Don Foster discovered and lifted a large teak pulley block, which had a big steel hook built into it and when stood up, it measured just over 1m in length. Don says that this is probably the wreckage of some type of barge, that was possibly used for salvage work, but was certainly not a hopper.

Both wrecks are said to be difficult to locate. Many people find them by dragging an anchor about. The wrecks are only some fifteen minutes away from the launch site, so they are quite easy to fit into a visit.

Unknown Steamship Wreck, (Casseo-Pape)
Depth 7-9m
Reference 50-70m in line with the end of South Gare and almost in line with the lighthouse.

This is a shore dive, with access from the old slipway on the eastern side of the South Gare breakwater, where the diver will find a number of large 1.5 by 1.5m concrete blocks on the left hand side. Towards the end of the Gare, the blocks are all jumbled together on top of each other, leaving many cavities in and around them, where crustaceans can be found from spring to autumn and large shoals of sprat and mackerel in July and August.

Moving away from the blocks at the Gare-end, dispersed and scattered wreckage will appear. While there is no sign of the hull, there is lots of deck machinery to be seen, including big winches, steel beams, large piles of heavy chain, which looks as if it had just fallen out of a chain-locker and a little further out lie two large anchors. The site is said to be an interesting rummage dive where anything could turn up, following a storm. It appears to be a vessel that ran into the end of the Gare at sometime or other, but no records can be found to identify her. The B.S.A.C. Teeside 43 Branch call the wreck, the 'Casseo-Pape', after the two buddies who first found her, many years ago.

CLAVERING

Wreck ★★
Scenery ★★
Depth 4-8m
Reference N 54 38 480, W 001 08 420
$\frac{1}{3}$ mile off South Gare, Teesmouth.

The *Clavering* was a steel 3,300-ton steamship, registered in London and owned by E. Haslehurst of London. She had dimensions of approximately 105.9m length, by 13.5m beam and a draught of 5.6m, while her single iron propeller was powered by a three-cylinder, triple-expansion steam engine that used three boilers.

Under the command of Captain J. Scott, the *Clavering* left Middlesbrough on passage for Japan with a cargo of pitch, cast-iron ingots and a crew of sixty-two, but at 6 a.m. in the morning of 31 January 1907, she was just leaving the Tees mouth and ran into a force ten northerly storm. The mountainous seas and howling wind drove the vessel near to the North Gare breakwater where she stranded and huge waves pounded her from stem to stern. Seaton Carew's lifeboat *Charles Ingleby* was launched and managed to rescue fifteen of the *Clavering's* crew. However, further attempts to reach her were made impossible by the flooding tide. At 3.30 p.m., a tug with West Hartlepool Pilots on board, towed the *Charles Ingleby* as close as possible to the wreck, but could not get close enough to render assistance.

Hartlepool's No.1 self-righting lifeboat *Ilminster* was taken to Seaton Carew by road and when the tide turned both lifeboats made repeated, but unsuccessful, attempts to reach the *Clavering* until 2 a.m. the following morning. In freezing weather at daybreak, conditions had settled a little, so the two lifeboats went back out to the stricken vessel and between them, rescued the remaining twenty-four surviving crewmen. Of the twenty people who lost their lives seventeen were Lascar seamen and one passenger. The Coxswain's of both lifeboats, Shepherd Sotheran and John Franklin, were awarded the RNLI's silver medal for their gallantry.

Wreck-site
Many local divers are confused with the remains of the *Clavering* and refer to her as the steamship *Carlo*. The two wrecks are quite mixed together, but the cargo of iron-ingots and pitch shows where at least part of the *Clavering* lies. The wreckage covers a large area and the site is reported to be a first class rummage dive. However, she is also largely buried in the sand, lying in two parts and scattered on some spoil-ground on the outer end of North Gare Sands. In recent times, lots of trinkets and 'goodies' have been recovered, such as portholes, copper-plate, a nice engine-room telegraph, complete with all its cogs, and chains and bell, so who knows what else may lie concealed under the sand and debris. There are no boilers on site, as these were salvaged soon after the vessel sank, but the prop shaft

is still there. Although mostly covered by plates and beams, it can be traced along and makes a good reference point, giving the diver a clue to her overall layout.

The wreck-site is a big jumble of twisted beams and bent steel plates. By finning through the middle of her you come across the cargo of iron-ingots, which indicates the site is one of her holds. Beyond this point where the bottom is exposed in places and looks like smooth, flat rock, closer inspection reveals it to be part of her cargo of black pitch. In the centre of the debris there is a small Admiralty anchor, approximately one and a half metres long, with one fluke completely buried under heavy plate, but this is most likely to be from another vessel. A little away from this area some heavy lengths of chain can be spotted. A considerable number of small crustaceans can be seen around the wreck and under the rocks around the outer edge of the scour and Dead Man's Fingers cover some of the debris and rocks.

Visibility is reasonable after a spell of dry settled weather with westerly winds and during neap tides, but any wind blowing from the north and north-east usually makes diving impractical.

The wreck lies inside the mouth of the river Tees, just to the west side of the main channel and permission to dive should be first sought from the Harbour Master. The river and port are very busy and it is common to see large bulk carriers of over 10,000 tons using the channel and it can be nerve-racking to be underwater when one of these vessels passes by. Launching is possible from South Gare Marine Club slipway, only half a mile from the wreck-site, although non-members must pay a day-launch fee. Advice about the wreck can be sought from members of the Teeside 43 Branch of the BSAC, whose clubhouse overlooks the wreck-site.

CARLO

Wreck ★★
Scenery ★★
Depth 2-8m
Reference N 54 38 480 W 001 08 420
738 metres from South Gare Light

The *Carlo* was an iron 1,307-ton Norwegian registered steamship, that had dimensions of around 73m length by 9.5m beam and her single iron propeller was powered by a three-cylinder, triple-expansion steam engine that used one boiler.

On 30 January 1901, the *Carlo* was on passage from Bilbao for Middlesbrough, with a cargo of iron-ore, when she stranded in the mouth of the Tees and became a total loss, later being dispersed with explosives to seabed level.

Wreck-site
The wreck is now totally collapsed, broken up, decayed and well dispersed in depths between 2-8m. Local divers say her remains lie scattered on sand and spoil-

An early lifeboat crew at Whitby preparing to launch, with the help from sailors and volunteers. Courtesy of the Whitby RNLI Lifeboat Museum and Shop.

ground and are partially buried and jumbled up with those of the steamship *Clavering* on the outer-end of North Gare Sands. She is reputed to be an excellent rummage dive where lots of interesting finds have been discovered over the past few years. However, there is no boiler on site, because, along with the engines, this was salvaged when the vessel stranded. When part of the bridge section was located, some 30m away from the main wreck, the telegraph and compass were found still intact. The area is a massive scrap-bed of broken, bent and twisted iron and steel, which sometimes shelters the occasional crustacean. Various species of crabs can be seen and some of the rocks have Dead Man's Fingers attached to them.

Visibility is reasonable after a spell of dry settled weather with westerly winds and during a neap tide, but any wind from the north and north-east usually makes diving difficult. The wreck lies inside the mouth of the Tees, just to the western side of the main channel and permission to dive should first be sought from the Harbour Master. Launching is possible from South Gare Marine Club slipway, only half a mile from the wreck-site, although non-members must pay a day-launch fee. Advice about the wreck-site can be sought from members of the Teeside 43 Branch of the BSAC.

VICTORY

Wreck ★
Scenery ★
Depth 12m
Reference N 54 39 04 W 001 07 48
½ mile E.-N.E. of South Gare light.

The *Victory* was a small British iron steam tug that was built in 1877 and registered in London. She was owned by G. Petrie of Middlesbrough and had a single iron propeller, powered by a two-cylinder, compound steam engine that used one boiler.

On 25 November 1897, the *Victory* was seeking towage from her base at Middlesbrough, under the command of Captain J. Lawson, when she foundered and was lost, following a collision with the Dutch-registered steamship *Durward*, just off the South Gare light, at the mouth of the river Tees. One of her five crewmen was lost in the incident.

Wreck-site
What remains of the *Victory* lies on a seabed of dirty sand in a general depth of around 12m, a quarter of a mile east-north-east of South Gare light. The wreck is more or less level with the seabed in a small depression in the sand, but all of her basic hull shape can still be made out, including the iron bottom plates, ribs and keel. However, the boiler, engine and superstructure are said to have been dispersed and little else is left.

Tidal streams are moderate and you can visit the site at most stages of the tide. Visibility is also at the whim of the river so the best time would be after a long spell of dry settled weather during the summer months.

H.M. TRAWLER REPRO

Wreck ★
Scenery ★
Depth 10m
Reference N 54 39 085 W 001 07 802
½ mile N.E. of South Gare Light.

The *Repro* was a steel 230-ton British steam fishing trawler that had dimensions of 35.7m length and a beam of 6.7m. She was built in 1910 by Cook, Welton & Gemmell in Yard 197 at Beverley and was launched on 13 April and registered as trawler GY510, No 127857 on 9 June by the new owners George F. Sleight of Grimsby. Her single steel propeller was powered by a three-cylinder, triple-expansion steam engine that developed 63hp, using one boiler, which gave the vessel a recorded speed of ten knots. Her machinery and engine were built by C.D. Holmes. In February 1915 the *Repro* was requisitioned by the Royal Navy and converted to HMT mine-sweeper No FY-1138.

On the 26 April 1917, the vessel was on Admiralty duties when she foundered and was lost just off Tod Point in the Tees Estuary, after detonating a mine laid by the German submarine *UC-41* a week earlier. Records do not show if any of her crew was lost when the vessel went down.

Wreck-site

This wreck, possibly that of H.M. Trawler *Repro*, lies on a dirty sand and stone seabed in a general depth of 10m. She is totally collapsed, partially buried and well broken up. It is believed that the vessel was dispersed or salvaged after she sank. Just bare remnants are left to be seen, which include sections of steel frame, part of the bows and pieces of broken engine and boiler.

There is very little interest to be found, however, the sand often moves following a storm which may reveal some long lost hidden artefacts. Tidal streams are reasonably moderate, except on a spring tide, while the underwater visibility varies with the amount of fresh water and effluence flowing down the river Tees. Very little marine life is to be found, except the occasional crab and a few small coley.

TEESDALE

Wreck ★★★
Scenery ★
Depth 35m
Reference N 54 39 052 W 000 58 553
4 miles N.E. of Redcar.

The *Teesdale* was a steel 2,470-ton British steamship, registered at West Hartlepool. She had dimensions of 94.48m length, by 13.46m beam and a draught of 6.19m, was owned at the time of loss by Sir Robert Ropner and built in 1904 by Ropner & Son, at Stockton-on-Tees. Her single propeller was powered by a three-cylinder, triple-expansion steam engine that developed 258hp, using two boilers. Her machinery was built by Blair & Co. Ltd at Stockton-on-Tees. She had one deck, five watertight bulkheads and a superstructure consisting of a 8.8m poop-deck, 56.1m bridge-deck and 11.3m forecastle.

On 15 June 1917, the *Teesdale* was on a voyage through the English Channel when she was torpedoed by a German submarine. Fortunately, the crew were able to take the vessel into shallow water, where she was beached and temporary repairs were made to the damaged hull and was refloated some weeks later. However, on 2 August, on the way to the river Tees for docking and repairs, she foundered and was lost, presumably due to the torpedo damage, about four miles north-east of Redcar.

Wreck-site

The wreck of the steamer *Teesdale* is reported to have sunk in position N 54 39 W 00 59 and the position given above shows a wreck or obstruction almost in the same place, so it is possible that this could be the vessel in question. She is said to be partially buried, with only some two metres of her structure showing above the seabed of sand and mud, in a general depth of 32m, the lowest astronomical depth. The wreck will now be well broken up, decayed and quite dispersed. Little else is known about the wreck-site, but it should be well worth investigating.

HARRATON

Wreck ★
Scenery ★
Depth 18m
Reference N 54 39 155 W 001 05 120
1.78 miles E.N.E. South Gare Light

The *Harraton* was an iron 669-ton British steamship, registered Sunderland and built in 1868 for Lord Lambton, the Rt Hon. Earl of Durham. Her single iron propeller was powered by a two-cylinder, compound steam engine that used one boiler.

On 19 April 1896, the *Harraton*, under the command of Captain J. Burton and carrying a crew of sixteen, was on passage from Sunderland for London with an unspecified cargo of coal, when she foundered, following a collision with the London-registered steamship *Engineer*.

The following is a statement from the Evening Gazette Records, researched by Stan Barnett, the Diving Officer of Teeside Branch of the B.S.A.C.

North Eastern Daily Gazette, Monday 20 April 1896

'Collision off the Tees Mouth.'

Yesterday a serious collision occurred off the Tees Mouth between the steamer *Harraton* belonging to the Earl of Durham's Collier Fleet and another vessel named the *Engineer*. The *Harraton* was observed about 10 o'clock making for the West Scar Rocks near Redcar with her stern almost level with the water's edge and shortly after was seen to sink about a mile off Coatham Pier, the crew took to the boats.

A large three masted Steamer appeared on the scene, after the vessel sank and picked up the whole of her crew.

It is considered that the Captain of the *Harraton* finding his vessel considerably damaged, made for the West Scar Rocks to get out of deep water. The weather at the time of the collision was very thick.

Captain While of Redcar Coastguard Station, along with several Fishing Boats went off to the wreck, took her bearings and brought back hatchings and other floating wreckage.

Harraton was the same vessel which a few months ago, ran down a Fishing Smack off Scarborough, when ten lives were lost.

Wreck-site

The wreck was dispersed in July 1896. On examination by divers on 3 July 1929 it was found to be levelled down to the seabed, except for her propeller and shaft, with one blade which was standing three feet above ground level.

The wreck is now well dispersed and very little now remains to show it was actually a steamship. Only a few rusting iron plates and framework are left, concreting into the seabed. However, sometimes after the winter storms, a few bits of relics may appear, but generally speaking the wreck-site is not really a very worthwhile dive, except maybe for the few large crustaceans that make their way to the odd pieces of wreckage, which provides them with a temporary shelter. Tidal streams are moderate and you can dive the site at most states of the tide, but it is best done on a low, slack neap.

JOHN MILES

Wreck ★★★
Scenery ★
Depth 45m
Reference N 54 39 902 W 000 50 121
6½ miles N.N.E. of Skinningrove

The *John Miles* was a steel 687-ton British steamship, registered in London and had dimensions of 49.98m length, by 9.14m beam and a draught of 3.58m. She was owned by Stephenson & Clarke & Co. and built in 1908 by S.P. Austin & Son at Sunderland. Her single screw propeller was powered by a three-cylinder, triple-expansion steam engine that developed 113hp, using one boiler.

The day she sank, on 22 February 1917, the *John Miles* was steaming at 8.25 knots, on passage from Newcastle-upon-Tyne for Shoreham-by-Sea, under the command of Captain W. Kelsey and carrying a 870-ton cargo of coal and a crew of fourteen. The chief engineer, being the senior surviving officer, stated in his report that a violent explosion took place on the port side, abaft of the main hatch at 12.35 p.m. The ship sank by the stern in two minutes and those of the crew who were on deck at the time were washed overboard. He and four others clung onto floating wreckage for about thirty minutes before they were picked up by a Royal Navy minesweeper and taken to Hartlepool.

Unfortunately, nine men, including her captain, died in the sea and one of the five rescued, the second engineer, died on board the minesweeper.

Wreck-site

The wreck lies orientated in an east to west direction, on a dirty seabed of sand, gravel, shells and mud, in a general depth of 45m, the lowest astronomical depth. She is reported to have collapsed down and to be well broken up, with the highest point being around her boiler and engine, which stands about 3.5m high and both are visibly exposed. Her donkey-engine and condenser also lie close to the boiler and engine with a mass of broken machinery and twisted steel plates surrounding them.

There are quite a number of large, flattened and bent copper pipes which protrude out of the heap of steel debris, along with some twisted handrails and part of a broken derrick. A number of fair sized cod of around five or six kilos and a large wolf-fish were observed close to the engine block area, so the wreck should be a good boat-angling venue. Tidal streams are very strong and visibility is reported to be very poor to dismal, making this wreck-site only suitable for very experienced divers.

H.M. TRAWLER RECEPTO

Wreck ★
Scenery ★
Depth 12m
Reference N 54 40 36 W 001 08 16
Near Long Scar buoy, Tees Bay

The *Recepto* was a steel 245-ton British steam fishing trawler that had dimensions of 36.7m length by 6.55m beam and a draught of 3.73m. She was trawler No 136991, built by Cook, Welton & Gemmell at Beverley in Yard No 299, launched on 6 June and registered at the port of Grimsby as GY254 by her new owner George F. Sleight of Grimsby on 23 July 1914. Her single steel propeller was powered by a three-cylinder, triple-expansion steam engine that developed 80hp, using one boiler, which gave the vessel a registered speed of ten and a half knots. Her engine and machinery were built by C.D. Holmes. In November 1914 the trawler was requisitioned by the Royal Navy and converted to become HMT mine-sweeper No FY-47.

On 16 February 1917 H.M. Trawler *Recepto* was on Admiralty duties in Tees Bay when she foundered and was lost off the Long Scar buoy after detonating a mine laid four days earlier by the German submarine *UC-30*.

Wreck-site

The wreck lies on a seabed of sand and stone in a general depth of 12m, the lowest astronomical depth. It is now totally collapsed and well dispersed, with just the battered remains of the engine, a few steel plates, frames, ribs and sections of the bows protruding above the dirty seabed in half a metre of scour. Except for a few small coley, very little marine life lives on or around the wreck-site. However, a few small crabs and the occasional lobster can be found in the early months of spring. Tidal streams are not too severe, but they pick up substantially during a spring tide, while the underwater visibility varies from nil to a few metres, depending on the wind direction and the amount of fresh water and effluence coming down the river Tees.

BURNHOPE

Wreck ★
Scenery ★
Depth 12m
Reference N 54 40 972 W 0001 09 104
2 ½ miles N. of North Gare Breakwater.

The *Burnhope* was a steel 1,941 British steamship, registered at Newcastle-upon-Tyne and had dimensions of 82.9m length, by 12.19m beam and a draught of 5.35m. She was owned by the Burnett Steam Ship Co. Ltd and built by Wood Skinner & Co. Ltd at Newcastle in 1907. Her single steel propeller was powered by a three-cylinder, triple-expansion steam engine that developed 200hp, using two boilers.

On 14 December 1916, under the command of Captain J. Rodger, the *Burnhope* had just set out on a voyage from Hartlepool to London with a 2,600-ton cargo of coal and was swinging to starboard before altering course in Hartlepool Bay, when she struck a German-laid mine. The pressure and blast from the enormous explosion that followed smashed the ship's wheelhouse windows and even the glass in the compass binnacles.   A second explosion beneath the port bow followed seconds later, which so seriously damaged the vessel that she began to sink by the bows. The captain immediately ordered the ship's starboard lifeboat to made ready and swung the ship to port-side in order to reach shallow water. After twenty minutes her bows touched ground and a minesweeper towed her stern-end round into the shallower water. However, when she took on a big list to port at 9.30 a.m., her crew, except for the captain, abandoned ship. Gradually the list got so bad that by 10.15 a.m. she went over onto her side and the captain had to be picked up out of the sea by the crew of the minesweeper. Unfortunately, he suffered a heart attack and died soon afterwards.

Wreck-site
The wreck of the *Burnhope* was dispersed using explosives and what was left of her lies in a general depth of 12-13m on a flat sand seabed, with the majority of her being covered by several metres of sand. There is a deep scour around the wreck where steel plating, ribs, frames and broken machinery protrudes out of the sand and other debris lies scattered around on the top. Winter storms often expose much of the ship's remains, only to cover them up soon after. Except for a few crabs, very little marine life is attracted to the wreck-site.

Tidal streams are generally very moderate and it is possible to dive the site at most states of the tide. Visibility is usually at the whim of the river Tees, but can be reasonable during the summer months, after a spell of dry weather.

The steamship Africander *came ashore near Redcar in January 1892. However, it is believed that she was refloated later that week. Note the teams of horses that were brought in to lighten her load.* Courtesy of the Zetland Lifeboat Museum, Redcar.

PATRIA

Wreck ★★★★
Scenery ★
Depth 35.5m
Reference N 54 41 987 W 001 02 802
Also: N 54 42 000 W 001 02 150
5 miles N. E. of South Gare light.

The *Patria* was an iron 838-ton Russian steamship, registered in the port of Wasa. She had dimensions of 62.68m length, by 8.76m beam and a draught of 4.59m. She was built at Port Glasgow by Murdock & Murry in 1882 and owned by Wasa Nordsjo Angf Aktieb in Wasa. Her single iron propeller was powered by a two-cylinder, compound steam engine that developed 93hp, using one boiler. Her machinery was built by Kincaid & Co. at Greenock. She had one deck, four watertight bulkheads and a superstructure, consisting of a 20.7m quarter-deck, 17m bridge-deck and an 8.5m forecastle.

On 29 December 1917, the *Patria* had left Newcastle with a cargo of coal for an unknown destination, when she struck a mine, laid by the very successful German submarine, *UB-21*, off Whitby. The vessel was badly damaged by the explosion, but managed to keep going under her own power for a further twenty miles, back towards the safety of the Tees. However, with vast quantities of seawater flooding into her hull, the pumps could not cope. She took on a heavy list and was only five miles off the Tees when the weight of water became too much; she keeled over onto one side and within three minutes, went down to the bottom.

Wreck-site
The wreck lies orientated in a east-north-east to west-south-west direction with her bows to east-north-east, in a general depth of 35.5m, the lowest astronomical depth, and within one mile of a further five wrecks. Unfortunately, the site is also rather close to the spoil-ground, an area of five to six square miles, which is used by the river Tees dredgers for dumping sludge, so visibility is usually very poor.

Peter Hale of Teeside says the wreck is a fantastic dive, because the hull is still intact and sitting upright on the seabed. The bridge and quarter-deck area of the ship are missing as they were classed as a navigation hazard to large vessels and dispersed by explosives, leaving just a large hole and broken framework around where they once were. The wreck stands around 4m high and is almost complete. However, she has collected a number of nets, including monofiliment ones. They can be a very serious hazard in the eerie, dim light.

There is also a 1.5m scour around the wreck-site, caused by the very strong tidal streams which sweep over and around her. Like all deep wrecks, this one also needs careful dive planning The best time to visit her would be at low, slack water on a neap tide and after a spell of settled weather.

OCEAN

Wreck ★★★★
Scenery ★
Depth 35m
Reference N 54 41 671 W 001 02 318
5 miles N.E. of South Gare Light.

The *Ocean* was a steel 1,442 ton, British steamship, registered in London and had dimensions of 75.28m length, by 10.74m beam and a draught of 4.72m. She was built by S.P. Austin & Son at Sunderland for Corry Colliers Ltd in 1894. Her single steel propeller was powered by a three-cylinder, triple-expansion steam engine that developed 155hp, using one boiler. Her machinery was built by North East Marine Engineering Co. Ltd. in Sunderland. She had one deck, four watertight bulkheads and a superstructure consisting of an 8.5m poop-deck, 19.1m quarter-deck, 13.85m bridge-deck and an 8.2m forecastle.

On 23 November 1917 the *Ocean*, under the command of Captain H. Norman, was torpedoed by the *UB-21*, while on passage from Granton to London, with an unspecified cargo of coal.

Wreck-site
The wreck of the *Ocean* lies orientated in a north-east to south-west direction, is

The Santiago was a Spanish-registered steamship, built in 1888, with a single propeller powered by a three-cylinder triple expansion steam engine and two boilers. On 8 November 1911 she was en route from Newcastle to Puillac with a cargo of coal and a crew of twenty-four when she foundered off Hartlepool, following a collision with the Hartlepool registered steam trawler Cairness, which also sank. Courtesy of the Zetland Lifeboat Museum, Redcar.

upright and in two substantial sections, with both the stern and bow sections standing proud of the seabed. The midships section, connecting the two together, where the bridge and forecastle were, has collapsed and inverted in on itself, down onto the engines and boiler. The depth to the top of the stern section is about 25m, with the top of bows at around 28m. Peter Hale says the wreck is very impressive and a top quality dive site.

However, very often, monofilament nets and/or trawl nets hang over her like a shroud and, combined with the usually poor visibility, which seems to prevail off the mouth of the Tees, a great deal of caution and planning are required when diving this wreck. Cod and large ling have been seen on numerous occasions and it is not unusual to see big lobsters under the wreckage. With a number of other wrecks in this vicinity, the *Ocean* is well worth looking at as a boat-angling venue. Being so far offshore, the tidal streams are fairly strong, making this a low, slack water dive.

MOTOR

Wreck ★★★
Scenery ★
Depth 35m
Reference N 54 41 971 W 001 02 225
5½ miles N.E. of South Gare Light

The *Motor* was a steel 312-ton British sailing ship built by Jarrow Steel in 1907, at Jarrow-on-Tyne, later converted to steam, and registered in North Shields. She had dimensions of 42.06m length, by 7.92m beam, a draught of 2.76m and was

The wooden barque Samarang *built in 1857 and owned by T. Emmerson of Newcastle-on-Tyne. On 10 October 1884 under the command of captain J.S. Goudie, she was en route from Quebec to Newcastle with a cargo of wood and twenty crew when she drove ashore on Marske beach, south of Redcar, in a force five northerly wind. Rocket brigades and lifeboats could not reach her and two men were lost when they took to their own boats, just before she broke up. The vessel was a total loss.* Courtesy of the Zetland Lifeboat Museum, Redcar.

owned at the time of loss by George W. Todd of Jarrow-on-Tyne. Her single steel propeller was powered by a three-cylinder, triple-expansion steam engine that developed 30hp, using one boiler.

On 16 January 1915, the *Motor* was on passage from Rosedale, Yorkshire, for Jarrow with a cargo of iron stone when she foundered five and a half miles east of the Heugh at Hartlepool. The reason the vessel sank is not explained, but it is thought that she may have struck a German-laid mine and sank with the loss of her crew of six.

Wreck-site

The wreck-site believed to be that of the steamship *Motor* lies fairly close the spoil-ground and also close to the other two very substantial wrecks of the *Patria* and *Ocean*, on a seabed of sand, mud and gravel, in a general depth of 35m, the lowest astronomical depth. The wreck is collapsed, well broken up and decayed, standing around 3m high around her now exposed boiler and engine. The area here is a mass of twisted steel plates and ribs, sections of hollow broken masts, non-ferrous pipes and lots of unrecognisable machinery and steel debris.

The wreck-site is very dark and gloomy, which usually requires a good torch to see anything. Tidal streams are strong and visibility nearly always poor to grim. The wreck-site is a fair way out to sea, so a sharp lookout is also required when either diving or fishing.

3. Tees to the Wear

SCANDIA (ex-EASTERN STAR)

Wreck ★★★★
Scenery ★
Depth 45m
Reference N 54 42 882 W 00 57 054
9 $\frac{1}{2}$ miles E. of The Heugh, Hartlepool.

The *Scandia* was an iron 1,153-ton Swedish steamship, registered in Helsingborg and had dimensions of 70.25m length, by 9.9m beam and a draught of 4.16m. She was built as the *Eastern Star* in 1884 by R. Thompson & Sons, at Sunderland and owned at the time of loss by H. Horndahl of Helsingborg in Sweden. Her single iron propeller was powered by a two-cylinder, compound steam engine that developed 120hp, using one boiler. Her machinery was built by J. Dickinson & Co. Ltd at Sunderland. She had one deck, four watertight bulkheads, and a superstructure consisting of a 27m quarter-deck, 17.3m bridge-deck and 7m forecastle.

On 23 December 1899, the *Scandia* was in ballast, steaming north from London for Sunderland, under the command of Captain F.P. Moller, when she collided with the steamship *Headland* and foundered 9 $\frac{1}{2}$ east of Hartlepool. It is most probable that her crew were rescued by the *Headland*, because the records make no mention of any of her crew of seventeen being lost in the incident.

Wreck-site
The wreck of the *Scandia* was discovered in 1998 when divers from the Dawdon Sub-Aqua Club located her remains. Her bell was recovered, which showed her to be the *Eastern Star*, which caused some confusion to the ship's identity. It was some months later that the author saw the bell in a dive-centre and traced her through records to be the *Scandia*.

She is reported to be lying on a seabed of fine-sand, mud and black-shells, in a general depth of 45m, the lowest astronomical depth. The wreck is fairly high at the stern-end for about 15m and from there she is collapsed down with the boiler and engine exposed. The rest of the wreck is collapsed, smashed to pieces and decayed, with pipes, bollards, frames, ribs, and pieces of broken derricks and hollow masts intermingled and spread all over the seabed. Dead Man's Fingers lighten up and cover the stern-end where her iron propeller is still attached. It is also covered with a series of trawl nets. Tidal streams are very strong and underwater visibility is seldom more than a couple of metres, even at the best of times, so this is not a dive-site for the inexperienced or faint hearted. There are no reports of marine life around the site, but most wrecks collect a few fish and crustaceans as residents.

The cargo passenger steamer Ficaria *came ashore near Redcar in June 1915, but was later refloated.* Courtesy of the Zetland Lifeboat Museum, Redcar.

BUTE

Wreck ★★★
Scenery ★
Depth 51m
Reference N 54 43 18 W 000 51 55
13½ miles E. of The Heugh, Hartlepool.

The *Bute* was a steel 176-ton British steam fishing trawler, registered at the port of Hull and had dimensions of 33.02m length, by 6.55m beam and a draught of 3.5m. She was owned at the time of loss by the Hull Steam Fishing & Ice Co. Ltd and built in 1905 by Earle's Company Ltd at Hull. Her single steel propeller was powered by a three-cylinder, triple-expansion steam engine that developed 39hp, using one boiler. The *Bute* had one deck, four watertight bulkheads and was ketch-rigged as a back-up to her engine.

On the 14 July 1916 the vessel was in ballast on a voyage to the fishing grounds from her temporary base in Tynemouth when she was stopped and captured by a German submarine. The submariner's forced her crew to abandon ship and she was sunk by explosive scuttling charges placed below the deck.

Wreck-site
The wreck, probably that of the steam-trawler *Bute*, lies orientated in a north-north-west to south-south-east direction, on a seabed of sand, mud and shells, in a general

depth of 51m, the lowest astronomical depth. She is now collapsed in on herself, but stands some 3m high around midships, where her boiler and engine are located. The propeller is visible and still attached to the shaft at the north-north-west end, however very little else is recognisable apart from her winch at the bows section. Tidal streams are rather strong and visibility usually poor, but it improves during the summer months after a spell of dry settled weather and neap tides. Very little marine life lives on and around the remains so she is hardly worth looking for to fish over.

TALISMAN

Wreck ★★★
Scenery ★
Depth 47m
Reference N 54 43 298 W 000 57 192
Also: N 54 43 190 W 000 57 19
4½ miles E. of The Heugh, Hartlepool.

The *Talisman* was a small, iron 153-ton British steamship, registered in Glasgow and had dimensions of 34.13m length, by 5.51m beam and a draught of 2.54m. She was built by W. Watson at Greenock in 1882 and owned by W. McLachlan & Co. The single iron propeller was powered by a two-cylinder, compound steam engine that developed 50hp, using one boiler.

On 6 August 1917, the *Talisman* was in ballast, on a voyage from Greenock to Grimsby, under the command of Captain N. Hyndman, when she was stopped by a German submarine. Her crew was forced to abandon ship in the lifeboat and then she was scuttled by the German sailors, using explosive charges.

Wreck-site
The wreck believed to be the *Talisman*, lies on a seabed of fine sand, mud and shell, surrounded by a three-quarter metre scour, in a general depth of 47m, the lowest astronomical depth. Her bows face north-west and the wreck, orientated in a south-east to north-west direction, is fairly intact, standing around 2.5m high and lying on her starboard side. She is starting to decay and is collapsing in on herself, with her boiler visible through what used to be the small bridge superstructure. The site does not see many divers, so it should be a good one to explore.

Soft corals encrust the highest sections, while a couple of large angler-fish have been observed in the scour close in to the wreck side, although other fish congregate on and over the wreck. Tidal streams are rather strong, making this a low, slack water dive for very experienced divers only. The site is fairly close to the spoil-grounds, so the wreck collects more than its fair share of sediment, so the visibility is always very murky and eerie, until you get close to the bottom. It is also a long way offshore, so great care should be taken by the surface cover, because the site is close to the main shipping lanes and large ships pass very close-by.

The sailing ship Gerbruder *came ashore during a force nine gale on the afternoon of 13 November 1901. She was later refloated.* Courtesy of the Zetland Lifeboat Museum. Redcar.

ROSELLA (ex-FEDERAL)

Wreck ★★★
Scenery ★
Depth 48m
Reference N 54 44 131 W 000 55 971
10½ miles E.N.E. of The Heugh, Hartlepool.

The *Rosella* was a steel 243-ton British steam fishing trawler, that had dimensions of 36.7m length, by 6.7m beam and a draught of 3.58m. She was built as No.125058 in Yard 136 by Cook, Welton & Gemmell at Beverley, launched as the *Federal*, on 14 February 1907 and registered as trawler GY272 at the port of Grimsby on 8 May 1907 for her new owners the Pelham Steam Fishing Co. Ltd. Her single steel propeller was powered by a three-cylinder, triple-expansion steam engine that developed 70hp, using one boiler and her machinery was built by C. D. Holmes & Co. Ltd at Hull. She had one deck, four watertight bulkheads and a quarter-deck of 22.7m. her name was changed to *Rosella* when she was sold to Thomas Baskcomb of Grimsby on 14 January 1911, who were the owners at the time of loss.

On 29 October 1914, the *Rosella* was in ballast, on passage from the Faroe Islands for Grimsby, under the command of Captain W. Harvey, when she foundered and was lost after detonating a German-laid mine twenty-five miles south-east of the Tyne.

Wreck-site

The wreck, believed to be that of the *Rosella*, lies in a general depth of 48m, the lowest astronomical depth, and very close to three other wrecks. She is collapsed, decayed, partially buried and well broken up, standing from 1m to around 3.5m at the highest point, with her boiler and engine exposed. The wreck lies orientated in an east-south-east to west-south-west direction with the remains of her bows to the east-south-east and no scour around her. It is not a very startling wreck, but worth a visit. However, it is only for very experienced divers.

Tidal streams are very strong and visibility is usually pretty grim, often being no more than half a metre. Also, there are at least a couple of trawl nets fouling the stern end of the wreck. A number of soft corals have taken hold on the upper structures, but few other kinds of marine life are to be seen. The wreck-site is in the main shipping lanes and a long way from shore, so a good lookout is required at all times.

DAFNI (ex-HOLSTEIN)

Wreck ★★★
Scenery ★
Depth 27.5m
Reference N 54 44 478 W 001 09 267
3 miles N.N.E. of The Heugh, Hartlepool.

The *Dafni* was a steel 1,190-ton Greek steamship, registered in the port of Piraeus and had dimensions of 73.15m length, by 10.79m beam and a draught of 5.79m. She was built as the *Holstein* in 1881 by Howaldtswerke at Kiel and owned at the time of loss by the Pandelis Brothers in Piraeus. Her single steel-screw propeller was powered by a three-cylinder, triple-expansion steam engine that developed 146hp, using one boiler.

On 16 December 1917, the *Dafni* was in ballast, on passage from Rouen for Sunderland, under the command of Captain C. Vldstaris when she was torpedoed and sunk by the German submarine *UB-34*, some three miles north-north-east of The Heugh at Hartlepool.

Wreck-site
The wreck, believed to be that of the steamship *Dafni*, lies orientated in a north-north-west to south-south-east direction, on a well-swept seabed of pebbles and stones, in a general depth of $27\frac{1}{2}$ m, the lowest astronomical depth. She is collapsed and well broken up, with the highest point of 3-4m being around her boiler, condenser and engine in amidships. Much of the wreck has a covering of hard, white, marine worm casings and soft corals have taken hold on the most exposed parts of her.

The wreck covers an area of seabed about 75 by 12m. There are signs of battered copper pipes and brass showing through the mound of steel debris. Visibility is usually rather poor, but improves during the summer months, however a good torch is still essential. A shoal of pout-whiting have adopted the boiler/engine area and can be seen at most times, however most of them weigh no more than half a kilo in weight and will hardly be worth the effort of fishing. Tidal streams are rather strong and a good lookout is required by the boat crew, because the wreck-site is in the shipping lanes.

EUCLID

Wreck ★★★
Scenery ★
Depth 34m
Reference N 54 45 825 W 001 09 045
5 miles N.N.E. of The Heugh, Hartlepool.

The *Euclid* was an iron 686-ton British steamship, registered in Sunderland and had dimensions of 59.84m length, by 8.86m beam and a draught of 5.02m. She was owned at the time of loss by E.J. Weatherly of Sunderland and built in 1866 by T.R. Oswald & Co. in Sunderland. Her single iron propeller was powered by a two-cylinder, compound steam engine that developed 90hp, using one boiler and her machinery was built by George Clark at Sunderland. She had one deck, four watertight bulkheads and was classed at Lloyds as 100 A1.

On 17 April 1890, the *Euclid* was on passage from Sunderland for Rochester with a cargo of coal, under the command of a Captain C. Knott when she foundered, following a collision with the London-registered steamship *Winslice*, during wind conditions south-east, force five. The vessel sank within minutes and four of her crew of fourteen were lost. The rest are believed to have been taken on board the other vessel and possibly landed at Hartlepool.

Wreck-site
The wreck, believed to be that of the *Euclid*, lies on a seabed of sand, pebbles, gravel and mud in a general depth of 34m, the lowest astronomical depth. She is partially buried, but collapsed, well broken up and badly decayed, standing no more than 3m high around the midships section where her boiler and engine are located.

The wreck faces north to south with a small scour around her and is rather dispersed, covering an area of about 50 by 10m. The iron plates, engine, boilers and broken machinery are covered in hard, white, marine worm casings and are fairly concreted together. There are also signs of non-ferrous metal pipes and brass flanges and unrecognisable instruments and equipment lying among the jumbled pile. A couple of decent-sized lobsters and a few cod have been observed around the wreck-site, but nothing worth spending any time angling for.

Tidal streams are fairly strong: the best time to dive would be on a low, neap tide after a spell of dry settled weather. Visibility is usually poor, but improves during the summer.

TANGISTAN

Wreck ★★★★
Scenery ★
Depth 55m
Reference N 54 46 132 W 000 53 321
12½ miles E.N.E. of The Heugh, Hartlepool.

The *Tangistan* was a steel 3,738-ton British steamship, registered in London and had dimensions of 106.6m length, 14.93m beam and a draught of 4.87m. She was owned at the time of loss by Frank C. Strict & Co. of London, owner of the Strick Line Ltd and built by William Gray & Co. at Hartlepool in 1906. Her single steel-screw propeller was powered by a three-cylinder, triple-expansion steam engine that used three boilers.

On 9 March 1915, the *Tangistan* was on passage from Benisaf for Middlesbrough with 6,000 tons of iron-ore and a crew of thirty-nine, when she was lost after being torpedoed by the unseen German submarine *U-12*. Only one of her crew, a Mr J. O'Toole, survived when the ship went down.

Mr O'Toole said later in a statement that the steamer had arrived off Middlesbrough too early for the tide to enter and was going very slowly. Then at 12.30 a.m. she was brought up in a huge shock and explosion. The lights all went out and the crew rushed up onto the deck, but before they could launch the lifeboats, the ship went down with a rush, on a perfectly even keel. Mr O'Toole said he was sucked down with the ship, but came up to the surface again and swam around for some two hours or so before being picked up by the steamship *Woodville* and landed at West Hartlepool.

The *Tangistan* was reported to have sank nine miles north of Flamborough Head, in position N 54 15 42 W 000 05 08, but there has been no record of any diving being carried out on this site, so it will be interesting to see what information comes up from the wreck.

The question remains: why would the *Tangistan*, after having arrived too early for the tide at Middlesbrough, go all the way back to Flamborough Head? Probably the most logical thing to do, was to stay close to the Tees, but to keep moving and that is why it is believed that this is her wreck-site.

Wreck-site

The wreck, believed to be that of the *Tangistan*, is very broken up and scattered over an area of 105m by 30m. She stands some 6m high, is orientated in a north-west to south-east direction, on a seabed of mud, fine-sand and black-shell, in a general depth of 55m, the lowest astronomical depth, with no scour. The wreck

The Otra, *an iron, full-rigged Norwegian sailing ship, built in 1878, was on a voyage from Libau to West Hartlepool, with a crew of fifteen and a cargo of pit-props, when she stranded in heavy seas at West Hartlepool on 5 June 1912. The vessel was a total loss and broke up soon after.* Courtesy of the Zetland Lifeboat Museum, Redcar.

is very substantial, although the hull and superstructure have totally collapsed, leaving the three boilers, condenser and engine visibly exposed, with broken machinery, huge bent and twisted copper pipes and brass fittings left sticking out of the debris in every direction. The highest point is reported to be the north-western end of the wreck, which is probably the bow section, where a number of portholes can be seen within easy reach, however much of the debris is now starting to concrete into the seabed.

A number of large cod, weighing about 10kg, were observed near the boilers and a small shoal of golden striped pout-whiting hovered around the top of the wreck-site. However, the wreck is a long way from land, so surface conditions would have to be fairly smooth for anyone contemplating fishing over her. The tidal streams are very strong and visibility is usually poor to grim, but after a neap tide and a spell of settled westerly winds and dry weather, this should vastly improve during the summer months.

H.A. BRIGHTMAN

Wreck ★★
Scenery ★
Depth 21m
Reference N 54 46 40 W 001 45 45
2½ miles N.E. of Blackhall Rocks.

The *H.A. Brightman* was an 850-ton three-mast British iron steamship, which was registered in North Shields and had dimensions of 76.2m length, by 8.86m beam and a draught of 5.28m. She was owned at the time of loss by T. Sutton of North Shields and built by Schlesenger, at Newcastle-upon-Tyne, in 1869. Her single iron propeller was powered by a two-cylinder, compound-inverted steam engine that developed 99hp, using one boiler and her machinery was built at Newcastle-upon-Tyne by T. Clark & Co. She had one deck, five watertight bulkheads and a superstructure, consisting of a 9.1m forecastle, 18.2m bridge-deck and a reinforced 10m quarter-deck.

On 17 January 1879 the steamer was carrying a cargo of coal and a crew of twenty-one, on passage from the Tyne for Alexandria, under the command of Captain G. Whatly, when she stranded on Blackhall Rocks in thick fog and heavy seas (other sources report her as stranding at Staithes in North Yorkshire). Records do not report what happened to her crew, so presumably they got off the vessel safely. The ship is then said to have drifted off later and sank in deep water, becoming a total loss.

Wreck-site
Local divers in the region believe that this wreck is that of the *H.A. Brightman*. The wreck lies in a general depth of 21m, the lowest astronomical depth. It is totally collapsed, well broken up, decayed and dispersed, with much of the remains lying under the thick layer of colliery waste that covers the seabed in this region. Only the boiler and engine and about a 1-2m section of hull is all that stands proud of the dirty sand, stone seabed. After about 6m in any direction, nothing else remains visible. Although covering a small area the boiler and engine are well worth looking at, as they are absolutely covered in soft-corals with shoals of small pout-whiting and coley swimming around, making it a very photogenic site.

The dive will only take around ten minutes to complete, but makes an excellent second or novice dive. Tidal streams are often rather strong, although nothing too much to worry about, while the visibility is usually poor at most times.

VESTRA

Wreck ★★★★
Scenery ★
Depth 35m
Reference N 54 47 625 W 001 05 720
Also: N 54 47 602 W 001 05 652
7½miles N.E. of The Heugh, Hartlepool.

The *Vestra* was a steel 1,021-ton British steamship, registered in Grangemouth and had dimensions of 65.73m length, by 9.75m beam and a draught of 4.29m. She was built by Ramage & Ferguson Ltd of Leith, in 1897, for J.T. Salveson & Co. and her single iron propeller was powered by a three-cylinder, triple-expansion steam engine, that developed 99hp, using one boiler. She had one deck, four watertight bulkheads and a centrally positioned superstructure, consisting of an 8.2m poop-deck, an 11.5m quarter-deck, a bridge-deck of 17.6m and forecastle measuring 9.1m.

On 6 February 1917, under the command of a Captain G. Ross, the *Vestra* was on a voyage from the Tyne to Rouen when she sunk, with the loss of two lives, after being torpedoed by the German submarine, *UB-35*.

Wreck-site
The wreck of the *Vestra* lies just outside the Hartlepool spoil-ground, on a seabed of dirty mud and fine-sand, in a general depth of 35m, the lowest astronomical depth and surrounded by a one metre scour. It has totally collapsed, but is still fairly substantial, standing 7m high in the midships section, where the superstructure was before it fell down and in. Her wreckage covers an area of about 75 by 20m, with the wreck orientated at an angle of 165 by 345 degrees, nearly north to south. It is draped with nets, both monofilament and trawl nets, making it rather unsafe in the poor, murky, dim light. There is quite an array of soft corals adorning the highest structures, where the tide sweeps over and around the wreck-site. The ship's bell was recovered last year and although she was supposed to be carrying a cargo of coal, it is rumoured that there is a hold full of live ammunition shells.

Tidal streams are very strong and underwater visibility is normally quite poor, especially in the last few metres, near to the seabed. The best time to dive on the wreck is during a neap tide, at low slack water, after a spell of settled dry weather. This wreck is also a long way from land, so anyone contemplating diving on it should do a lot of pre-planning.

AZIRA

Wreck ★★★★
Scenery ★
Depth 34m
Reference N 54 48 400 W 001 09 655
Also: N 54 48 400 W 001 09 705
5½ miles E.S.E. of Seaham

The *Azira* was a steel 1,144-ton Norwegian steamship, registered in Bergen and had dimensions of 70.4m length, by 10.38m beam and a draught of 4.11m. She was built in 1907 by Trondhjems Mek Vaeks, at Trondheim and owned by Pelton Steam Ship Co. of Newcastle-upon-Tyne. Her single steel propeller was powered by a three-cylinder, triple-expansion steam engine that developed 106hp, using one boiler.

On 4 September 1917, the *Azira* was on passage from Newcastle for Cherbourg, under the command of Captain J. Traasdahl, carrying a cargo of coal and a crew of eighteen, when she was attacked and sunk by the German submarine, *UB-22*.

The vessel was about six miles south-east of Seaham Harbour when the first mate on watch saw the periscope of the U-boat about 550m off the port bow, but thought it was a dan-buoy marking the safe channel. However, the vessel had only travelled a short distance further when it was rocked amidships by an exploding torpedo, which killed the ship's carpenter. The steam tug *Bureaucrat* was just 100m away from the *Azira* at the time. Her crew had already seen the torpedo heading towards the *Azira*, so they wasted no time in reaching the stricken ship. Twelve of the *Azira's* crew got away in a lifeboat, but the rope snapped, leaving five of the crew stranded. Another ship, the steamer *Aberline*, launched her lifeboat and successfully rescued four of the men, but the captain, who was last off his ship, was taken on board the tug, *Bureaucrat*, only minutes before the *Azira* went down to the bottom.

All that was ever seen of the submarine was her periscope. It was not until German records were released after the First World War that the *UB-22* was found to be responsible for sinking the *Azira*.

Wreck-site
The wreck lies on a seabed of fine-sand, stones and mud, in a general depth of 34m, the lowest astronomical depth, some five and a half miles east-south-east of Seaham Harbour. Her hull and superstructure has collapsed in on herself, but she is still very substantial, standing around 4-5m high, while the bow section is quite intact and has a huge array of Dead Man's Fingers growing on it. The wreck used to be full of live shell cases, but they have been removed. There are lots of large copper pipes, brass valves and a number of portholes that can be seen around the wreck.

Shoals of pollack and cod have also adopted the wreck site as their home, along with a few crustaceans. Unfortunately, trawl nets can be a bit of a hazard in the dim, gloomy light, so a great deal of caution is called for. Tidal streams are very strong, so the best time to dive the site is at low, slack water on a neap tide, after a dry spell of weather. The wreck will also make a good boat-angling venue, when conditions are right, especially when there are two large wrecks in close proximity.

Adjacent wreck
Peter Hale from Middlebrough, who gave the report, says that just 100m inshore of the *Azira* lies another very large wreck, bigger than the *Azira*, with two boilers, standing in position: N 54 48 55 W 001 09 66. It appears to have been a large iron built collier loaded with a cargo of coal. However, she will remain a mystery ship until someone is able to identify her.

The wreck has collapsed down but appears equally as substantial as that of the *Azira*. This particular wreck has not been dived on as much as the *Azira*, so there may be more interesting equipment still remaining.

ACHIEVEMENT

Wreck ★★★
Scenery ★
Depth 44m
Reference N 54 48 932 W 001 05 935
9½ miles E.S.E. of Seaham Harbour.

The *Achievement* was an iron 133-ton British fishing trawler, registered at North Shields and had dimensions of 30.17m length, by 6.22m beam and a draught of 3.35m. She was owned at the time of loss by the Scott Brothers of Sunderland and built in 1866. Her single iron propeller was powered by a two-cylinder, compound steam engine that used one boiler.

On 25 March 1884, the vessel was in ballast, *en-route* from her home base at Sunderland to the fishing grounds, when she foundered and was lost, following a collision with the Sunderland-registered steamship *Dunelm*. It is believed that her skipper, Captain J. Brown, and the other six crew members were taken on board the *Dunelm* and landed back at Sunderland.

Wreck-site
The wreck lies orientated in a north-west to south-east direction, on a seabed of fine-sand and mud, in a general depth of 44m, being the lowest astronomical depth. She is now totally collapsed, well broken up, badly decayed and partially buried. Much of her machinery and rusting remains have begun to concrete together into the surrounding seabed. The highest 2m section is around the

centrally-positioned boiler and engine and the whole wreck-site of debris only covers about 20m by 8m and is covered in sediment.

Very little marine life can be seen, although the site is very dark and gloomy and requires a good torch to see anything. Tidal streams are fairly brisk and in general the wreck is not worth visiting for either diving or fishing, but a closer inspection may reveal the odd goodie that could still be lying around.

TEAL

Wreck ★★★
Scenery ★
Depth 26m
Reference N 54 49 310 W 001 14 080
Also: N 54 49 310 W 001 14 515
3 miles E.S.E. of Seaham Harbour.

The *Teal* was a steel 766 tons British steamship with dimensions of 67.08m length, by 8.66m beam and a draught of 4.47m. She was built in 1876 by M. Pearse & Co. at Stockton and owned at the time of loss by the General Steam Navigation Co. Ltd. Her single iron propeller was powered by a two-cylinder, compound steam engine that developed 174hp, using one boiler. The machinery was built by Blair & Co. Ltd in Stockton and she had two decks and her superstructure consisted of a 23.4m poop-deck and a forecastle of 13.7m.

On 29 April 1916, under the command of Captain W.A.W. Hove and carrying a crew of nineteen, the *Teal* was on passage from Leith to London with a general cargo, when she was attacked by the German submarine, *UB-27*. The *Teal* was steaming south when the U-boat suddenly appeared out of a fog bank, on her starboard beam and fired a torpedo. However, Captain Hove saw the torpedo's track and took evasive action by putting the helm hard over to port. The missile missed the ship by a few feet, but then the submarine began shelling her with its deck gun. Realizing they had little chance of escape, the skipper stopped the *Teal* and ordered his crew into the boats. The U-boat then went alongside and the submarine's crew placed explosive timing devices in her at 8.20 a.m. Then she left the area to chase after another merchant ship. The crew of the *Teal* watched as every one of the scuttling charges exploded, but their little vessel refused to sink. Fifty minutes later, the *UB-27* reappeared and fired a second torpedo. This time it did not miss and the *Teal* went up in a huge explosion. The submarine headed east out to sea, while the survivors were able to make their way back in the ship's boats, landing at Hartlepool later that same day.

Kapitan Stein, skipper of the *UB-27*, ran out of luck the next year. On 29 July, the submarine's periscope was sighted by the crew of the torpedo-gunboat HMS *Halcyon* off Winterton-on-sea, in Norfolk. The gun-boat made her full speed of seventeen knots over the top of the U-boat and probably struck her conning tower as a sudden violent collision was felt. At the same time as she ran over the

U-boat, the *Halcyon* dropped two 500lb depth charges, which brought masses of oil and air up to the surface, sending the *UB-27* and her crew down to the bottom forever, where they now lie in a general depth of 45m.

Wreck-site
The wreck lies on a seabed of coarse-sand and pebbles in a general depth of 26m, the lowest astronomical depth. Keith Lawrence of Seaham reports that the wreck is well broken up, having totally collapsed down on top of itself, except for the stern section, which is relatively intact, with her iron propeller still attached. The boiler, condenser and engine are now exposed among the jumble of steel framework, ribs and plates, which are intermingled with long, twisted, copper pipes and brass flanges. The highest point of the wreck is the boiler, which with the stern-end are ablaze with soft corals. She also has at least one trawl net draped over her, which makes the murky visibility even poorer.

Quite a few large lobsters have been seen and occasionally, shoals of pout-whiting visit the wreck-site during the summer months. Tidal streams are very brisk and the best time to dive the wreck would be at low, slack water on a neap tide. The wreck may also be a good boat-angling venue.

MEREDITH

Wreck ★★★
Scenery ★
Depth 42m
Reference N 54 49 472 W 001 09 425
6½ miles E.S.E. of Seaham Harbour.

The *Meredith* was an iron 976-ton British steamship, registered in London and had dimensions of 67.18m length, by 8.89m beam and a draught of 5.18m. She was built in 1871 by Iliff, Mounsey & Co. at Sunderland and owned at the time of loss by R. Thorman of Seaham Harbour. Her single iron propeller was powered by a two-cylinder, inverted compound steam engine that developed 99hp, using one boiler.

On 31 March 1891, the *Meredith* was in ballast on passage from London for Sunderland, under the command of Captain R.T. Humble with a crew of seventeen, when she foundered and was lost, following a collision with the Sunderland-registered steamship *Longnewton*. Wind conditions were a choppy north-east force four at the time of the incident, but the reason for the collision is not known. It is believed that the crew of the *Meredith* were taken on board the *Longnewton* and landed at Sunderland.

Wreck-site
The wreck, possibly that of the *Meredith*, lies orientated in a north-west to south-east direction, on a seabed of fine sand and mud, in a general depth of 42m, the

lowest astronomical depth. The wreck is badly decayed, well broken up and completely collapsed. The highest section of 4m at midships, where her engine, boiler and condenser are located and openly visible, are surrounded by a large mound of broken machinery, iron plates and framework. By the way things are lying around, it appears that the vessel may have turned upside down, before collapsing and breaking up.

Soft corals cover much of the exposed parts of the wreck and a shoal of pout-whiting can be seen around her midships area, so she may make a good boat angling venue, when conditions are right. Tidal streams are fairly strong and the visibility is usually very poor. The site is also in the shipping lanes, so a good lookout will be required at all times.

TATIANA (ex-CLAUDIUS)

Wreck ★★★
Scenery ★
Depth 61m
Reference N 54 50 05 W 000 56 57
Also: N 54 50 082 W 000 57 032
13½ miles N.E. of The Heugh, Hartlepool.

The *Tatiana* was a steel 285-ton British steam fishing trawler, registered at Grimsby and had dimensions of 41.63m length, by 7.01m beam and a draught of 3.68m. She was owned at the time of loss by A. Bannister and built as the *Claudius* in 1909 at Selby by Cochrane & Sons Ltd. Her single steel propeller was powered by a three-cylinder, triple-expansion steam engine that developed 87hp, using one boiler. Her centrally-positioned machinery was built by Amos & Smith Ltd at Hull. She had one deck, four watertight bulkheads, a 21.9m quarter-deck and 6.7m forecastle.

On 31 July 1916, the *Tatiana* was in ballast on a voyage from her base at Grimsby to the fishing grounds, under the command of Captain W.F. Jenner, when she was stopped and captured by a German submarine. The crew of the *Tatiana* were ordered to abandon ship and their vessel was sunk by explosive scuttling charges that were placed below decks.

Wreck-site
The wreck, believed to be that of the *Tatiana*, lies orientated in a east-north-east to west-south-west direction, on a seabed of fine sand, broken shells and mud, in a general depth of 61m, the lowest astronomical depth. She is partially buried, totally collapsed, decayed and well-broken up, standing just over 2m high at midships, where her boiler, condenser and engine are exposed and surrounded by a small mound of debris that covers an area of about 10 x 5m.

Possibly, all of her interesting instruments and machinery are still around, but they may be buried beneath the silt and debris. At over 61m there are much better wrecks to dive and it is very doubtful whether the wreck would be even worth fishing over, being so small and so far out from shore. Tidal streams are very strong, but the visibility is usually good during the summer months, even if the wreck-site is very dark. Only divers with experience and expertise should consider diving on wrecks at this depth.

HELVETIA

Wreck ★★★
Scenery ★
Depth 42m
Reference N 54 50 460 W 001 10 660
4 miles E. of Seaham.

The *Helvetia* was an iron 167-ton British steam fishing trawler, registered at Grimsby and had dimensions of 30.98m length, by 6.29m beam and a draught of 3.37m. She was owned at the time of loss by the Great Grimsby & East Coast Steam Fish Co. and was built by Cook, Welton & Gemmell, at Hull, in 1898. Her single iron propeller was powered by a three-cylinder, triple-expansion steam engine that developed 50hp, using one boiler and her machinery was built by C. D. Holmes & Co. at Hull. She was classed as 100 A1 at Lloyds, had one deck, three watertight bulkheads and a superstructure consisting of a 14.3m quarter-deck and a 5.8m forecastle.

On 1 August 1916, the *Helvetia* was in ballast, on a return voyage from the Faroe Islands to Grimsby, when she was stopped and captured by a German submarine. Captain W.H. Brennan and his crew were forced to abandon ship, then she was sunk by explosive scuttling charges placed below deck.

Wreck-site
The wreck, believed to be that of the steam-trawler *Helvetia*, lies on a seabed of black-shells, coarse sand and gravel, in a general depth of 42m, the lowest astronomical depth, and very close to the two wrecks of the steamships *Llwyngwair* and *Vianna*. Very little is known about this wreck, except that she stands 3m high, which will probably be around the boiler and engine area. The rest of her will almost certainly be totally collapsed, decayed and rather flattened. Being a fairly small vessel of 167 tons, there will not be much to see. However, there are no reports of her ever being dived, so the remains will definitely be worthy of an investigation.

Tidal streams are fairly strong and visibility usually very poor, but during the summer months it significantly improves during neap tides and after a spell of dry settled weather and westerly winds.

EIDENT

Wreck ★★★
Scenery ★
Depth 44m
Reference N 54 50 838 W 001 08 485
7½ miles E. of Seaham Harbour.

The *Eident* was an iron 1,520-ton British steamship, registered at Sunderland and had dimensions of 79.37m length, by 10.36m beam and a draught of 5.66m. She was owned at the time of loss by J. Westoll of Sunderland and built by Short Brothers at Sunderland in 1880. Her single iron propeller was powered by a two-cylinder, compound steam engine that developed 178hp, using one boiler and her machinery was built by T. Richardson & Sons at Hartlepool. She had one deck, five watertight bulkheads and a superstructure consisting of a 30.5m quarter-deck, 18.8m bridge-deck and 9.1m forecastle.

On 24 October 1902, the *Eident*, under the command of Captain J. Martin, was on passage from London for South Shields with a cargo of iron, when she foundered and was lost, following a collision with the Norwegian-registered steamship *G.M.B.* It is believed that her eighteen crew members were taken on board the *G.M.B.* and landed at Sunderland.

Wreck-site
The wreck lies orientated in a north-west to south-east direction, on a dirty seabed of sand, mud, broken shells and gravel, in a general depth of 44m, the lowest astronomical depth. The wreck is partially buried, with her bows to the north-west. She is totally collapsed, well broken up and badly decayed, with the highest 3m section around her boiler, condenser and engine, which are all exposed to the strong tidal streams and covered in Dead Man's Fingers. Masses of iron debris, bent and flattened copper, lead pipes and decayed broken machinery surround the boiler and the engine, but little else is recognizable. However, all of the vessel's interesting instruments will be lying somewhere among the scattered debris.

Visibility is very poor, usually only a metre or so, but it significantly improves during the summer months, after a spell of settled weather and neap tides. Very little marine life is visible and the wreck will probably be of little interest to the boat-angling fraternity.

NORMAN

Wreck ★
Scenery ★
Depth 4-6m
Reference 54 51 400 W 001 20 052
300m south of Ryhope Dene

The *Norman* was an iron, full-rigged, 420-ton (516 tons gross) British steamship, registered in London. She was owned by Messers Bremer, Bennett & Bremer of Mark Lane, and built in London by Rotherhithe in 1854. Her single iron-screw propeller was powered by a two-cylinder compound-steam engine that developed 60hp, using one boiler and her machinery was built by Summers & Day Ltd, at Southampton.

On 10 June 1881, the *Norman* was under the command of Captain S.H. Smith, on passage from Danzig for Stockton-on-Tees with a cargo of wheat, when she stranded inshore, during a south-south-east gale and heavy seas, just south of the Ryhope Dene. The coastguard committee and chief officer at Seaham called out the emergency services at 2 p.m. and Seaham Volunteer Life-Brigade arrived on the scene.

At their second attempt the life-brigade managed to fire the rocket apparatus over to the stricken vessel and prepared to take off her crew by breeches buoy. However, when the seventeen crew and two passengers saw Seaham boat, *the Sisters' Carter of Harrogate* approaching, they said that they would prefer to wait for the lifeboat. She took ten of the men, the Captain's wife and a female passenger off the *Norman*, leaving her captain, first mate and five crewmen on board the ship. Shortly after, one man was taken off using the apparatus and Bosun's Chair. Then, after an interval, the rest of the crew was taken off in the lifeboat, along with the crew's belongings. The captain stayed on board until she began to break up in the surf and had to be abandoned, eventually becoming a total wreck.

Wreck-site

What remains of the *Norman* lies on rocky ground, intermingled with patches of sand. Very little is recognizable, except her battered boiler, a few pieces of scattered iron plating, an anchor and her iron propeller, which protrudes half out of a patch of sand and rock. Tidal streams are very moderate and it is possible to dive the wreck-site at any stage of the tide. However, high water is preferred, because as the wreck is so shallow it is subjected to surface waves.

Visibility is usually poor, but improves after a spell of dry, settled weather. There is very little marine life about, except for a few Green Shore crabs and one or two small flatfish, but during the winter, many anglers fish off the beach for cod around this area.

On 31 December 1898, the small, iron 389-ton Danish registered steamship *Niord* came ashore during heavy seas and thick fog, around 200m south of the steamer *Norman*. Seaham's lifeboat, *Skynner* was launched at 12.08 a.m on New Year's Day 1899. In rough seas her Coxswain, William Miller, took the lifeboat in towards the stricken vessel and dropped anchor at 1 a.m. The lifeboat veered towards the steamer and eventually came alongside, where all eleven of the steamer's crewmen were taken off safely and landed back at Seaham Harbour. The captain Smith wrote a letter of appreciation and thanks for the rescue of his crew to the local newspaper, where it appeared a few days later.

The *Niord* was on a voyage from Randers/Fredrikshavn to Newcastle-upon-Tyne, with an unspecified cargo, under the command of Captain C.F.W. Rasmussen and carrying a crew of fourteen. Her single propeller was powered by a three-cylinder, triple-expansion steam engine, using one boiler.

MONICA

Wreck ★★★
Scenery ★
Depth 62m
Reference N 54 51 588 W 000 50 109
20 miles E. of Seaham Harbour.

The *Monica* was an iron 1,312-ton British steamship, registered in London and had dimensions of 71.73m length, by 9.88m beam and a draught of 5.41m. She was owned by F. Gordon & Stamp and built in 1878 by Austin & Hunter, both of Sunderland. Her single iron propeller was powered by a two-cylinder, compound-inverted steam engine that developed 120hp, using one boiler. Her machinery was built by Black, Hawthorn & Co. at Sunderland.

The *Monica* had one deck, five watertight bulkheads and a superstructure, consisting of an 18.5m reinforced quarter-deck, a 12.8m bridge-deck and a 7.3m forecastle. She was classed as 100 A1 at Lloyds.

On 14 September 1883, the *Monica* foundered and was lost twenty miles east of Seaham Harbour, following a collision with the London-registered steamship *John McIntyre*. She was carrying a crew of seventeen and a cargo of coal under the command of Captain J. Bowman, on a passage from South Shields to Hamburg. Weather conditions were fine at the time of the incident, as only an easterly force two was blowing. It is believed that her crew were taken on board the *John McIntyre*.

Wreck-site
The wreck lies on a dirty seabed of fine sand and mud, in a general depth of 62m, the lowest astronomical depth. She is partly buried, but standing about 4m high in the midships section, where her boiler, condenser and engine block lie exposed and surrounded by a mass of collapsed, decayed and badly broken iron plates and flattened machinery. Much of the vessel's bridge equipment and a number of brass portholes, with iron back-plates, can be seen among the jumble of rusting, iron debris and bent, copper and lead pipes. A few very large cod have been observed, which would make this wreck-site an excellent boat-angling venue. However, she

The SS Ottercaps, owned by Lambton Collieries, was built by Robert Thompson of Sunderland in 1878, registered at Sunderland, had dimensions of 65.9m length, 9.7m beam and 4.9m draught. On 10 August 1890 the SS Ottercaps went aground near to the old south pier. All her crew and two passengers were saved by the Sunderland Southside Volunteer Life Brigade, but the ship had damage to her stern post and rudder. John Crown of the Strand Slipway was given a contract to get the vessel off the beach and on 14 August she was towed off by the tugs Ben Ledi, Snowdrop and Her Majesty and dry docked by S.P. Austin. In 1903 the SS Ottercaps sank with the loss of all her crew after being wrecked at Feunteot at Raz De Seins in France, while on a voyage from Sunderland to Bilbao via St Nazaire in France. Courtesy of the Roker Volunteer Life Brigade.

is a long way out to sea and there are other large wrecks nearer to shore.

Tidal streams are fairly strong, but quite reasonable near to the bottom, while the underwater it is very murky and eerie, making a powerful torch essential. This wreck is only for the most experienced, technical divers and will require a lot of careful pre-planning.

ABASOTA

Wreck ★★
Scenery ★★★
Depth 8-9m
Reference N 54 53 51 W 001 19 58
Whitestones Reef, Sunderland.

The *Abasota* was a steel, 1,550-ton Spanish-registered steamship owned by the Montevideo Co. She was built to carry passengers and a 2,500-ton cargo at

Newcastle-upon-Tyne in 1903. Her single steel propeller was powered by a three-cylinder, triple-expansion steam engine that used two boilers.

On 19 October 1908, the *Abasota* was on passage from Algiers, via Bilbao for the Tyne with 2,500 tons of iron ore, under the command of Captain Learete, with a crew of twenty-four on board, when she struck the Whitestones Reef, one mile south-east of Sunderland. She was enduring gale-force winds and blinding rain in massive seas, while hugging the coast-line, when, suddenly, she ground to a halt on this submerged, offshore reef.

The *Sunderland Echo* reported the following news on 20 October 1908:

> The Spanish ship *Abasota* on her way to the Tyne from Bilbao came inshore too close in heavy rain and big seas where she was carried into a dangerous position and ultimately dashed onto the Whitestones with great force. The Life-Brigade mustered from both north and south of the river, among them was Dr Beattie and W. J. Oliver, Secretary of the Royal Lifeboat Society who ordered the North Dock and Hendon Beach-boats out. The Wearmouth Coal Company's steam tug *Marsden* under the command of Jos. Scott on seeing the vessel in danger, steamed out to it and on the way met two boats containing men from the *Abasota* who had abandoned her and were making for the shore. These were with difficulty picked up by the tug which afterwards went alongside and took off the remainder of the crew. The boats from the first men were allowed to be swept away in the angry sea, being tossed about in the corner just behind the Patent Fuel Works. All the crew were saved but had no time to pick up their belongings. The steamer was pitching heavily and the stern frequently in the air and there was considerable danger of the boilers bursting. The *Marsden* had just sheered away to make her way back when a boiler went BANG. The steamer settled down in such a way she was immovable despite the battering from heavy waves and which washed her decks. The lifeboats had just got out of the cable-line when Mr Johnson received word that they were not needed. The tide was high and sea so great that the lifeboat crew had to ride out the sea until a suitable opportunity arose later. The men were landed at the North Basin at South Docks where they were given dry clothing and food. They were all Spaniards and their vessel was built at Newcastle in 1903.

The *Marsden* was a steel 131-ton steam-paddle tug, that had a length of 28.9m and a beam of 2.7m. She was built in 1906 by J.P. Reynoldson & Sons, at South Shields, at a cost of £4,975, for Sunderland Towage Co. Ltd. Her two paddles were powered by a two-cylinder, side-lever steam engine that developed 350hp, using one boiler. The *Marsden* was hired by the Royal Navy in 1915 and was wrecked at Suvla Bay, Gallipoli, in Turkey, in October 1915.

Wreck-site

The remains of the *Abasota* were discovered on the Whitestones Reef in 1995, after a search using a magnetometer. The wreck is well smashed up, decayed and scattered among the short kelp and rocks, in a general depth of 3-5m, the lowest astronomical depth. One of her square boilers was found lying on its side and the splattered remains of another was spread around close-by, among the boulders, together with lots of big pieces of lead piping and bits of broken machinery. A good search of the area is still on the agenda, as we did not have enough time and air when the wreck was discovered.

Tidal streams are moderate and it is possible to dive the area at any state of the tide, although the current becomes quite strong on a spring tide. Visibility is usually only a metre or two, but it significantly improves during the summer on a neap tide and after a spell of dry settled weather. Vast shoals of saithe (coley) swim over and around the Whitestone in the spring and summer months and the area is well used by local lobster and crab fishermen. Depths vary between 5-15m around the Whitestones Reef.

GRAN

Wreck, stern section ★★
Bow section ★★★
Scenery ★★
Depth 15-18m
Reference N 54 53 871 W 001 19 512
1½ miles S.E. of the river Wear

The *Gran* was a steel 1,153-ton Norwegian steamship, registered at the port of Lyngor in Norway and had dimensions of 69.82m length, by 10.69m beam and a 4.8m draught. She was built in 1907 by Bergen M.V., in Bergen and owned at the time of loss by Adgesidins Redero Akties. Her single steel- propeller was powered by a three-cylinder, triple-expansion steam engine that developed 106hp, using one boiler.

On 23 May 1917, the *Gran* was in ballast, on passage from Rouen for Newcastle-upon-Tyne, under the command of Captain A.T. Anderson, when she foundered one mile east of Ryhope, after detonating a mine laid by the German submarine, *UC-40*. The *Gran* was blown in two by the explosion and the halves sank about 200m apart, in a position just to the northern end of the Whitestones Reef. However, my records do not show if any of her crew were lost. This vessel was insured against war risks on the London market for a total sum of 960,000 kroner.

Wreck-site
Stern Section
The stern section of the wreck, where you can find the boiler, a steel propeller, two large winches and the remains of her engine, lie to the southern end, in a

general depth of 18m. They are scattered around and everything is well concreted into the seabed, with hard, white, marine-worm casings covering the few remaining pipes and plates. All in all, it is a rather dismal dive, as no marine life could be seen around the surrounding rocks and seabed.

During the summer, coley shoals can be seen all around this area and it is popular with local angling boats. This end of the wreck has also been professionally salvaged, so there are very few, if any, items of interest to be found. Visibility is usually very poor, due to the amount of suspended sediment in the water from the River Wear and the proximity of the local sewer pipe. However, during the summer, after a spell of light, westerly winds and no rain, underwater visibility can extend over 10m, at times.

Bow Section and Decking
The rest of the wreck, which accounts for two-thirds of the ship, lies approximately 200m north-west of the boiler and engine, in a general depth of 15-18m, the lowest astronomical depth of about 11-13m. However, there are some huge boulder reefs, just to the south-east, that gave misleading information on the echo-sounder. The wreck lies up against the base of the reef, orientated in a south-west to north-east direction, on hard, flat, rocky ground.

The flat, steel decking accounts for seventy percent of the wreck and lies more or less flush with the seabed. There are still a few large, brass valves bolted solidly onto the decking. At the head of the flat decking, is what appears to have been the wheelhouse, which is the highest structure left. There are no visible signs of any brass artifacts around. They must lie under the surrounding pile of steel debris. However, the clapper from the ship's bell was discovered. You can see into the wheelhouse, but it would be impossible to enter, due to the twisted steel plates and girders and the very narrow entrance. This is the more interesting section of the wreck, although it is not the best that can be found. The area is often fished with monofilament gill nets, so extra caution should be taken at all times. It is possible to dive at any state of the tide, but it is best in low, slack water after westerly winds.

DENHAM

Wreck ★★★
Scenery ★
Depth 44m
Reference N 54 54 078 W 001 12 832
6 miles N.E. of Seaham Harbour.

The *Denham* was an iron 869-ton British steamship, registered at Newcastle-upon-Tyne and had dimensions of 64m length, by 9.19m beam and a draught of

4.87m. She was owned by J.H. Reah of Newcastle and built by Wigham, Richardson Ltd, at Newcastle-upon-Tyne, in 1878. Her single iron propeller was powered by a two-cylinder, compound-steam engine that developed 98hp, using one boiler. Her machinery was built at Newcastle-upon-Tyne by J. Shaw & Co. She had one deck, four watertight bulkheads, a 6.7m poop-deck, 11.9m bridge-deck and 7.9m forecastle.

On 22 February 1894, the *Denham* foundered and was lost six miles north-east of Seaham Harbour, following a collision with the Danish-registered steamship *Rolf*. She had been on passage from the Tyne for Rochester, under the command of Captain F. Rochester and was carrying a cargo of coal and a crew of seventeen. There are no reports of any crew being lost. It is believed that they were taken on board the *Rolf* and landed at Sunderland.

Wreck-site

The wreck, believed to be that of the steamship *Denham*, lies on a seabed of fine-sand, mud, gravel and broken shell, in a general depth of 44m, the lowest astronomical depth. It is partially buried, well broken up, badly decayed and dispersed over an area of around 55m x 9m. The highest section of the wreck, at around 2m, is the boiler, which lies alongside her broken engine and machinery, which are covered in a coating of hard, white, marine worm casings. Everything of interest will still be somewhere in the wreck-site, but with so much concreted debris and in such a depth they will take some searching for.

Tidal streams are fairly strong and visibilty usually dismal, making a powerful torch essential to see anything. This is also a dive-site only for very experienced divers who know what they are doing.

JAMES

Wreck ★★★★
Scenery ★
Depth 54m
Reference N 54 53 62 W 001 05 23
10½ miles E.N.E. of Seaham Harbour.

The *James* was an iron, British steamship of around 1,800 tons and had dimensions of approximately 80m length, by 11m beam and a draught of 5m. She was registered at the port of Sunderland and was built in 1882. Her single, iron propeller was powered by a three-cylinder, triple-expansion steam engine that used two boilers and the vessel had a centrally positioned superstructure.

On 27 January 1910, the *James* was in ballast on passage from Rouen for the Tyne, carrying a crew of eighteen, when she foundered and was lost following a collision with the Dartmouth-registered steamship *Vanessa*.

Wreck-site

The wreck, believed to be that of the steamship *James*, lies orientated in a north-west to south-east direction, on a dirty seabed of mud and broken shells in a general depth of 54m, the lowest astronomical depth. She is still quite substantial, but appears to be upside down and standing some 6m high around her midships section, where the hull has collapsed onto the boilers and engine, all of which are now exposed and covered in a profusion of soft corals. Very little is recognizable, but most of her interesting instruments will be somewhere under the pile of iron debris. A number of portholes are clearly visible, as well as an anchor windlass, a large winch and some lengths of heavy copper piping that protrude out of the wreckage. Quite a number of fish were picked up on the echo-sounder around the wreck-site, so she may be worth marking down for a day's boat angling.

Tidal streams are rather strong and visibility is usually very poor, but it improves significantly during the summer months. The wreck-site is also a long way from shore, so careful planning is required by anyone contemplating either diving or fishing on this wreck. Lion's-mane jellyfish will be a nuisance during the months of July and August as well.

GENERAL HAVELOCK

Wreck ★
Scenery ★★★
Depth 6-8m
Reference N 54 53 64 W 001 19 45
½ mile offshore, inside Whitestone's Reef.

The *General Havelock* was an iron 670-ton British steamship, registered at Sunderland and owned by Messrs R.M. Hudson & Sons of John Street in Sunderland. She was built in 1868 as a passenger and general cargo vessel, equipped with a single iron propeller said to have been powered by a three-cylinder, triple-expansion steam engine, using one boiler, although this would have been very early for that type of engine and it may have been a two-cylinder, compound steam engine.

On 27 September 1894, under the command of Captain J.G. Stock, the *General Havelock* was on her return voyage from London to Sunderland, with thirty passengers and a crew of twenty-one, when she foundered after striking the offshore rocks at Hendon in Sunderland.

This was the report in the Sunderland Echo the following day:

'General Havelock wrecked'
The *General Havelock* went ashore at 9.40 p.m. on the rocks near to the old Spelter Works at Hendon. Built in 1868 for passengers and general

The Arendal *was a Norwegian-registered wooden brig of 275 gross tons (255 tons net) and had dimensions of 31.4m length, 8m beam and 4.9m draught. She was built in 1855 and owned by B. Jacobsen of Arendal. She was en-route from Tonsberg to Sunderland with cargo of pit props and eight crew, under the command of H. Hansen and at approximately 9.30 a.m. on 2 March 1906, she attempted to enter the harbour during a north-east gale when she ran ashore just inside the harbour. The volunteer life brigade was summoned, but owing to the great distance from the shore the rocket line was useless. The vessel was drifting towards the North Pier and the crew had to be rescued by the lifeboat, except for the captain and first mate who remained on board. The steam tugs* Stag *and* Devonia *eventually succeeded in connecting a tow and brought the vessel into port.* Courtesy of the Roker Volunteer Life Brigade.

cargo, she was trading between London and Sunderland calling at Scarborough during the summer months, being occasionally held up for repairs. On the afternoon of Wednesday she left her wharf in London at about 4 p.m. for the return journey to Sunderland. Pleasant weather was experienced and she called into Scarborough to discharge passengers for that watering place and take other passengers to Sunderland. The journey was delayed because of contrary winds and she passed Ryhope at 9 o'clock. Those on board felt the vessel grating on rocks and soon seen the vessel was holed and before they realised the ship was fast, it began to list. Four boats were lowered then the *Havelock* listed so badly that it was impossible to stand. Among 30 passengers on board Captain Stock and the Officers succeeded in allaying their fears. The Captain and Mate were the last to leave the ship. The second boat, which included passengers and ladies began to fill up with water and the passengers were in a bad plight. A tug-boat, that proved to be the *Norfolk*

Hero from Sunderland was sighted and bore down and enabled everyone to get aboard. It then landed them ashore, some suffering from fright and some fainted when they got ashore. Every assistance was given by the Docks Master and his assistant. The *Havelock* filled up with water overnight and next morning there was very little to see but the engine and boiler. The passengers' and crews' luggage and effects were washed ashore during the early hours and were taken by a crowd of men and women, but the police were called. The vessel belonged to Messrs Hudson of John Street and it was 670 tons.

In an earlier incident on 24 April 1884, the *General Havelock* was in collision with the wooden Runswick fishing coble *Peace*, two miles east-north-east of Runswick Bay, in light, easterly winds. Owned by the skipper, Mr J. Hutton, who was on board at the time, both he and his other crewman perished when the *Peace* went down.

Wreck-site
The remains of the *General Havelock* have almost disappeared now and all that remains are a few bits of twisted, iron framework and girders, a boiler and her iron propeller. The seabed around this area is comprised of small reefs and rocks, covered in sediment and what appears to be excrement from the nearby sewer out-fall a little to the north. Tidal streams are very moderate and it is possible to dive the wreck at any state of the tide, however visibility is usually poor, except sometimes during the summer months after a spell of dry settled weather and westerly winds.

CORNWALL

Wreck ★★
Scenery ★★
Depth 10-11m
Reference N 54 53 65 W 001 20 44
$\frac{1}{3}$ miles south of the old dock entrance.

Built at Sunderland for the Lambton Coal Company in 1873, the *Cornwall* was a small, iron steamship of 677 tons gross, registered at the port of London and owned by H.T. Morton of Durham. Her single iron propeller was powered by a two-cylinder, invert-compound steam engine that used one boiler.

On 9 September 1884, the *Cornwall*, with sixteen crew and one passenger, was on route from London to Sunderland, under the command of a Captain G. Bell. She was steaming steadily north, just off Scarborough in a thick fog, when at 1 a.m., the 3,000-ton iron steamer *Stanmore* of Liverpool, accidentally rammed into her stern end, close to the engines. The force of the impact left a huge gash all the way down the side of the *Cornwall*, below the water-line and she immediately began to fill up with water. Most of her crew scrambled to safety over the bows of

Sunderland South Volunteer Life Brigade in the early twentieth century. Courtesy of Captain Fred Roberts, Roker VLB.

the *Stanmore*, which stayed with the damaged ship until the arrival of a large sea-going tug, that assisted and accompanied the *Cornwall* on her remaining passage to Sunderland.

Unfortunately, the extent of the damage proved too much for her, because at 9 a.m. and within a few hundred metres of her destination, the *Cornwall* went to the bottom. The tug rescued the remaining crew members and landed them safely ashore at Sunderland. Although the wreck was lying in only 10-11m of water, very close to shore and not far from the Hendon paper mills, she was never salvaged. She quickly succumbed to the elements.

Wreck-site

The wreck lies approximately 575m directly south of the old and now disused south harbour entrance to the South Docks at Hendon. The seabed around the area where the *Cornwall* lies in 10-11m on a seabed that consists mostly of flat rock and small reefs, with a few short strands of kelp and a heavy coating of sediment. As would be expected in this depth of water and so far in shore, her remains are well smashed up and almost level with the bottom. However, when the wreck was first discovered, huge copper pipes and bronze valves were scattered everywhere and a number of portholes were lying between the debris, just waiting to be picked up.

Now, mostly twisted, jagged framework and iron pipes, that are gradually concreting into the seabed, cover an area of around 50 x 20m. The highest point is a jumble of decayed iron plates and pipes that stand some 2m high, which lie close to the remains of an iron condenser, which has burst open, leaving a matted heap of thin brass tubes strewn around. There is no sign of her propeller. At first it was thought that the ship may have been a paddle-steamer. The boiler is also missing, but, because the seabed is rather flat, this may have been rolled inshore during the winter storms or broken up.

Visibility is usually very poor, due mostly to the close proximity of the Hendon sewers and the river Wear. However, during the summer months the visibility can sometimes reach as much as ten metres, with the boat-cover visible on the surface. The seabed is often carpeted with starfish in this area, obviously attracted by the sewer out-fall, but most other forms of marine life are rather conspicuous by their absence, while currents are very moderate.

The wreck is fairly level to the seabed, but it still makes an interesting rummage dive, as you never know what hidden artifact the winter storms may turn up.

SARA (ex-ANT)
Wreck ★
Scenery ★★★
Depth 8-10m
Reference N 54 54 17 W 001 19 90
S.W. side of Hendon Rock

The *Sara* was an iron 1133-ton steamship and had dimensions of 68.58m length, by 9.57m beam and a 4.49m draught. Originally called the *Ant*, she was built by W. Gray & Sons of Hartlepool in August 1883 for H. Martini & Co. of Glasgow. Her iron propeller was powered by a two-cylinder, inverted-compound steam engine that developed 99hp, using one boiler. Her machinery was built by Blair of Stockton.

In 1886 she was sold to G. Jamieson of Liverpool and resold in 1902 to a Norwegian company, Aktieselsk Sara (H. Skougaard). She was then fitted with a larger engine of 113hp and re-registered under the name of *Sara* at the port of Langesund in Norway. She had one deck, four watertight bulkheads and a superstructure consisting of an 8.2m poop deck, 15.8m quarter-deck, 17.6m bridge-deck and 9.4m forecastle.

On 22 November 1915, under the command of Captain J. Jensen, she was on passage from Gothenburg for Sunderland with a cargo of pit-props. The *Sara* was making her way to the old South Dock entrance of the port in heavy fog, when she stranded on the Hendon Rock at 7 a.m. (This is a huge rock, which is permanently submerged, some two and a half metres beneath the suface, on a low spring tide.) Four tugs attempted to re-float her on the incoming tide without success, as she had a gaping hole in her side and a severe starboard list.

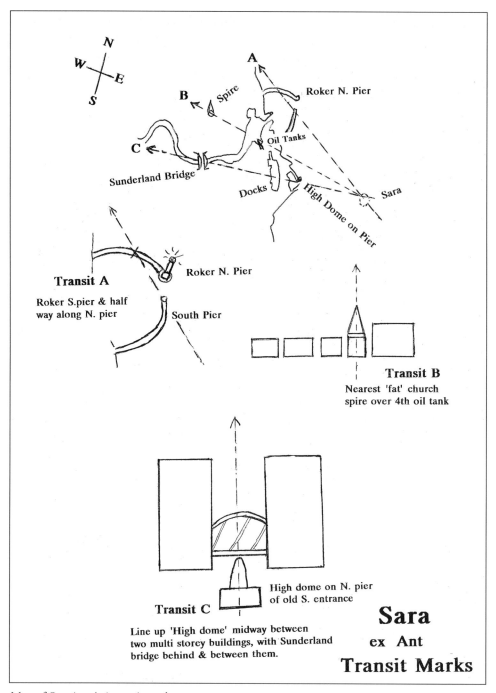

Map of *Sara* (ex-*Ant*) transit marks.

Eventually, she filled up with water and slipped down to the bottom. One of the tugs rescued her crew at 3 p.m, just before she sank, and put them safely ashore. The buoyant cargo, combined with the pressure of water, quickly burst open the hatch covers and the ship's cargo of pit-props covered the sea's surface. The following day, Hendon and Ryhope beaches were littered with timbers, keeping the local people's home fires burning for many months, thanks to the unfortunate mishap.

Wreck-site
The wreck was discovered by the author and one of his colleagues, Rolf Mitchinson, while systematically searching all of the high rocky protrusions from the seabed with an echo-sounder in 1975. At the time of the discovery, the wreck, although smashed to pieces by the forces of nature, was virtually untouched by salvers or divers. The seabed to the south-west of her boiler was strewn with iron ribs, frame-work, decking and copper pipes of every size, massive crushed lead pipes, varying shapes of bronze valves, a brass donkey boiler lying close to the condenser and lots of intact brass portholes. The ship's bell, bearing the inscription 'ANT, 1883, Glasgow', was recovered by the author in 1978. It was found lying buried in a concretion of coal-dust and small stones, with only the brass loop showing above the debris, between the ship's ribs, looking for all the world like the end of a brass cannon.

All that remains of her today is her boiler, standing upright, close to the south-western side of Hendon Rock, in 8-10m and the twisted iron ribs and framework, plus at least three iron propellers lying among the concretion of coal dust and pebbles. However, she is still an interesting dive, because strewn around her wreckage and the large kelp-covered boulders, there is evidence of at least one other wreck, hence the concretion of coal dust and extra propellers. Tides can be fairly strong, but it is possible to dive at any state of the tide. Visibility is usually poor, from 0-3/4m, due to the effluence from the river Wear and the out-flow of a nearby sewer. Occasionally, during the summer months, after a dry spell, small tides and a run of westerly winds, the visibility can reach as much as ten metres. The seabed and kelp beds always have a coating of sediment, since the sewer-pipe was built a few years ago, but cod, wrasse, shoals of coley and crustaceans are a fairly common sight.

QUILLOTA (ex-BRAHMIN)

Wreck ★
Scenery ★★
Depth 12m
Reference N 54 54 40 W 001 19 60
½m off Hendon, Sunderland.

The *Quillota* was a very large iron, full-rigged French sailing ship of 1,335 tons, registered at the port of Dunkirk and had dimensions of 70.51m length, by

The Maliano *(ex* Godolphin*) was a steel 1,558 ton Spanish-registered steamship with dimensions of 76.2m length, by 10.7m beam and a draught of 5m. She was built by Grangemouth dockyard at Alloa in 1889 and was owned by Aznar y Cia of Bilbao. Her single iron propeller was powered by a three-cylinder, triple-expansion steam engine that used one boiler and her machinery was built by Hutson & Corbett of Glasgow. On 23 March 1900 the* Maliano *was on a voyage from Bilbao, with a cargo of iron ore and a crew of twenty-three. After attempting to enter the harbour at Sunderland in a strong easterly wind and with corresponding seas, steerage was lost and she stranded on Roker Beach, 50m from the pier, at the harbour entrance. The ship heeled over with her decks to the sea, which broke over her in great ferocity. The volunteer life brigade was quickly on the scene and effected communications with the vessel. However, the crew got the apparatus and breeches buoy tangled up and it travelled half way over to the vessel before jamming. William Hennen, divisional carpenter of the coastguard, elected to go on board and try to put matters right. He hauled out as far as possible, then went hand over hand along the hawser to reach the vessel. Once the gear was free the crew were quickly landed, twenty-three of them in around thirty minutes, with Hennen the last to leave. He was later awarded the bronze medal by the Board of Trade for his brave actions. The crew was so grateful to the brigade and the coastguard that they left momentoes at the Brigade House. The* Maliano *was later refloated. It was reported to be still around in the 1920s.* Courtesy of the Roker Volunteer Life Brigade.

11.06m beam and a draught of 6.62m. She was built as the *Brahmin* in 1876 at Greenock by R. Steele and Company and owned at the time of loss by A.D. Bordes & Sons of Dunkirk. She had two decks, one bulkhead and a superstructure consisting of a 13.4m poop-deck and a 10.7m forecastle. She was also classed as 100 A1 by Lloyd's of London.

Amongst seafarers and people interested in the days of sail there has always been a great debate about the variations of rigs on sailing vessels and the different names given to them. However, the 'full rigged ship', is technically the only sailing vessel entitled to be called a ship. She would have had been square rigged on all three, or possibly more masts and have had a gaff sail on the mizzen.

The *Quillota* had been trading between South America and France. On 12 November 1901, under the command of Captain C. Delepine, she was in ballast on passage from Nantes for North Shields to pick up a cargo of coal, with a crew of twenty-two and a pilot, when she grounded and was lost at Hendon during raging, force ten winds, from east-north-east.

The following were headlines, followed by a report, on a full page of the *Sunderland Echo* on 11 November 1901:

> The Storm, the barometer went down with great rapidity, strong gales blowing accompanied by sheets of rain, the streets washed cleaner than they have been for some considerable time and only those forced to go out, do so. It is many years since our port was the scene of such disaster. 'Loss of the *Harriott* of Goole'; 'Exciting Scenes, two men drowned'; 'Wreck at Whitburn, 4 saved several drowned'; 'Huge seas off Tyne'; 'Barque in distress'; 'Third ketch ashore'; 'Atlantic Hurricane'.

Headlines and reports on one full page of the *Echo* on 12 November 1901 read:

> 'Wreck on South Pier, two drowned, Schooner Founders, boat swamped, loss of nine lives'; 'Death Toll in Wear, 34 men drowned in five vessels'; 'Disaster off Scarborough, ship lost with all hands'; 'Disaster off the Tyne, loss of big ship and 16 lives'; 'Wreck ashore at Seaham'; 'Steamer beaches at Redcar'; 'Wreck at West Hartlepool, three lives lost'; 'Vessels founder off Tyne'; 'Another wreck at Seaham'; 'Lifeboat capsizes at Great Yarmouth; 9 or 10 men drowned'; 'Eight men drowned at Seaham'.

Headlines and report in the *Echo* on 13 November read:

> 'Wreck of French Ship', 'The *Quillota* in ballast for the Tyne had been trading between South America and France was thought to have come to anchor and for a while she was stationary and would weather the gale. At times she was hidden from sight in huge depressions and masses of spray. By night the vessel was burning distress signals, but nothing could be done for she was beyond the reach of rockets and no small craft could live in that seething sea.
>
> From that time there seemed very little hope. She gradually drove in and touched bottom. The men had been all washed off the ship and only five of its crew of twenty-two, including the pilot had been saved.
>
> C. Delepine Captain, the mate Parn and two seamen. Delepine and Ollivier Francole had reached terra firma some time after the vessel stranded. They were ill clad to withstand the rigours of such a night and wandered about the beach with cut and bleeding feet until they managed to climb up the embankment and on to the signal cable in

the N.E.R., whence they were taken by the coastguard to the Toll Bar Inn. The manager John Lawther gave them food and warm drinks.

The captain was dressed in an oil-skin, jacket, lining and shirt while the seaman had on trousers and lining but neither had on shoes or socks. Shortly after 1 o'clock another crewman who gave his name as Leinel Francole was found in Commercial Road with a life-belt round him. He was soaking wet and taken by a man named Carter to Hendon Police Station. Here he was given hot coffee and Inspector Sanderson furnished him with clothes. He said he was from the *Quillota* and was battling with angry waters for some considerable time before reaching shore.

The vicinity of Ryhope was thickly strewn with wreckage, but the *Quillota* had completely disappeared unless a spar which was just visible at low water really belonged to her. Close to this was a name board of the *Harriot* lost yesterday. Two men were found buried in sand/clay and were noticed when a hand waved to someone and they were dug out but one died later.

The surviving seaman called Leinel Francole told one of the reporters 'the vessel was going to the Tyne for a cargo of coal and got caught in the full force of the tempest so the Captain dropped the two anchors but they dragged as the day went on and the ship gradually drifted towards the beach. The men huddled together in the poop and could not hear for the howling wind and they got drenched from the heavy rain and spray I got caught in a big wave and washed into the sea in my trousers and bare feet, but with a life-belt around me. I swam hard and scarcely knew where I was going and was thoroughly shattered when I was thrown onto the shore. After I got my breath, I succeeded in scrambling up the cliff, but no one was about so I walked towards the lights where I met a man in Commercial Road.' That was the man that took him to the police station.

Apparently, the South Side Volunteer Life Brigade mustered on Hendon Beach, but the ship was too far out. The lifeboat crew were in favour of going out to help the crew, but they needed a tug to tow them and the tug skipper refused, saying it would be suicidal in those conditions.

Seventeen people were lost altogether on the *Quillota*. The wind raged for almost three days between the nights of 11 and 14 November 1901. At least seventeen vessels foundered and were lost in the horrendous conditions. They were the 288-ton snow *Cambois* at Whitburn; the schooner *Harrriot* at Sunderland; the ketch *Europa* at Sunderland; the Russian 141-ton schooner *Alcor* at Seaham; the 155-ton brigantine *Cornucopia* at Hartlepool; the 180-ton brigantine *Constance Ellen* at South Shields; the 247-ton Swedish schooner *Sirius* off Hawthorn; the 156-ton ketch *Dauntless* at Hartlepool; the ketch *Impel* off Seaham; the 417-ton Norwegian barque *Christiane* at South Shields; the 128-ton schooner *Miss Thomas* near Hawthorn; the 237-ton barquentine *Lile* off Sunderland; the 100-ton schooner *Hannah & Jane* at Blackhall Rocks; the steam trawler *Retriever* off Tynemouth; the 471-ton barque *Trio* at Seaton Carew; the German ketch *Catharina* at West Hartlepool; the steam tug *Countess Vane* at her moorings in Seaham Harbour; the 196-ton brigantine *Florence* at Hartlepool; the 222-ton brig *John Roberts* in Marsden Bay; the 325-ton Guernsey-registered barque *Wave Queen* at West Hartlepool and the 467-ton iron dump barge *Loch-na-gar* off Seaham.

The total number of people who died is uncertain, but at least sixty-five are known to have drowned or were lost at sea in those ships alone, while six more vessels were lost north of the Tyne during those two to three days and another four lost south of the Tees.

Wreck-site

The wreck of *Quillota* lies in a general depth of 10-12m on a seabed of hard rock and surrounded by small reefs, so it is difficult to pick up with an echo sounder. The easiest way to find her is with the use of a magnetometer. However, these are not so easy to come by. The wreck, which is well smashed up and decayed, is spread over a wide area and the outline of her hull is stands about $1\frac{1}{2}$ m high. However, the iron is now concreting into the seabed rocks. She was found by accident, when we were exploring the area with a magnetometer and on inspection we thought she was just an old iron barge, because there was no sign of boilers or an engine, so the area was not properly looked at. Further investigation is needed which should have been carried out by the end of the year 2000.

Visibility is usually poor, but can be as much as 10m after neap tides, a dry spell and light westerly winds, during the summer months. Tidal streams are fairly strong, although it is possible to dive at other states of the tide, but it is best left alone on springs. Lion's-mane jellyfish are also a nuisance during the months of July and August.

POVENA

Wreck ★★
Scenery ★★
Depth 16m
Reference N 54 54 094 W 001 18 733
1 mile S.E. of river Wear entrance.

The *Povena* was a steel 2,104-ton Spanish well-deck steamship, registered at the port of Bilbao and had dimensions of 83.9m length, by 12.7m beam and a draught of 5.3 m. She was built by William Gray & Company at yard No 553, West Hartlepool, in May 1898 and was owned by Ramon de la Sota of Bilbao, who owned a fleet of twenty-four steamers. Her single steel propeller was powered by a three-cylinder, triple-expansion steam engine that used one boiler and her machinery was built by Central Marine Engine Works Ltd at Sunderland.

On the afternoon of 3 June 1899, the *Povena* was on passage from Bilbao for the Tyne with a cargo of iron ore when she struck the Whitestones Reef, one and a half miles south of the river Wear at Sunderland. She was refloated on the following tide and steamed on to the Tyne, but foundered and was lost soon after, possibly on 5 June.

Her sister ship, the *Algota* that was launched on 9 February 1898, was sunk by a German U-boat off Ushant on 29 January 1917.

Wreck-site

The wreck of *Povena* lies on a well swept rocky seabed in a general depth of 16m just north, and outside of the Whitestones Reef at Sunderland. She was salvaged some ten years ago when the wreck was found untouched since the day she sank in 1899. Her boiler stands upright next to her engine, which lies on its side and the brass and copper condenser lies beneath the engine. The bell, stern equipment, propeller, shaft, anchor, chains and most non-ferrous items have all been removed now, but the wreck is still worth a good rummage dive. There are a number of small reefs about one metre high at the stern end of the wreck-site, which may produce one or two crustaceans, while huge shoals of saithe (coleys) can be found all around this area during the summer months.

Tidal streams are moderate, but can be quite severe during spring tides, while the visibility is usually only 1m or so, but improves significantly during the summer when it is possible to see as much as 10m on a good day. The best time to dive the wreck site is on a neap tide, at low, slack water and after a spell of dry, settled weather.

4. Wear to the Tyne

ORION

Wreck ★
Scenery ★
Depth 3m
Reference N 54 55 28 W 001 21 41
Inside the north pier, Sunderland.

The *Orion* was a steel 2,164-ton German registered steamship, built in 1901. Her single steel propeller was powered by a three-cylinder, triple-expansion steam engine that used three boilers.

On 21 November 1913, the *Orion* was on passage from Sunderland for Libau with a cargo of coal and a crew of eighteen when she stranded inside the north pier, at the entrance to the river Wear. The crew was taken off by the Volunteer Life Brigade. The vessel stood in the shallow water for some time before she broke in two becoming a total loss.

Wreck-site
Major salvage work was carried out on the *Orion* soon after she broke up, but part of her top frames lie mixed up with what remnants of the steamship *J.B. Eiminson*

Above and previous page: *The 2,164 ton German steamer* Orion *stranded near the north pier of the River Wear on 21 November 1913. Later she became a total wreck and broke in two in shallow water. Parts of the wreck are still visible at low spring tides and lies mixed up with the remains of the steamer* J.B. Eminson.

and just break the surface on a low spring tide. All that remains of the two wrecks lies about 50m south, and half way along the inside of the north pier, on a rather dirty sand seabed, in a general depth of 3m, about the lowest astronomical depth. The iron and steel plates, top frames and pieces of box sections are covered in small brown and red seaweeds. Sometimes they harbour the occasional edible crab or lobster, but most commonly seen are the hordes of scurrying green-shore crabs, butterfish, flatfish and colourful little blennies.

There are no strong currents to worry about, but the visibility is at the mercy of the river Wear. The best time to visit the wreck-site is at low tide, after a long spell of dry settled weather during the summer, when visibility may reach a few metres, then you can swim out from the beach between the piers.

J. B. EMINSON

Wreck ★
Scenery ★
Depth 3m
Reference N 54 55 28 W 001 21 41
Inside north pier, Sunderland.

The 1,031 ton British steamship J.B.Eminson *stranded next to the north pier of the River Wear on 7 February 1881, after attempting to enter the river during a strong southerly gale. The wreck now lies mixed up with the remains of the steamer* Orion *and parts of her can be seen during a low, spring tide.*

The *J.B. Eminson* was an iron 1,031-ton British steamship registered at Sunderland and had dimensions of 67.5m length, by 9.44m beam and a draught of 5.2m. She was owned at the time of loss by the Marquis of Londonderry, (although another report says she was owned by J.O. Clazey of Sunderland) and built in 1875 by Short's Co. Ltd at Sunderland. Her single iron propeller was powered by a two-cylinder, compound-steam engine that developed 90hp, using one boiler and her machinery was built by T. Richardson & Sons Ltd at Hartlepool.

Under the command of Captain J. Rutherford, the *J.B. Eminson* was on a return voyage from London to Sunderland in ballast, when, on 7 February 1881, she grounded close to the north pier at Sunderland. A strong southerly gale was blowing when the steamer tried to enter the river at 8 p.m. that evening and the sea was heaving with white curling water. As soon as it was realised, the Roker Division of the Volunteer Rocket Brigade effected communications with the heaving cane, while the South Division fired a rocket, but missed. The crew was eventually landed by a ladder onto the pier and the breeches-buoy was used only to land one out of the sixteen crew on board.

Several steam tugs arrived and tried desperately to tow the stranded vessel off the pier rocks, but each attempt failed and the tug *Rescue* lost her smoke-stack when she fouled the warps. The *J.B. Eminson* became a total loss and was eventually left to the elements.

Wreck-site

The ship's remains lies mixed up with the remnants of the steamship *Orion* which came ashore in the same area in November 1913. She dries on a low spring tide and lies about 50m south of the middle of the north pier at Sunderland, on a seabed of dirty sand, in a general depth of 3m, the lowest astronomical depth. All that remains now are some flattened iron and steel top frames, plates and small pieces of box sections, which are covered in brown and red seaweed. Edible crabs or the occasional lobster can sometimes be found, but most common are the multitudes of scurrying green-shore crabs, butterfish, flatfish and colourful little blennies.

There are no strong currents to worry about, but the visibility is at the mercy of the river Wear. The best time to visit the wreck-site is on a low spring tide, after a long spell of settled weather and westerly winds during the summer months, when you can actually swim out from the beach and snorkel around the remains.

UC-32

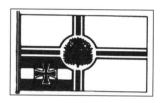

Wreck ★★★
Scenery ★
Depth 12-13m
Reference N 54 54 521 W 001 19 320
Also: N 54 54 510 W 001 19 621
4½ miles N-E of south pier, river Wear.

The *UC-32* was a UC11 Class German submarine of 511 tons, built and launched in Germany on 12 August 1916 and commissioned on 13 September. She had dimensions of 52m length, with a beam of 5.2m and was armed with one 88.8mm deck gun, three bow and one stern torpedo tubes, (sized 483mm by 178mm and 76mm by 102mm). She also had six vertically inclined mine tubes and carried eighteen UC-200 mines. Her twin bronze propellers were powered by two oil engines that developed between 460hp and 620hp and she ran submerged on an electric motor, powered by rows of lead/acid batteries. She was reported to be capable of about 12 knots surface speed and 7.4 knots submerged.

During the First World War, *UC-32* was a mine-laying submarine and had a general patrol area from the Humber to the Tyne. Also, she used to harass trawlers at the mouth of the river Wear. She would lie in wait until vessels left the river, then she would surface and sink them with her deck gun and submerge before any ship or plane could catch her. However, the Royal Navy got together with the fishermen and armed a steam fishing trawler with a large deck gun (a Q ship) and kept it camouflaged until the submarine surfaced. Then they took the covers off and let blaze at the U-boat. Taken by surprise, she immediately crash-dived, leaving one unfortunate sailor still on her deck. The submarine got away that time, but the sailor drowned.

The UC-59 *is seen standing next to the British 'K' class submarine K-6 in December 1918 or early 1919, after surrendering to the Allies at the end of the First World War. The* UC-59 *was a sister ship of German submarine* UC-32 *which blew up and sank off Sunderland after detonating one of her own mines.* Courtesy of the Royal Navy Submarine Museum, Gosport.

On 23 February 1917, *UC-32* was just starting to lay her mines off the river mouth, in 12m of water, when she accidentally struck one of her own mines. The vessel blew up and sank, killing nineteen of her crew, but the captain, Oberleutnant zur See Herbert Breyer and two sailors were rescued by an examination vessel. It was thought that a plug that held the mine to the sinker must have dissolved too quickly, releasing the mine, which exploded under her stern-end.

A diving colleague of mine, Rolf Mitchinson, said that his father had told him that when he was a young boy of nine years old, he lived in a house overlooking the Sunderland docks, from where he watched three of the U-Boat's rescued crew being brought ashore, under armed guard. He said he could remember the hatred many of the local people who lined the docks felt for the German sailors, because the people jeered and spat at them as they stepped onto the quay.

Apart from trawlers, *UC-32* also sank the 1,112-ton Norwegian registered ship *Jerve* off the Yorkshire coast, near Flamborough Head, on 1 February 1917, only three weeks before she blew herself up. Then on 6 May after she was lost, the 904-ton steamship *Hebble* also foundered off Sunderland, after detonating one of her mines.

Wreck-site

Fifteen years ago a substantial amount of the wreck was still intact, including her twin bronze propellers, which had inscribed on them 'Vulcanwerke, Volcad Works, Rubel Bronze, 29-7-1916 and Durchmess, Steigung. When she was found, the complete periscope and about five whole telegraphs were also there, along with her two bronze propellers, however they are now long since gone, taken when the wreck was first discovered.

In about 1993-1994, a diver from a Sunderland Sub Aqua club, 'rediscovered' the wreck and told the media about what he had found. The German Embassy got involved and it was designated as a war grave. Because the wreck was close to the shipping channel and there were still live mines and torpedoes on board, the Royal Navy brought in divers to examine her and decided to disperse it. Now, the police launch from the river Wear warns off any diving boats moored anywhere near her.

The wreck lies approximately 400m north from the north pier lighthouse at Sunderland in 12-13m. There is still a substantial amount of her left, in three main sections and lots of copper and brass to be seen along with dozens of giant lead batteries standing in rows The torpedo tube also still has a live torpedo in it too, just ready for firing.

Underwater visibility is at the whim of the river Wear, because it is directly in line with the out flowing fresh water on the ebb tide, however during dry spells in the summer months visibility can reach 10m and you can dive at any state of the tide. It should be remembered that at the moment this site is classed as a war grave.

ABBOTSFORD

Wreck ★★★★
Scenery ★
Depth 58m
Reference N 54 55 295 W 001 06 235
10 miles E. of river Wear.

The *Abbotsford* was an iron British steamship of around 1,000 tons. She was built in 1870, registered at the port of Leith and had dimensions of some 66m length and a beam of 9.50m. She was owned at the time of loss by G. Gibson & Co. in Leith and her single iron propeller was powered by a two-cylinder, compound-steam engine that used one boiler.

On 22 October 1906, the *Abbotsford* was carrying a general cargo on passage from Ghent for Leith when she foundered and was lost, following a collision with the Hull-registered steam trawler, *Helen McGregor*. It is believed that her crew of eighteen and her master, Captain A.G. Bridges were taken on board the trawler and landed at the Tyne.

Wreck-site

The wreck, believed to be the that of the steamship *Abbotsford*, lies orientated in a north to south direction on a seabed of mud and black shells in a general depth of 58m, the lowest astronomical depth. The wreck is now totally collapsed, well broken up, decayed and surrounded by a field of debris, with the highest section of 3m at midships, where her boiler and engine are exposed. The outline of the wreck is still clearly defined, although most of it is a jumbled mass of broken machinery. A number of large lengths of copper pipe, brass valves, an anchor windlass, two anchors and a propeller can be seen in the debris. The wreck-site, an area of some 60 x 15m, is said to be very dark and eerie and has a layer of muddy silt covering everything, with very little obvious marine life to be seen.

Tidal streams are very strong and visibility is usually poor, but it will improve during neap tides and a spell of dry, settled weather and westerly winds.

ZEELAND

Wreck ★★★★
Scenery ★
Depth 48m
Reference N 54 55 396 W 001 09 455
7 miles E. of river Wear

The *Zeeland* was a steel 1,293-ton Dutch steamship, registered at Rotterdam and had dimensions of 70.46m length, by 10.46m beam and a draught of 4.47m. She was owned at the time of loss by Scheepvaart-en Steenkolen Maats NV and built in 1907 by Werf v/h Rijkee & Co. at Rotterdam. Her single steel propeller was powered by a three-cylinder, triple-expansion steam engine that developed 147hp using two boilers.

On 1 August 1916, the *Zeeland* was on passage from Methil for Rouen, under the command of Captain J.J. Schutt and carrying an unspecified cargo of coal, when she was stopped by the German submarine *UB-39*. Her crew was forced to abandon the vessel that was then sunk by gunfire, seven miles east of Sunderland.

Wreck-site

The wreck, believed to be that of the steamship *Zeeland* lies on a well swept seabed of sand, mud and broken black shells in a general depth of 48m, the lowest astronomical depth. She is still very substantial and intact, standing over 6m high in the midships section. However, her bridge structure is now collapsed and part of the hull close to midships has inverted. The wreck is said to be very exciting, but will require a number of dives to explore properly. The upper structures have a colourful array of soft corals coating them. However, trawl nets have become entangled with the stern-end creating a serious obstacle when descending the shot-line in the murky, dark green light. Not surprisingly the wreck-site is very dark and gloomy, but this far out to sea the visibility can sometimes be fantastic near to the seabed, at certain times of the year.

Although no fish were seen during the dive, a number of very large fish were picked up on the fish-finder close to the wreck, so she should make a good boat angling venue, when conditions are right. Tidal streams are strong and anyone contemplating diving the wreck-site, should take extra precautions with the surface boat cover, as it is in the main shipping lanes.

PRESTO

Wreck ★★★
Scenery ★
Depth 17m
Reference N 54 55 44 W 001 19 02
1½ miles E. of river Wear entrance.

The *Presto* was a steel 1,143-ton British steamship, registered at Newcastle-upon-Tyne and had dimensions of 69.59m length, by 9.8m beam and a draught of 4.31m. She was owned at the time of loss by the Pelton Steam Ship Co. Ltd and built by J. Crown & Sons Ltd at Sunderland in 1905. Her single steel propeller was powered by a three-cylinder, triple-expansion steam engine that developed 135hp, using one boiler. Her machinery was built at Sunderland by G. Clark Ltd. She had one deck, a well-deck, four watertight bulkheads and a superstructure consisting of a 5.8m poop-deck, 18.5m quarter-deck, 14.6m bridge-deck and 8.5m forecastle. The vessel was also armed with a stern-mounted deck gun that fired 2.72 kg (6lb) shells.

On 6 April 1917, the *Presto* was in ballast on passage from London for Newcastle-upon-Tyne, under the command of a Captain Lowery, when she foundered and was lost, one and a half miles east of the river Wear. She was making about 9.5 knots when it is believed she detonated a German-laid mine under her No.1 hold, which caused a violent explosion and killed four of her crew, (another report says six crew) at 9.40 am. The ship immediately began to sink by the head. Her surviving crew abandoned ship in the boats and the examination vessel, which happened to be close-by at the time, picked them up and took the *Presto* in tow by the stern. Two tugs also came out from the Wear and assisted in the tow. However, at 11 a.m. she had taken in so much water that the fore part actually struck the seabed about one and a half miles from Roker lighthouse, where she was abandoned, settling on the bottom in 17m of water.

Wreck-site

The wreck, believed to be the steamship *Presto*, lies fairly close to the remains of the *Hebble* on a well swept seabed of hard stone and sand, in a general depth of

17m. The wreck is in line with the main shipping channels for the river and appears to have been dispersed with explosives at some time or other, because she is reported to be totally collapsed, badly broken up, rather flattened and concreting into the seabed. The highest section of about 3m is around the boiler and engine, which is covered in soft corals, but there is little else of interest to be seen. Shoals of pout-whiting have adopted the remains and a number of crustaceans can be found. However, during the months of July and August Lion's-main jellyfish can be a real nuisance in the brisk tidal streams.

Visibility is no more than a couple of metres, but it significantly improves on a neap tide and after a spell of dry, settled weather and westerly winds, during the summer months.

HEBBLE

Wreck ★★★★
Scenery ★★
Depth 17m
Reference N 54 55 466 W 001 18 820
1 ½ miles E. of river Wear entrance.

The *Hebble* was a steel 904-ton British steamship, registered at Goole and had dimensions of 68.58m length, by 9.6m beam and a draught of 4.69m. She was built in 1891 by W. Dobson & Co. at Newcastle-upon-Tyne for the Lancashire & Yorkshire Railway C. Her single steel propeller was powered by a three-cylinder, triple-expansion steam engine that developed 181hp, using two boilers and her machinery was built by the Wallsend Slipway Co. Ltd of Newcastle-upon-Tyne. She had one deck, five watertight bulkheads and a superstructure consisting of a 9.1m poop-deck, a bridge-deck of 16.4m and a forecastle of 10m.

At 11.50 a.m. on 6 May 1917, under the command of Captain Flower, the *Hebble* was on passage from Scapa Flow for Sunderland when she struck a mine laid by the German submarine *UC-32* and foundered almost at once (earlier that year, the *UC-32* was lost after she struck one of her own mines on 23 February). The *Hebble* was on government service as Ammunition Stores Carrier No 3, at the time and was carrying a full cargo of explosives. Out of her compliment of sixteen crew, the chief engineer and four seamen died in the explosion, but the other eleven crewmen were rescued by a motor launch and landed at Sunderland (another source states that eight crew died).

Wreck-site
The *Hebble*, or what remains of her, lies on a flat seabed in a general depth around 17m, the lowest astronomical depth and one and a half miles almost due east of Roker pier at Sunderland. The wreck is very difficult to locate because of her size. The boilers, condensers and engine stand upright, but are concreted together, amid

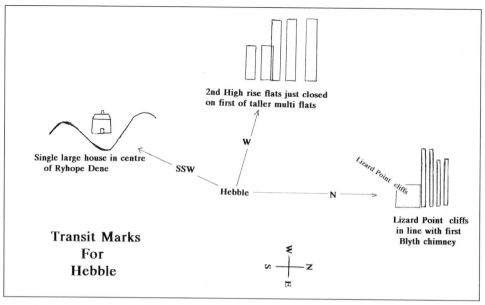

2nd High rise flats just closed on first of taller multi flats

W

Single large house in centre of Ryhope Dene

SSW

Hebble

N

Lizard Point cliffs

Lizard Point cliffs in line with first Blyth chimney

Transit Marks
For
Hebble

Map of transit marks for Hebble.

a mass of huge copper pipes and steel framework. The whole area of wreckage only covers some 20m or so in diameter. The bow section of the ship, which was blown off by the exploding ammunition, is missing, and probably there will be very little left of it. However, it cannot be far away from the main part of the wreck.

However, it is worth visiting as it is completely carpeted in beautifully coloured soft corals. Over the top of the wreck, swarms of pout-whiting, pollack, saithe and cod swim in a dense cloud, while large conger, crab and lobsters are to be found hiding under the twisted mass of metal. There are no interesting artifacts to be found, and the big lumps of copper and brass which can be seen sticking out all over, are well concreted into the pile of debris. This is a really fabulous dive because of the amount of marine life to be seen.

The surrounding seabed is hard, flat, stony ground, so if the tide is running and the anchor does not catch onto something quickly, you will soon drift away from the wreck. On average, visibility is not very startling and you would normally only expect 2-3m. However, during the summer, on a neap tide, after a dry spell, sometimes it is even possible to see the cover-boat on the surface. You can dive the wreck at most states of the tide, but the flow on a spring tide is fairly strong and diving is not recommended.

During the summer months, Lion's-mane jellyfish swarm with the tide in huge numbers and they can be a real diving hazard, not just when descending and ascending. Their long, stinging cells get caught up all over the wreckage. At this time of year, when wreck diving off this coast, it is always advisable to carry a bottle of vinegar in the boat, because vinegar neutralizes the poison and helps to relieve the burning sensation from a sting.

RAVENSBOURNE

Wreck ★★★★
Scenery ★
Depth 44m
Reference N 54 55 54 W 001 14 33
Also given: N 54 55 90 W 001 14 60
4½ E. of river Wear entrance.

The *Ravensbourne* was a steel 1,240-ton British steamship registered at the Port of London and had dimensions of 70.1m length, by 10.87m beam and a draught of 4.72m. She was built at Campbeltown in 1916 by the Campbeltown Shipbuilding Co. and owned by the South Metropolitan Gas Co. Her single steel propeller was powered by a three-cylinder, triple-expansion steam engine that used two boilers. Her machinery was built by D. Rowan & Co. at Glasgow. She had a superstructure consisting of a 24m quarter-deck, a bridge-deck of 14.6m and a 7.9m forecastle. She also was armed with a 2.72 kg (6lb) stern-mounted deck gun.

On 31 January 1917, the *Ravensbourne* was steaming south at 9½ knots on passage from Newcastle for London, with a crew of nineteen, when she detonated a German-laid mine at 0.40 p.m. A violent explosion rocked the midships section on the port side, blowing a massive hole into the engine room that killed the chief engineer, the second engineer and a donkeyman. The surviving crew abandoned ship in the starboard boat, as the vessel immediately began to sink, the port boat having been totally wrecked in the explosion. They had just cleared away from her, when the *Ravensbourne* went down, eight minutes after striking the mine. The Danish steamship *Ajax* picked up the sixteen survivors soon after and landed them on the Tyne quay at 5 p.m.

Wreck-site
The wreck, believed to be that of the *Ravensbourne* is quite substantial and lying on a seabed of sand and stone in a general depth of 44m. The bridge structure and hull have collapsed down around the two boilers and are carpeted in lots of soft corals However, the stern-end stands fairly intact with her deck gun and propeller still in place and lots of twisted steel plates, framework and copper pipes protrude from midships section, around the engine area. Lengths of her twisted and warped deck-railings lie criss-crossed over the wreck-site and a number of intact portholes can be seen amongst the debris.

The occasional 5lb lobster has also been observed, albeit impossible to extract, and shoals of large fish, mostly cod and pout-whiting, have adopted the wreck, so it will be a good boat angling venue, when conditions are right. Tidal streams are very strong and a lot of pre-planning is called for by anyone wishing to dive the wreck-site. It is also a very dark and gloomy site and the presence of trawl nets floating above her like shrouds at the stern-end add to the safety problems.

ATLANTIC (ex-HORACE)

Wreck ★★★★
Scenery ★
Depth 25-26m
Reference N 54 56 232 W 001 18 149
2 miles and 12 degrees N-E from Roker pier.

The *Atlantic* was an iron 1,601-ton Russian steamship, registered at Wiborg and had dimensions of 79.09m length, by 10.49m beam and a draught of 5.89m. She was owned at the time of loss by Rederi Acktiebolager Ocean in Viborg and built as the *Horace* at John Redheads & Co. Ltd at South Shields in 1878. The single iron propeller was powered by a two-cylinder, compound-steam engine that developed 164hp, using two boilers. She had one deck, four watertight bulkheads and a centrally positioned superstructure that consisted of a 29m quarter-deck, 18.2m bridge-deck and 9.1m forecastle.

On 17 September 1902, the *Atlantic* was on a voyage from Sunderland to Crondstadt with a cargo of coal and twenty-one crew, under the command of Captain P.G. Lindroos, when she foundered and was lost, following a collision with the Newcastle-registered steamship *Twizell* two miles north-east of Sunderland.

Wreck-site
Very few local people have even heard of the *Atlantic*, yet in her time she was quite a substantial vessel. She lies partially buried, on a seabed of dirty sand and gravel, in a general depth of 26m, the lowest astronomical depth, just to the north of the Sunderland spoil-ground. The wreck has now totally collapsed into a pile of debris, with the highest point being about 3m around her two boilers and engine, which are covered in silt, visibly exposed and surrounded by a pile of decayed, twisted plates and broken machinery.

The depth is very reasonable and it is within the range of the majority of sport-divers. However, tidal streams are fairly strong, making the site a low, slack water dive. A Russian ship's bell would make a very interesting souvenir, although the bell on this wreck will almost certainly be called the *Horace*. Very little marine life has been observed, but she may attract a few crustaceans. A good torch will be required, as visibility is not good.

MAINDY BRIDGE (ex-BEGONIA)

Wreck ★★★★
Scenery ★
Depth 39m
Reference N 54 56 25 W 001 15 56
Also given: N 54 56 69 W 001 15 80
3 miles E. of Wear entrance.

The *Maindy Bridge* was an iron 3,653-ton British steam collier with dimensions of 84.8m length, by 12.5m beam and a draught of 5.5m. She was built as the *Begonia* in 1899, possibly managed by Jenkins, Richards & Evans Ltd of Cardiff and owned at the time of loss by the Maindy Shipping Company Ltd. Her single iron-screw propeller was powered by a three-cylinder, triple-expansion steam engine that used two boilers.

On 8 December 1917, the *Maindy Bridge* was in ballast, on passage from Middlesbrough for the Tyne, when she was foundered after being torpedoed by the German submarine *UC-49* and two of two of her crew were lost.

Wreck-site
The wreck, believed to be that of the *Maindy Bridge*, is very substantial, lying on a seabed of dirty sand and stone, in a general depth of 39m, however there are also some other non-wreck objects on the seabed, in the vicinity of the wreck, which are probably clumps of rock. She stands around 6m high, with the rear quarter section still intact, very similar to that of the *Sunniva*. Her rear-mounted deck-gun points downwards, because the decking is sloping and damaged underneath. The central midships section has collapsed down onto the boilers and engine block and the whole area is strewn with large copper-pipes, pieces of broken masts or derricks, twisted steel plates and broken machinery. Very little diving has taken place on the wreck so most of her interesting bridge equipment and navigational instruments should still be around, making the wreck-site much more exciting to visit.

Lots of soft corals cover the higher and most exposed parts of the wreck, while quite a fair number of large crustaceans can be seen under the iron debris, and the stern-end has been adopted by a large shoal of pout whiting.

Tidal streams can be very strong and visibility is usually rather dismal, making this a definite low, slack water dive. Nets float around like curtains on the stern section, so extreme care should be taken when diving this site. The wreck may be worth noting as a boat-angling venue too.

CLEMATIS

Wreck ★★★
Scenery ★
Depth 43m
Reference N 54 56 295 W 001 15 008
4½ E.S.E. of Souter Point.

The *Clematis* was an iron 1,234-ton British steamship, registered at West Hartlepool and had dimensions of 70.15m length, by 9.75m beam and a draught of 4.67m. She was built in 1884 by R. Cragg & Sons at Middlesbrough and owned at the time of loss by J. Lilly of West Hartlepool. Her single iron propeller was powered by a two-cylinder, compound-steam engine that developed 99hp, using one boiler. Her machinery was built by Westgarth, English & Co. at Middlesbrough.

On 18 April 1894, the *Clematis* was in ballast on passage from Stockton-on-Tees for Blyth, under the command of Captain T. Batty and carrying a crew of sixteen, when she foundered and was lost following a collision with the London-registered steamship *Beamish*.

Wreck-site
The wreck, possibly that of the *Clematis*, lies orientated in a north to south direction, on a seabed of dirty sand, in a general depth of 43m, the lowest astronomical depth. She is totally collapsed, well broken up, badly decayed and partially buried. The highest section at 3m is around her boiler and engine at midships. An anchor, windlass, bollards, lengths of chain and a large winch, covered in soft corals, can be seen at the northern end of the wreck, while her propeller and part of the shaft are visible at the stern. Lots of battered copper pipes and lumps of lead can be seen near the centre. The wreck is covered in silt, but most of her interesting instruments should still be around, along with the bell, which would positively identify her as the *Clematis*. Tidal streams are strong and visibility is usually very poor, but it improves during the summer months after a spell of settled weather and neap tides. Lion's-mane jellyfish can be a nuisance between the months of July and September when decompressing on a shot-line.

SAGA

Wreck ★★★★
Scenery ★
Depth 40m
Reference N 54 56 475 W 001 15 918
4 miles E.N.E. of Wear north pier.

The *Saga* was a steel 1,143-ton British steamship, registered at Newcastle-upon-Tyne, built in 1901 and owned by Robinson, Brown & Co. of Newcastle. At the time of loss she was owned by The Shipping Controller. Her single steel propeller was powered by a three-cylinder triple-expansion steam engine that used one boiler.

One report says that on 1 August 1915 the *Saga* was in ballast on passage from Marseilles for the Tyne when she was torpedoed and sunk by the German submarine *U-28*, four miles east-north-east of the river Wear. Ten of her crew are said to have died, but the book British Vessels Lost at Sea reorts that no lives were lost.

A further report by A.J. Tennent in his book British Merchant Ships Sunk by U-boats in the 1914-1918 War says that on 14 February 1918, the *Saga* was on passage from Sunderland to Rouen, with a cargo of coal when she was torpedoed by the German U-boat and sunk four miles east-north-east of Sunderland.

On 2 September 1917, the *U-28* was off North Cape in the Arctic when she torpedoed the steamship *Olive Branch*. She then closed in to finish her off with her deck gun. However, after firing just one shot, the steamship exploded so violently that it sank the *U-28*, too. (No olive branch offered there.)

Wreck-site
The wreck lies on a seabed of fine sand and mud in a general depth of 40m, the lowest astronomical depth. She is quite substantial, but most of the vessel has now collapsed, exposing her boiler, engine, condenser and donkey-engine. The highest section of 5m is around midships and her bows, which are covered in soft corals. Lots of broken machinery, bollards, winches, anchors, large sections of hollow mast and various pipes lie scattered among the collapsed steel plates.

The wreck is reported to be very interesting, with large numbers of cod to be seen under and over the debris, so she should be well worth visiting as a boat angling venue. Tidal streams are fairly strong and visibility is usually very poor, but it significantly improves after a spell of dry, settled weather, during the summer months.

CORDOVA

Wreck ★★★
Scenery ★
Depth 52m
Reference N 54 56 602 W 001 10 212
7½ miles E. of Wear, north pier.

The *Cordova* was a large iron barque of 650 tons that had dimensions of around 52m length and 9m beam. She was owned at the time of loss by G. Wakeham and registered at the port of Liverpool. The barque had three masts, but was square-rigged on only fore and main masts. Her mizzen mast was fore and aft, (gaff rigged), which is sometimes referred to as a 'spanker'. The barque's highest sails, known as royal-sails, were often removed in latter days. Sometimes the vessel was built in this way to reduce the number of crewmen required. When this was done, the barque was then referred to as being 'bald-headed'.

On 3 May 1893, the *Cordova* was on passage from Sunderland for Iquiqui, under the command of Captain T.I. Gill, with a cargo of coal, a crew of twenty and six passengers, when she foundered and was lost, following a collision with the Newcastle-upon-Tyne steamship *Knarwater*. Wind conditions were north-north-east, force two at the time. Unfortunately, it is not known at what time of day the collision happened, if there was any fog or whether there were any casualties on either vessels.

Wreck-site

The wreck, believed to be that of the *Cordova*, lies orientated in an east to west direction, on a dirty seabed of mud, fine sand and broken shells, in a general depth of 52m, the lowest astronomical depth. The wreck is totally collapsed, well broken up and badly decayed. The highest 2-3m part is around her midships section, includes quite a few large sheets of iron hull and broken debris, covering an area of about 40 x 15m.

The wreck is also partially buried and well covered in silt, although a number of Dead Man's Fingers have attached themselves to the mound of iron. A good search of this wreck may produce a positive identity and the ship's bell will certainly make a very interesting talking point and valuable souvenir. Very few fish have been observed around the wreck-site. Tidal streams are quite strong and visibility usually very poor, so a good torch is essential.

CHAMOIS

Wreck ★
Scenery ★★
Depth 4m
Reference N 54 56 605 W 001 21 035
North of Whitburn Steel.

The *Chamois* was an iron and steel 2,100-ton British steamship, registered in London and had dimensions of some 87.5m length, by 11.8m beam and a draught of 5.8m. She was built in Sunderland in 1890 and owned at the time of loss by Messrs Cory & Co. of London, however another report said she was built in 1900 and was owned by W. Jackson of London. Her single iron propeller was powered by a three-cylinder, triple-expansion steam engine that used two boilers.

On 8 January 1903, the *Chamois* was in ballast on passage from Rotterdam for the Tyne, under the command of Swanseaman Captain Geo. Jeffries and carrying a crew of twenty-one, when she drove ashore during thick fog and heavy weather. The vessel could just be dimly seen offshore from the beach near Whitburn Steel, with her head pointing to the north-north-west. The coastguard raised the alarm in response to signals from the stranded vessel and very quickly the lifesaving apparatus was set up by the rocket brigade, under Chief Officer Parks R.N. The seabed at the point where the *Chamois* grounded is rather flat, and fairly far offshore, proved too great a distance for the rocket lines. An immediate request was made for the new lifeboat *William Charles* to be launched was made. She had just made her first trial run the day before, under the command of Captain Holmes, the Inspecting Officer of the R.N.L.I.

Reports at the time say, 'she was a smart boat in every respect, the wheels of the carriage running on iron planes which loosely encircled the rims. In this way a flat surface is presented to the soft yielding sand and the device worked admirably'. The lifeboat went out in a nasty and dangerous ground swell and rescued the twenty-one crew, including Captain Jeffries and brought them safely ashore. Several tugs made a number of unsuccessful attempts to pull the vessel off the rocks, but the heavy ground swell had taken its toll and left her badly holed. With her hull full of water and orientated at an impossible angle, the wind and sea having swung her round to N.N.E., she was written off and became a total loss. Some salvage work took place on the vessel's top structures, but the rest of her was left to the elements.

Wreck-site
The wreck lies just north of the Whitburn Steel on a seabed of rocks and small reefs, in a general depth of 4m, about the lowest astronomical depth. She is now totalled smashed up, except for a few twisted, decaying plates, ribs, frames, pieces of broken machinery and a little section of her bows. Very little else of the *Chamois* is recognisable, today.

Tidal streams are very moderate and visibility is reasonable on neap tides during the summer, after a spell of dry settled weather.

INGER (ex-BEN LOMOND)

Wreck ★
Scenery ★★
Depth 5m
Reference N 54 57 273 W 001 20 803
½ mile S.S.E. of Souter Point

The *Inger* was an iron Danish-registered steamship of around 750 tons and had dimensions of some 55m length, by 8.5m beam. She was owned at the time of loss by Messrs N.K. Stroyberg of Aalborg of Denmark and built in Sunderland as the *Ben Lomond*, in 1871, for a North Shields company. Her single iron propeller was powered by a two-cylinder, compound-steam engine that used one boiler.

At 7 p.m. on 4 January 1906, the *Inger* was in ballast on passage from Aalborg for Sunderland, under the command of Captain E.S. Thorkelin, when she ran aground during thick fog, heavy seas and a massive ground swell. The Whitburn Volunteer Life Brigade rushed to the scene, but the vessel was too far off shore to render assistance. However, the Sunderland lifeboat *William Charles* had been called and managed to get alongside the stricken vessel to rescue the one passenger and crew of eighteen Danish seamen. All attempts to refloat her were made impossible when the engine room flooded through the badly-holed hull plates and it wasn't long before she began to break up, eventually to become a total wreck. It is believed that the vessel was partly salvaged, but the rest was left to the elements.

Wreck-site
The wreck lies on a hard, weed-covered seabed of rocks and boulders, in a general depth of 5m, about the lowest astronomical depth. Very little of the vessel remains now, except for some twisted iron plates, keel and rib sections and her iron propeller. However, some five years ago, a porthole and some short lengths of copper piping were recovered. The wreck, however, is now gradually concreting into the seabed and rocks.

Visiblity is often in the region of 5m during the summer months, after a spell of dry, settled weather, while tidal streams are very moderate. Green-shore crabs, winkles, blennies, small coleys, the occasional small edible-crab and even lobsters can sometimes be found under the larger boulders and in the many small reefs.

POLTAVA (ex-GEORG, ex-GEORGE R.)

Wreck ★★★★
Scenery ★
Depth 39m
Reference N 54 57 472 W 001 17 295
3 miles E.N.E. of Souter Point

The *Poltava* was an iron 945-ton steamship with dimensions of 65m length, by 9.6m beam and a draught of 4.3m. She was built in 1889 for H. Schuldt by Rostocker Act. Ges. at Rostock in northern Germany and called the *Georg* On 6 August 1914 she was captured by *H.M.S. Comorant* and taken to Gibraltar. In 1915 she was sold to Tyzack & Branfoot of Newcastle-upon-Tyne and renamed *George R*, but later in 1915 she was acquired by Kaye, Sons & Co. Ltd, the owners at the time of loss and renamed *Poltava* (Official No.139078). Her single iron propeller was powered by a two-cylinder, compound-steam engine that used one boiler.

On 19 April 1917, the *Poltava* had set out on a voyage from the Tyne with a cargo of coal, but detonated a mine laid by the German submarine *UC-44* just off Souter Point. The vessel foundered within minutes, however none of her crew was lost.

Wreck-site

The *Poltava* is quite a substantial wreck, lying on a seabed of dirty fine sand and mud in a general depth of 39m, the lowest astronomical depth. It is upright and standing up to 4m high in the midships section, though partially buried. Unfortunately, the top upper structures and most of the hull have now collapsed in on itself. Although she has not been positively identified, the wreck's location and size makes it most likely that it is the *Poltava*. However, there is the possibility that she is in position N54 58 250 W 001 16 402, the location of the steamship *Rotha*.

Lots of copper pipes are visible through the jumble of twisted iron plates and debris, as well as iron bollards, pieces of lifeboat-davits, broken hatch-covers and hundreds of soft corals that have taken hold at the most exposed ends of the wreck.

Cod and large shoals of pout-whiting are in abundance, making this an excellent boat angling venue and a number of lobsters could be clearly seen among the wreckage. The wreck is very little dived and all of the interesting bridge equipment should still be around. However, it may possibly be lying underneath the pile of collapsed wreckage. Tidal streams are strong and visibility is usually very poor, making this a very dark and gloomy dive-site.

A great deal care should be taken when diving this site because of monofilament trammel nets, which hang like spiders webs all over one end.

CECILIA

Wreck ★★
Scenery ★★
Depth 6m
Reference N 54 58 13 W 001 21 37
Lizard Point, near Whitburn.

The *Cecilia* was an iron 612-ton sailing barque, registered at Liverpool and had dimensions of 49.6m length, by 8.55m beam, with a draught of 5.66m. She was owned at the time of loss by P. Nelson & Co. of Liverpool and built by MacKern in 1863 at Preston. She had two decks, two watertight bulkheads and was classed as Lloyd's 100 A1.

On 3 March 1881, the *Cecilia* was under the command of Captain T.B. Nelson and carrying a cargo of coal on passage from Newcastle-upon-Tyne for Valparaiso, when she was driven ashore at Lizard Point and lost with her crew of eighteen, during a force ten south-easterly storm.

Wreck-site

This wreck is believed to be that of the iron barque *Cecilia*, although some divers refer to her as the *Angela Madre*. This was a 122-ton British registered sailing vessel, possibly a schooner, that had dimensions of 28m length, by 7m beam and a draught of 3.3m. Records available do not show whether she was built of wood, iron or steel.

At 8.53 p.m. on 5 May 1917, the *Angela Madre* was on passage from the Thames for Newcastle-upon-Tyne with a cargo of burnt ore when she was seen to blow up and sink, with the loss of her master and crew of four. It is believed that the vessel detonated a German laid mine three miles south-east of the Tyne.

The wreck lies orientated in a east to west direction in a general depth of 6m, about the lowest astronomical depth, just south-east of Souter lighthouse and 200m east of the small shingle beach. The site can be approached along a footpath leading away to the south-east from the car park on the cliff tops, which is located at the north side of the Souter lighthouse. Since the National Trust took over the area, divers have a quarter mile hike along the twisting cliff path to the first small sand, shingle and rock beach. The wreck lies in an easterly direction, about 200m out from the beach.

She is now totally collapsed, decayed and well broken up, with just her anchor, ribs, keel and iron plates dispersed along a deep, silty gully, covering an area of around 40-50m. A number of artefacts have been recovered in recent years, including three small, brass portholes, a brass deck wash-port and four dead-eyes, but little else of obvious interest. Large angler fish are fairly common during the summer months and will quite often follow divers around, especially if they have been prodded or touched by divers. A large cavernous mouth full of needle sharp teeth coming after you, can be rather unnerving.

Tidal streams are usually just moderate, however, on a shore dive, it is always best to leave enough air to come back along the bottom, where the current is less strong. Visibility is usually poor, but improves significantly during the summer months when you may experience over 10m visibility.

ROTHA

Wreck ★★★★
Scenery ★
Depth 42 metres
Reference N 54 58 260 W 001 16 424
Also: N 54 58 250 W 001 16 402
3 miles E. of Souter Point

The *Rotha* was steel 1,108-ton British steamship, registered at Newcastle-upon-Tyne and had dimensions of 67.05m length, by 9.49m beam and a draught of 4.69m. She was owned by Sharp & Co. at Newcastle and built in 1893 by J. Laing at Sunderland. Her single iron propeller was powered by a three-cylinder, triple-expansion steam engine that developed 156hp, using one boiler. Her machinery was built by North East Marine Engineering Co. Ltd in Sunderland. The vessel was classed as 100 A1 at Lloyds and she had one deck and a superstructure consisting of a 28m, poop-deck, 28m quarter-deck, 13.4m bridge-deck and a 6.7m forecastle.

The Star of Hope *was a wooden brig of 239 tons and had dimensions of 29.87m length, 6.5m beam and 4.676m draught. She was owned by W. Falkinbridge of Whitby and registered at of Whitby. On 6 December 1882 the* Star of Hope *was in ballast on a voyage from Dieppe to South Shields under the command of Captain J.R. Walker and carrying a crew of six when, during wind conditions east-north-east force eight, she was deliberately run ashore at Whitby on the falling tide. The crew were rescued by the lifeboat, but the vessel became a total wreck.* Courtsey of the Whitby Literary and Philosophical Society.

In less than an hour of leaving the river Tyne on 23 February 1902, the *Rotha* foundered and was lost three miles east of Souter lighthouse, following a collision with the Danish-registered steamship *Skjold*. The *Rotha* was on passage for Devonport, under the command of Captain J. Hay, with fourteen crew and an unspecified cargo of coal. With a light south-westerly wind blowing, weather conditions were very good, however the records do not show whether it was day or night when the collision occurred.

Wreck-site
Bob Scullion of Marsden Dive Centre informed me that the wreck is very old and badly decayed and appears to be pre-date the First World War. She is believed to be that of the steamship *Rotha*. However, there has been no positive identification of the vessel and there is the possibility that she lies in position N 54 57 472 W 001 17 295, the location of the steamship *Poltava*. The wreck lies on a seabed of dirty sand, mud

The Southwark of London, *a small steamer ashore near Whitby in 1893. The photograph shows the men employed to make her safe. She was successfully refloated later that week.* Courtsey of the Whitby Literary and Philosophical Society.

and broken shells in a general depth of 42m, the lowest astronomical depth. She is still rather substantial, but totally collapsed and very broken up. Her bows are fairly intact and lying at an angle of about sixty degrees.

The hold section is still intact and it is possible to swim into it, but the wreck is generally a jumbled pile of twisted girders, steel plates, big lengths of loose bent and flattened copper pipe and broken machinery. Her boiler and engine are openly visible in the centre of the wreckage and close to them is a massive, complete, iron steering wheel lodged solid. Every thing is covered in a heavy coating of sediment.

A number of small cod, pout-whiting, blennies and a medium sized eel were observed and the whole wreck is covered in an abundance of urchins and Dead Man's Fingers. Tidal streams are fairly strong and visibility is usually rather poor, but can be excellent on a neap tide, following a spell of dry settled weather and light westerly winds.

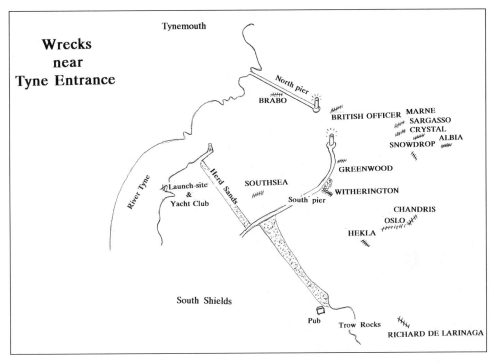

Wrecks
near
Tyne Entrance

Tynemouth

North pier

BRABO

BRITISH OFFICER MARNE

SARGASSO

CRYSTAL

SNOWDROP ALBIA

GREENWOOD

SOUTHSEA

WITHERINGTON

South pier

CHANDRIS

OSLO

HEKLA

River Tyne

Launch-site
&
Yacht Club

Herd Sands

South Shields

Pub Trow Rocks

RICHARD DE LARINAGA

Wrecks near Tyne entrance.

ILIOUS

Wreck ★★
Scenery ★
Depth 22m
Reference N 54 58 725 W 001 20 764
½ mile E. of Souter Point

The *Ilious* was an iron 2,020-ton British registered steamship, with dimensions of 75.1m length, by 11.3m beam and a draught of 7.7m. She was built by Short Brothers in 1882 and owned by Lumsden, Byers & Co. Her single iron propeller was powered by a two-cylinder compound-steam engine that used two boilers.

On 16 December 1898, the *Ilious* foundered with the loss of twenty lives, three quarters of a mile east of Souter Point, following a collision with the steamship *Pierremont*.

Wreck-site
The wreck of the *Ilious* lies orientated in a north-west to south-east direction on a hard sandy seabed, in a general depth of 22m, the lowest astronomical depth. In 1971 the wreck was standing up some 8m high from the seabed, but alas she is now quite dispersed in comparison. Her bows are said to be reasonably intact and

have a covering of Dead Man's Fingers, however the rest of the wreck is totally collapsed and well broken up. Jeff Maine told me that her boilers are standing upright next to the engine block, which is rather smashed open and lying on its side, showing all of the large bronze bearings.

The wreck has been quite well salvaged. The anchor chain and prop shaft were removed some time ago, along with the ship's bell and many of the other interesting items, but it still makes an nice rummage dive. Bits of brass and copper pipe can still be found, as well as the occasional porthole under the piles of iron debris. A good torch is required most of the time.

Large cod up to 10kg are not uncommon and local angling boats regularly make good catches of cod, fishing over the top of the *Ilious*. Tidal streams are strong, but not severe, although the best time to dive on it is at low, slack water on a neap tide. Visibility always seems dark and dismal making this a very gloomy dive-site. Watch out for bothersome Lion's-mane jellyfish during the late summer months. Finding the wreck is quite easy, as the seabed is all sand, so dragging an anchor along, will usually pick up the wreckage.

MONKSEATON

Wreck ★★★
Scenery ★
Depth 25m
Reference N 54 59 492 W 001 20 884
Also given: N 54 59 421 W 001 20 793
1½ miles N.N.E. of Souter lighthouse.

The *Monkseaton* was a steel 965-ton British steamship registered at Newcastle and had dimensions of 68.19m length, by 9.27m beam and a draught of 5.28m. She was owned at the time of loss by J. Elliott & Co. of Newcastle-upon-Tyne and was built in 1870 by Smith at North Shields. Her single iron propeller was powered by a two-cylinder, inverted-compound-steam engine that developed 110hp, using one boiler. Her centrally positioned machinery was built by R. & W. Hawthorn at Newcastle-upon-Tyne. She had one deck, four watertight bulkheads and was classed as A1 at Lloyds.

On 8 December 1877, the *Monkseaton* was in ballast on passage from Rotterdam for the Tyne under the command of Captain W. Weightman when she foundered and was lost, following a collision with the North Shields-registered steamship *Jenny Otto*.

Wreck-site
The wreck lies orientated in more or less a north-west to south-east direction, on a dirty seabed of mud and sand, in a general depth of 25m, the lowest astronomical depth. She is completely collapsed, well broken up and badly decayed with the highest section of 3m being around her boiler and engine. Large lengths of flattened and bent copper pipes can be made out between the midships section to the stern-

end. Everything is coated in the hard white casings of marine worms and parts of the wreck have Dead Man's Fingers clinging to the most exposed structures.

Usually the wreck-site is very dark and dismal and requires a good torch to be able to see much. A number of crustaceans and the occasional cod have been seen hiding in the debris. However, there are much better wrecks than this one to spend any time fishing over. Tidal streams are fairly strong, but it would be possible to dive the site during neap tides on the ebb flow.

PROTECTOR

Wreck ★★★
Scenery ★
Depth 23m
Reference N 55 00 024 W 001 22 881
Also N 55 00 024 W 001 22 899
Also given N 55 01 054 W 001 22 170
1 mile N.E. of Tynemouth lighthouse.

The *Protector* was a steel 200-ton steam pilot cutter, rigged with sails, that had dimensions of 33.52m length, by 6.73m beam and a draught of 3.22m. She was owned by the Tyne Pilotage Commissioners and built by J.P. Rennoldson & Sons at South Shields in 1907. Her single bronze screw propeller was powered by a three-cylinder, triple-expansion steam engine that developed 50hp using one boiler.

On 31 December 1916, the *Protector* was lying off the Tyne entrance awaiting pilotage duties when she was seen to suddenly blow up and sink. It was believed that the vessel had detonated a German mine, just laid early that same morning. The explosion lifted the vessel clean out of the water and she sank almost immediately, taking Captain J. K. Parker and eighteen other people down with her.

Wreck-site
The wreck has not been positively identified as that of the pilot cutter *Protector* yet and two positions have been supplied. The first two sets of co-ordinates are for someone's 'secret wreck', that he claims is the *Protector*. However, there is no information to confirm this, but she will probably be well worth investigating.

The second set of co-ordinates, has the wreck orientated in a more or less south-south-east to north-north-west direction, on a seabed of dark, dirty sand and stone in a general depth of 21m, the lowest astronomical depth. She has totally collapsed down onto the seabed in a small 1m pile of twisted steel plates, frames and broken machinery, with the remains of her engine in the midst of it all, which is typical of a small wreck of this period. There are a few copper pipes, brass valves and flanges to be seen, but it is not known whether the vessel's bridge equipment: the telegraph, compass binnacle and bell are still around, as much of her has gone into the seabed. The wreck covers an area of around 35-40m long and 3m wide.

Tidal streams are fairly strong, so the best time to dive the wreck-site is at low slack water on a neap tide. Visibility is usually poor, being only a couple of metres or so, but it significantly improves during the summer months after a spell of dry, settled weather and westerly winds. Lion's-mane jellyfish are a real nuisance between the months of July and September and the wreck-site is in the main shipping lane, so a good look-out will be required by the boat crew.

HEKLA

Wreck ★★
Scenery ★
Depth 8m
Reference N 55 00 052 W 001 23 900
½mile S. of Tyne South Pier

The *Hekla* was an iron 1,126-ton Norwegian-registered steamship, built in 1874 and owned at the time of loss by D/S Hekla. Her single iron propeller was powered by a three-cylinder, triple-expansion steam engine that used one boiler.

On 23 April 1902, the *Hekla* was taking a cargo of iron-ore on passage from Bilbao for the Tyne, under the command of Captain H.S. Jespersen, when she was in collision with the unregistered steamship *Dilkira*, just south of the river Tyne. The *Hekla* tried to beach in shallow water, but foundered and was lost with seven of her seventeen crew.

Wreck-site
There has been no positive identification of this wreck to say she is that of the *Hekla*, however the position and details of her sinking make it highly likely. The wreck lies on a sandy seabed about 200m inshore from the western end and bow section of the wreck of the *Oslofjord*. The whole outline of the vessel's hull can be made out, with iron plates, ribs, double bottom sections, girders and broken machinery, most of which only stands about 1-1.5 m from the seabed and it is surrounded by a small scour. Her boiler stands upright, but is showing signs of breaking up. Quite a number of crustaceans can be found hiding amongst the wreckage, early in the summer months.

There are no real currents to worry about and you can dive the site at any state of the tide. However, if there is any surface swell, it very quickly stirs the sediment up and spoils the visibility, which is normally a couple of metres or so during the summer months.

5. Tyne to Blyth

GREENWOOD

Wreck ★
Scenery ★★
Depth 10-12m
Reference N 55 00 60 W 001 24 03
Outside of south pier, South Shields.

The *Greenwood* was an iron 928-ton British steamship, registered at Newcastle-upon-Tyne and owned at the time of loss by J.E. Tully of Newcastle. She was built in 1869 and had a single iron propeller that was powered by a three-cylinder, triple-expansion steam engine that used one boiler.

On 20 August 1900 the *Greenwood* was on a voyage from London to the Tyne in ballast, under the command of Captain J. Wilson, with a crew of fifteen and one passenger, when, just outside of the Tyne entrance, she was in a collision with the London-registered steamship *Ulysses*. Both vessels were seriously damaged, but the *Greenwood* was holed below the water-line and lost her power. The tide and light north-north-east wind blew her in against the south pier wall, where she foundered and was lost before tugs could pull her clear.

Wreck-site
The remains of the *Greenwood* are only about 50m away from the wreck of the destroyer, *Witherington*, but further out towards the pier end. She is now totally collapsed and well smashed up like that of the destroyer, but still worth a visit as a second dive. Her boiler stands upright in the midst of broken iron ribs and frames protruding from the silty sand, along with lots of thin, brass tubes scattered around the seabed that have come from the brass condenser that burst open. Not far away from these is an old iron anchor and iron propeller. Like the destroyer, she has lots of fishing lines, complete with weights and hooks criss-crossing over the wreckage, so a little care is required.

The tidal streams are rather more noticeable than they are on the *Witherington*, but you can dive at any state of the tide, with low, slack water or, better still, on a neap tide. Visibility is at the whim of the river Tyne, but it can be excellent after a dry spell of weather and light westerly winds. If there is any swell from the north or east, the site is best avoided, because there is usually a lot of back wash from the pier walls. Shellfish can often be found under the nearby large boulders, up against the pier wall.

SARGASSO

Wreck ★★★
Scenery ★
Depth 17 metres
Reference N 55 00 744 W 001 23 526
½ mile E. of Tyne south pier lighthouse.

The *Sargasso* was an iron 1,508-ton British steamship, registered in London and built in 1885. She was owned by the Sargasso Steam Ship Co. and managed by Messrs M. Isaacs of London. Her single iron propeller was powered by a three-cylinder, triple-expansion steam engine that used two boilers.

The *Sargasso* had just left Smith's Dock Co. works at North Shields after an extensive overhaul and repairs on 18 April 1912 and was leaving the Tyne for passage to Cartagena with a crew of twenty-one and a cargo of coal. She passed Lloyds hailing station at the Low Light, North Shields at 4.30 p.m. with the iron 116-ton steam paddle tug *Thames*, owned by Robert Stephenson Allen, taking her outside of the river. The paddle-tug cast the rope and ran alongside her at dead slow speed to take off the captain's wife and two daughters, who had been having a trip down river to the harbour mouth.

With the ladies safely on board, having said their goodbyes, they were waving handkerchiefs to the captain as the two vessels pulled apart. As the tug was swinging clear and beginning to head back up the river, the steamship *Mary Ada Short* came into view and smashed into the *Sargasso* with a terrific force, striking the her on the starboard side, alongside the number two hatch, almost cutting her in two. The *Mary Ada Short* remained in the breach for a minute or two, with her bows towering high over the stricken *Sargasso*, then they slowly drew apart.

The *Sargasso* heeled over almost immediately and settled down by the foreword. In addition to the North Shields-registered *Thames*, which was barely a hundred metres by then, the 75-ton North Shields tug *Triton* was also in the vicinity. So both vessels, along with a little Foy-boat, drew alongside the sinking ship. The bulk of the steamer's crew leapt aboard the *Triton*, but two engineers jumped onto the little Foy-boat, whose crew took a terrible risk and showed great daring in rowing up to the steamer, which may have capsized and dragged them down with her. The *Sargasso* sank in less than five minutes of being struck.

There was a roll-call of the *Sargasso*'s crew, who nearly all resided in the Tyne and Wear area. It was found that one man, an ordinary seaman called Alfred Prescott, was missing. A reporter from the *Newcastle Journal* interviewed some of the crew in the Sailor's Home in North Shields. One of them said that Mr Prescott had just finished his shift and was seen going to his berth in the foreword part of the ship, where the vessel had gone down first.

An hour after high water, the *Sargasso*'s mast was still showing in the fairway, a quarter of a mile to the south-east, just outside of the river's entrance. The steamer *Mary Ada Short*, owned by the Westoll Line of Sunderland, was a well known trader and had come to the Tyne in ballast from Brake.

The *Triton*, one of the tugs involved in the rescue, also had another unusual story to tell. She was an iron 75-ton screw-driven vessel, powered by a two-cylinder, compound steam engine that developed 40hp, using one boiler and had dimensions of 25.7m length, by 5m beam and a draught of 2.8m. She was built in 1883 for the Falmouth Fishery Co. Ltd, but owned by the Anchor Steam Tug Co. Ltd between 1903 and 1920.

On Whit Monday 16 May, 1910, two years before the rescue incident with the *Sargasso*, she was on the annual pleasure cruise, carrying thirty people, most of them belonging to the North Shields New Quay Water Rats, a name given to the riverside workers and water clerks of the tug companies. Visibility on the river was very poor at the time and the vessel was in a collision with the Tribal-class six smoke stacks destroyer HMS *Viking*, which was on sea-trials and had just been completed in Palmer's Shipyard at Jarrow. The *Triton* sank on the edge of the Black Midden rocks on the north side of the river, near to the entrance of the Tyne. Luckily, all of her passengers and crew, some who had sustained injuries, were picked up and returned to the quayside. The *Triton* was later salvaged and returned to service, but nothing is known of what happened to the piano and other musical instruments that were on board the tug at the time. She was broken up in May 1930.

Wreck-site

The wreck, believed to be that of the *Sargasso*, lies orientated in more or less a north-north-east to south-south-west direction on a seabed of dirty sand and stone, in a general depth of 15m, the lowest astronomical depth. She is well broken up, rather decayed and partly buried, standing only about $1\frac{1}{2}$-2m high, with the remains of her two busted boilers and engine block about the highest point. They are sitting amid the vessel's ribs and broken, twisted iron work. It appears that the wreck has been dispersed at sometime or another, which is not surprising, being in the shipping lanes. Much of the non-ferrous metal has long since gone, but as the wreck covers an area of about 68-70m x 25m, so it is still a worthwhile dive, because you never know what may turn up.

Tidal streams are moderate, but the site is best dived on a neap tide after a long spell of settled, dry weather when the visibility will be at a premium. Lobsters can be found among the wreckage and debris, while during the summer months, large shoals of coley and mackerel converge on the area.

ALBIA

Wreck ★★★
Scenery ★
Depth 15m
Reference N 54 00 452 W 001 23 050
½mile E. of Tyne south pier

The *Albia* was a steel 2,482-ton Spanish-registered steamship that was built on the Tyne in 1880 and owned at the time of loss by a Spanish shipping company. Her single iron propeller was powered by a three-cylinder, triple-expansion steam engine that used two boilers.

On 5 February 1915 the *Albia* was on a voyage from Sagunto to Jarrow with a crew of twenty-four, eight passengers and a cargo of iron ore, when she stranded on the Whitestones Reef, one mile south-east of Sunderland. The crew managed to refloat the vessel, which had damaged her hull in the grounding. Then the captain decided to make full speed for her destination. However, she was taking in water fast and by the time they reached the mouth of the Tyne, she was in immediate danger of sinking. A Tyne pilot cutter skipper who saw her predicament, rushed to her aid and took off twenty-one people in all. It is believed that the remaining people took to the boats, minutes before the *Albia* foundered just outside of the river mouth and close to the main shipping lane.

Wreck-site
The wreck is very substantial with some large box sections. However, she is well broken up and covered in many fishing lures and monofilament fishing lines. Her boilers are standing upright, along with her brass condenser and engine block and are surrounded by jumbled mounds of steel debris, masses of broken pipes and broken machinery, which are all covered in heavy sediment. Shoals of pout-whiting, saithe, pollack and cod can be seen over and around the wreck during the summer months, while lobsters and crabs are fairly common, too.

Tidal streams are reasonable, but visibility depends greatly on how much fresh water is coming down the river Tyne. However, during the summer months, visibility can sometimes reach 10m on a neap tide and after a spell of dry, settled weather. A good look-out is required by the boat crew, because the site is near to the main shipping lanes, where some extremely large vessels, including huge Scandinavian ferries, come in and out of the Tyne and the noise from their giant propellers can be very frightening to divers underwater. Lion's-mane jellyfish can also be a real nuisance between the months of July and September.

CRYSTAL

Wreck ★★★
Scenery ★
Depth 15-16m
Reference N 55 00 742 W 001 23 728
½ mile E. of Tyne south pier

The *Crystal* was an iron 2,613-ton British steamship, registered at Newcastle-upon-Tyne and built by J. L. Thompson & Sons at Sunderland for the Arrow Shipping Co. Ltd in about 1883. Her single iron propeller was powered by a two-cylinder, compound steam engine, that developed 300hp, using two boilers and the machinery was built by Wallsend Slipway Co. Ltd. She had two decks and seven watertight bulkheads.

On 7 January 1892, the *Crystal* was on passage from the Tyne for New York, under the command of Captain R.B. Stannard. She had just left the Tyne during a force nine easterly gale when her engine failed. Conditions were horrendous. With mountainous seas breaking over the vessel, she foundered a few hundred metres outside of the Tyne entrance.

Wreck-site
The wreck of the *Crystal* lies only about 500m seaward and east of the south pier at South Shields on a seabed of dirty sand and stone, in a general depth of around 15-16m. She is sitting almost in the direct shipping lane for the mouth of the river, so great care should be taken when diving the site. Huge ships pass very close to the wreck-site and the noise created by the enormous engines and propellers can be very nerve-racking. There is a substantial amount of the wreck left, although, as would be expected after all of these years, she is totally collapsed and well broken up. Bronze valves and copper pipes still attached to battered machinery can be found, while rusting steel plates, bent framework and girders lie in flattened heaps on top of each other.

The ship's 300hp engines are broken into a mashed heap However, it is reported that there is no sign of either boiler. The ship was carrying a general cargo, which must have included large stone, mill grinding wheels, because dozens of these lie stacked up in one section of the wreck. One or two crustaceans may be encountered among the framework and the occasional codling. However, the most unusual creature I have seen on the wreck was a large cuttlefish of about 35cm long, which was probably defending its eggs, hanging from a large pipe-end. Tidal streams are only moderate and you can dive the site at any state of the tide. However, the underwater visibility very much depends on the outflow from the Tyne.

RIO COLORADO (ex-SHEILA)

Wreck ★★
Scenery ★★
Depth 15m
Reference N 55 00 960 W 001 22 710
1 mile E. of Tyne, north pier.

The *Rio Colorado* was a steel 3,565-ton British steamship, registered in London and owned at the time of loss by the London-American Maritime Trading Company. She was built as the *Sheila* in 1903 by William Doxford & Sons Ltd at Sunderland and had dimensions of 103.65m length, by 15.29m beam and a draught of 6.85m. Her single steel propeller was powered by a three-cylinder, triple-expansion engine that developed 300hp, using three boilers.

At 5.45 a.m. on 22 March 1917, the *Rio Colorado* had just made the perilous voyage across the Atlantic from Montevideo to Newcastle-upon-Tyne, under the command of Captain A.G. Cromach when she detonated a mine laid by the German submarine, *UC-50*. She had been approaching the examination vessel just off the mouth of the Tyne with her valuable, much needed cargo of wheat, when she struck the mine amidships, blasting a massive hole in the side of her hull. Sea conditions were extremely rough at the time and the vessel foundered in just forty minutes. The chief officer, boatswain and two seamen drowned, while three firemen and the second engineer were lost, presumed drowned. The captain drowned while attempting to swim the short distance to the examination vessel, but the remaining nineteen crew and the pilot were picked up and taken to the New Quay at North Shields.

Wreck-site
The *Rio Colorado* lies orientated in an east to west direction on a seabed of dirty hard sand and stone, in a general depth of 15m, the lowest astronomical depth, about one mile east of the Tyne north pier lighthouse. Because of her position in relation to the shipping channel, the wreck was dispersed with explosives soon after she sank. Although she is totally collapsed and well flattened, the debris is spread over a wide area, covering 105m by 50m of seabed. Lots of twisted, steel plates, ribs, pipes and framework are jumbled together, surrounding her three upright boilers and the battered remains of the steam engine.

Shoals of small coley and large pollack often swarm around the wreck during the summer months and the odd cod and lobster can be seen under the steel plates. Visibility varies greatly throughout the year, but it is generally rather poor and seldom rises above a couple of metres, except maybe after neap tides and a spell of dry, settled weather during the summer months.

The wreck was originally sold to Mr T. Johnso. However, it is rumoured that Delta Divers now own her.

FIRELIGHT (ex-ROOKWOOD)

Wreck *****
Scenery *
Depth 36m
Reference N 55 01 213 W 001 19 155
2 miles E of Tyne, south pier lighthouse.

The *Firelight* was a steel 1,143-ton British steamship, registered in London and had dimensions of 71.93m length, by 9.73m beam and a draught of 4.49m. She was owned at the time of loss by The Gas Light & Coke Co. and built as the *Rookwood* in 1896 by J. Blumer & Co. Ltd at Sunderland. Her single steel propeller was powered by a three-cylinder, triple-expansion steam engine that developed 180hp, using two boilers and her machinery was built by J. Dickinson & Sons Ltd at Sunderland. She had one deck, four watertight bulkheads and a superstructure consisting of a 5.5m quarter-deck, 22.6m bridge-deck and a 7.9m forecastle.

On the morning of 1 May 1917, the *Firelight* had just left the river Tyne and was on passage from Newcastle-upon-Tyne for London with a cargo of coal, when she was torpedoed and sunk by the submerged German submarine, *UC-29*. The track of the torpedo was seen by the crew just prior to it striking the *Firelight* amidships on her port side at 8.25 a.m.. However, even before her crew, who immediately abandoned ship in their own boats, had left the vessel, the sea was washing over the upper decks. The U-boat's periscope was seen for a short time after the ship went down and the survivors were later picked up by the steamship *Collingwood* and landed at North Shields.

Wreck-site
This wreck, believed to be that of the *Firelight*, lies orientated in a north-east to south-west direction on a seabed of dirty sand, stone and colliery waste in a general depth of 36m, the lowest astronomical depth. She is sitting upright, fairly intact and standing up to 9m high, but with quite a bit of damage to the bow section at the south-western end. The highest part is said to be the stern to midships section, where a number of portholes are visible, all of which is covered in soft corals.

Sections of the bridge structure, although partially collapsed, are reported to be still in reasonable condition and it appears that there are many places where it would be possible to access the wreck's interior. It is not known if the vessel's interesting bridge equipment is still in place, or whether her bell has been recovered, but she will be well worth investigating.

There are lots of fish of various species shoaling over and around the wreck, especially cod and pout-whiting, so she should make an interesting boat angling venue. Tidal streams are rather strong and visibility is usually poor, but it significantly improves during the summer months after a spell of dry settled weather and light westerly winds. Lion's-mane jellyfish can be a nuisance when decompressing on a shot line between July and September.

SJOVIK (ex-SVEN, ex-ROSEHILL)

Wreck ★★★★
Scenery ★
Depth 39m
Reference N 55 01 683 W 001 18 968
3 miles E.S.E. of Tyne, south pier.

The *Sjovik* was an iron 1,596-ton Swedish steamship, registered at the port of Norrkopings and had dimensions of 79.14m length, by 10.97m beam and a draught of 5.84m. She was owned at the time of loss by Norrkopings Rederiaktieb in Sweden and built as the *Rosehill* in 1884 by J.L. Thompson & Sons Ltd at Sunderland. Her single iron propeller was powered by a two-cylinder, compound steam engine that developed 170hp, using two boilers and her machinery was built by T. Richardson & Sons at Hartlepool. She had one deck, a well-deck, four watertight bulkheads and a superstructure consisting of a 30.5m quarter-deck, 17.6m bridge-deck and a 7.9m forecastle.

On 18 October 1916, under the command of Captain C.S. Linggren, the *Sjovik* was on passage from Helsingborg for London, with a cargo of wood, when it is believed she foundered and was lost after detonating a German mine, three miles east-south-east of the river Tyne.

Wreck-site
Although not yet positively identified, it is believed that this could be the wreck of the Swedish steamship *Sjovik*. She lies on a well swept, hard sandstone seabed in a general depth of 39m, being the lowest astronomical depth. The wreck is standing upright, orientated in a north-north-west to south-south-west direction. It is very broken up, with the highest point being about 5m around the engine and boilers area where the iron bridge-structure has collapsed down on itself. Broken machinery, pieces of hollow broken masts, bollards, brass valves and copper pipes, with brass flanges attached, are protruding out of the iron debris and scattered everywhere.

Colourful, soft corals cover the highest structures and a fair number of crustaceans can be seen, although a good torch is essential. The wreckage covers an area of about 65m by 25m and her full outline is distinguishable. This wreck should also make an interesting boat angling venue when conditions are right. Tidal streams are fairly strong, but visibility is rather poor, but it improves significantly on a low neap tide, after a spell of dry settled weather and light westerly winds, however Lion's-mane jellyfish can be a nuisance when diving between the months of July and September.

BUTETOWN (ex-COOKHAM)

Wreck ★★
Scenery ★★★★
Depth 4-7 m
Reference N 55 02 343 W 001 25 472
Brown's Bay, Cullercoats.

The *Butetown* was a steel 1,594-ton British steamship that was registered in London and had a length of 75m. She was built as the *Cookham* at Milford Haven by J.R. Oswald & Co. in 1890 for the Lambert Brothers, who owned her until 1904 when she was sold to W. Cory. In 1916 she joined the Townline Co. Ltd, of London, who were the owners at the time of loss. Her single steel propeller was powered by a three-cylinder, triple-expansion steam engine that used two boilers.

On 4 December 1917, the *Butetown* was on passage from Blyth for Fredrikstadt with a crew of twenty-four and a cargo of coal when she stranded on the rocks at Cullercoats during heavy seas and a very strong, southerly wind. The Cullercoats 11.4m, self-righting, twelve-oared lifeboat, *Co-operator No.1* was launched at 5.15 p.m. and found one of the ship's boats, containing fourteen crewmen, about one and a half miles from the stranded vessel. They were taken aboard the lifeboat. The men told Coxswain Lisle that the other ten crewmen were in another of the ship's boats. After some searching they were found, and towed back to shore.

The lifeboat *Co-operator No.1*, had arrived at Cullercoats on 10 April 1907 and was the second boat of that name to be stationed there, the other having served for twenty-three years.

Wreck-site
The remains of the *Butetown* lie orientated in a north-west to south-east direction, in a general depth of 4-7m, depending on the size of the tide. It also lies on the north side and parallel to a large reef, which dries at low water and runs out from the shore for about 400m. The *Butetown* is totally collapsed and has been heavily salvaged over the last few decades, but is still a nice pleasant dive, where the pieces of wreckage and surrounding reefs provide shelter for a few tasty crustaceans. From her two boilers, which are situated about midships, steel cross-spars or ribs, about 5m in length, run at right angles across the wreck every metre or so and, with the collection of huge steel plates, provide a guide to the vessel's outline.

Nothing of real interest in the way of artefacts remain on the wreck-site, but good finds do occasionally turn up after the pounding of winter storms. Large pollack and cod can sometimes be seen among the dense carpet of kelp which grows all around this area and there is an interesting array of aquatic flora and fauna to be found. The best time to visit the wreck-site is after a spell of light westerly winds on a neap tide

The Dimitry, *Dracula's wooden barque of around 250 tons, ashore at Whitby in 1885. Note the rear mast has been removed from the ship and is lying on the beach, awaiting repairs. The two horse and carts are to help in unloading.* Courtesy of the Whitby Literary and Philosophical Society.

when visibility can often reach 10m. Access from the shore is quite easy too, by going down the steps on the promenade near Table Rocks, although it does entail a bit of a swim to reach the wreck-site, about 150m off-shore.

Members of the Deep Blue Dive Centre of 69a, Front Street at Tynemouth, regularly take their novice divers to the wreck-site on training exercises. They reckon that there are numerous ways to access the site from the shore. However, the best route, and most consistent method of locating the wreck from the entry point on the map, is to swim away from the shore and descend to avoid the worst of any surge that is especially noticeable close to the shore at high tide. Set off at a leisurely pace in an easterly direction for about three minutes, then reset your heading to south and continue for another minute or so until you reach a reef wall, which will be straight in front of you. (The reef is not obvious close to the shore and without the initial use of your compass, there is every chance that you will swim straight over it, missing it altogether. It should not be confused with the reef that can be seen at low tide from the main road, looking down into the sea, the wreck lies to the left of this).

Once you have located the reef wall, which is in among the kelp, keep it on your right-hand side and use it like a handrail continuing east for another couple of minutes until it disappears. Maintain your easterly heading until the reef reappears on your right hand side. There are several gaps in the reef wall over a distance of 30m, which allows you to swim through. On the other side of the wall, approximately four to six fin-kicks away, you will arrive at the wreck of the *Butetown*.

By continuing in a southerly direction from this point you will come across the main reef wall, which is visible from the shore at low water. A short swim or climb, depending on the tide, over this reef and you find the remains of the 4,796-ton steamship *Zepheros*. Unfortunately, the vessel was so very heavily salvaged, that all that remains of her now are some steel bottom plates and an angular plate, which can be seen from the road at very low water.

SPRAY (ex-FIRSBY, ex-DENABY)

Wreck ★★★★
Scenery ★
Depth 46 m
Reference N 55 04 061 W 001 19 015
5 miles N.E. of the Tyne

The *Spray* was a steel 1,072-ton British steamship, registered in Aberdeen and had dimensions of 68.58m length, by 10.16m beam and a draught of 4.31m. She was built as the *Denaby* by S.P. Austin & Son at Sunderland, in 1891 and owned at the time of her loss by Ellis & McHardy. Her single steel propeller was powered by a three-cylinder, triple-expansion steam engine that developed 136hp, using one boiler. Her machinery was built by J. Dickinson of Sunderland. She had one deck, four watertight bulkheads and a superstructure consisting of an 8.5m poop-deck, 15.2m quarter-deck and a bridge-deck of 13.4m.

On 14 April 1917, the *Spray* was in ballast on passage from Aberdeen for Sunderland, under the command of Captain C.O. Lawrence. At 6.15 a.m., she was steaming south at a steady ten knots when a huge explosion rocked the ship near to her stern. The aft section of the vessel was totally destroyed and as shattered steel plates and debris filled the air, she immediately began to fill up and go down by the stern. Captain Lawrence gave the order to stop the engine and abandon ship and she went down within twenty-five minutes. A torpedo-boat destroyer arrived shortly after and rescued all of her crew and landed them at North Shields.

Wreck-site
The wreck lies orientated in a north-east to south-west direction, in a general depth of 46m, the lowest astronomical depth. She is still fairly substantial, but is mostly well broken up, with some superstructure visible on the north side of the wreck, which stands over 7m high around midships, where her boiler and engine are located. Wreckage is spread over an 86 x 20m area of seabed and lots of copper pipes, brass valves, pieces of broken derrick, anchor, windlass and broken air-ducts can be seen. Her boiler, condenser and engine are both visibly exposed and soft corals have established themselves on the highest structures, while shoals of pout-whiting have adopted the boiler area as a haven.

Many of the interesting artefacts should still be around, because the wreck has not been dived very much, but it is starting to become increasingly popular with some local divers. The wreck-site always appears to be very dark, even when the visibility is good and tidal streams are fairly strong, making this a low, slack water dive. Extra care should be taken, because of the likelihood of nets covering part of the wreck and during the summer months the boat cover should keep a watchful eye out for large ships passing close-by and also for drifting salmon fishing boats, with their mile long nets.

JANET CLARK

Wreck ★★
Scenery ★★★★
Depth 5m
Reference N 55 04 25 W 001 26 60
N.E. side of St Mary's Island, Whitley Bay.

The *Janet Clark* (also referred to as the *Jane Clark*) was an iron-hulled 406-ton British steamship, registered at Glasgow and had a length of approximately 40m. She was owned at the time of loss by J. Bruce of Glasgow and built on the Clyde in 1883. Her single iron propeller was powered by a two-cylinder, compound-steam engine that used one boiler.

On 24 December 1894, the vessel was on passage from Drontheim in Norway for Swansea, under the command of Captain H. Parker, carrying fourteen crew and a cargo of copper-ore and iron pyrite, when she stranded at St Mary's Island during dense fog and a light south-westerly wind. The voyage should have taken just a few days, but severe gales set in shortly after she left port and the weather conditions delayed the ship for ten days, during which time food ran out and her crew of fourteen had to go hungry. The storm is said to have worsened and waves breached the vessel, carrying away her wheelhouse, bridge equipment and compasses. For some sixteen hours prior to her stranding, she was completely at the mercy of the sea, wind and weather. The crew had no form of navigation, and in the pitch dark and a dense fog she drove ashore at 3 a.m. in the morning, (there was no light on the island at this time). The following morning the crew made some unsuccessful attempts to refloat her, but she was hemmed in solid. Later that evening she broke in two and became a total wreck. The crew made a safe crossing over to the island and were taken to nearby Blyth.

Wreck-site
The wreck lies at a right angle to the reef and is now totally collapsed, broken up, decayed and rather dispersed in a general depth of 5m, about the lowest astronomical depth. The members of the Deep Blue Dive Centre at Tynemouth say the fore section is well smashed up and partially obscured by boulders and a jungle of kelp, while the stern-end with the propeller, is said to be almost complete and clear of the rocks in deeper water. Her boiler stands upright and

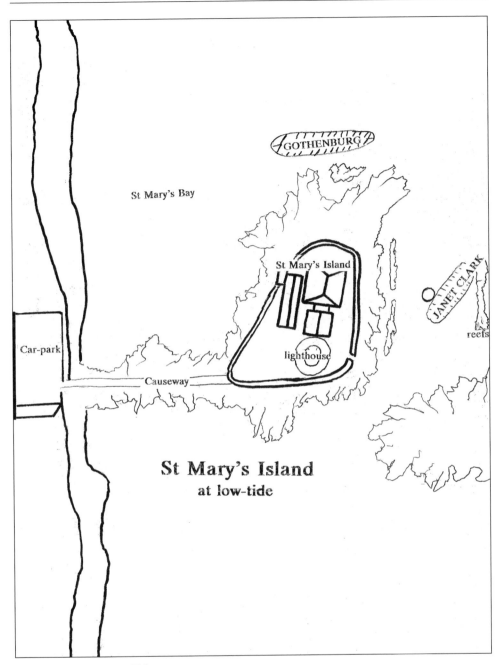

Map of St Mary's at Low Tide.

The Sylviana, a steamer of around 2,000 tons, ashore at Skinninggrove in 1901. She was believed to have been refloated later. Note the team of five to six horses at the ship's bows and the deep track marks made in the sand, obviously the cart was carrying something heavy. Courtesy of the Whitby Literary and Philosophical Society.

separate, just off the starboard side, while lots of iron plates lie scattered about, more or less at the base of the reef. The wreck covers an area of around 30m in length and is almost surrounded by reefs, where small codling, lump-suckers, pollack, saithe, wrasse and fair numbers of nice crustaceans can be found under the ledges and scattered wreckage.

Diving the wreck should only be done when the sea is fairly calm, with a light offshore wind, as the visibility can quickly deteriorate when there is any surface swell. Tidal streams, which flow north or south, also pick up considerably on spring tides, so more care should be taken. To get to the wreck-site from the island it is best to enter the water at it northern corner, preferably at low tide, which then entails a short swim straight out to where a marker buoy is usually floating over the wreck. After exploring the wreck-site and reefs, head in a south-easterly direction, by keeping the reef on your right hand side to just behind the lighthouse tower and into the gully where you can find a convenient exit point.

In June 1996, the area out to a depth contour of 20m, was designated a voluntary nature reserve to help establish an underwater nature trail. The reserve attracted a grant aid from the World Wide Fund for Nature and English Nature and is administered by North Tyneside Council. The trail runs out from the island to the wreck-site of the *Janet Clark* and back along the reef edge, over which distance there is a healthy array of marine life.

With two car-parks just over the causeway on the main land, there are adequate parking facilities, but this means that there will be quite a long walk at low tide, humping heavy diving equipment over to the island, so having a boat can be a big advantage.

Before visiting the island, it will also be worth checking with the Senior Warden of St Mary's Lighthouse Tel. 0191 2008654 or 0191 2008650.

GOTHENBURG CITY

Wreck ★★
Scenery ★★★
Depth 7-8m
Reference N 55 04 400 W 01 26 900
N.-N.W. side of St Mary's Island

The *Gothenburg City* was an iron 2,529-ton British steamship registered at West Hartlepool, and had dimensions of 91.87m length, by 11.58m beam and a draught of 7.21m. She was owned by C. Furness MP and built in 1884 by E. Withy & Co. both at West Hartlepool. Her single iron propeller was powered by a two-cylinder, compound steam engine that developed 300hp, using two boilers. Her machinery was built by T. Richardson & Sons of Hartlepool. She had two decks, three watertight bulkheads and a superstructure consisting of an 11m poop-deck, 23m bridge-deck and 8.7m forecastle.

Under the command of Captain John Harrison, the *Gothenburg City* sailed from Montreal for Newcastle-upon-Tyne on 13 June, with a cargo of deal, animals, cattle and phosphate rock. On 26 June 1891, she encountered heavy fog when close inshore off Northumberland and her speed was cut down to half, but she ran aground at St Mary's Island. Tugs were brought in to assist and Penny ferries unloaded 150 cattle out of the total of 476 animals on board, while another vessel took off part of her 400 standards of deal and 300 tons of phosphate rock. The ship's hull was badly damaged under her engine room and the amount of water that flooded in made the attempts by three tugs to pull her clear of the rocks, rather fruitless.

The following day, her remaining cargo was off-loaded to lighten the ship with a view to refloating her, but by this time her hull had filled up with water and it was found that her engine and boilers had actually moved. During the operation, a diving boat sank near to the stranded ship and a hard-hat (standard) diver was drowned. Further efforts to save the vessel were made impossible when heavy seas pushed her beam on to the rocks and huge waves pounded her for days. She was eventually written off as a total loss.

Wreck-site
What remains of the *Gothenburg City* lies just out from the north-north-western side of St Mary's Island, in about 8m of water. She is well broken up, with one boiler still remaining, lots of scattered iron plates, ribs, an anchor and chain and

173

The 2,259 ton steamer Gothenburg City *ashore at St Mary's Island on 26 June 1891.*

the propeller shaft. This is a good novice dive, which can be accessed from the shore at low tide, via the tidal causeway to St Mary's Island. Currents are very moderate, except during a spring tide and the surrounding reefs hold an interesting amount of marine life, including some good lobsters. Underwater visibility during the summer months can reach as much as 15m at times, after a spell of dry weather and light westerly winds.

LONGHIRST

Wreck ★★
Scenery ★★★
Depth 4-9m
Reference N 55 04 646 W 001 26 947
Outer-Bells, Hartley Rocks, near Whitley Bay.

The *Longhurst* was an iron 680 ton, three masted, British steamship, registered at Newcastle-upon-Tyne and had dimensions of 66.87m length, by 8.94m beam and a draught of 4.36m. She was owned by J. Elliot of Newcastle-upon-Tyne and built in 1873 by Smith at North Shields. Her single iron propeller was powered by a two-cylinder, compound-steam engine that developed 90hp, using one boiler and her machinery was built by Revenhill, Eastons & Co. She had one deck, four watertight bulkheads and a superstructure, consisting of a 21.3m reinforced quarter-deck and a 6.4m poop-deck. The vessel was also classed as A1 by Lloyds.

On 7 December 1878, the *Longhirst* was in ballast on a voyage from London to North Shields, under the command of Captain B. Blasby, when wind conditions north-east force six stranded and wrecked her on the reef known as the Outer-Bells, just north of St Mary's Island, near Whitley Bay.

Wreck-site
Keith Birtle informed me that what remains of the *Longhirst* lies in two gullies on the Outer-Bells reef. She is totally collapsed and well smashed up among the kelp, with her prop-shaft, lumps of iron plate and iron ribs concreting into the surrounding rocks, along with some very dispersed and broken machinery. Her boiler, which is now starting to disintegrate, lies close to the surface on a very low tide. A small pleasure yacht called the *Nora* struck the boiler and sank a few years ago, but was subsequently raised and salvaged.

The surrounding reefs make a good rummage dive for crustaceans. The Outer-Bells can be quite scenic during the summer months, with Dead Man's Fingers all over the rock walls. Tidal streams can be strong, but it is possible to dive the site at most states of the tide.

Large shoals of coley and individual pollack can be found all around this area, as well as the individual rock codling, especially during the summer months, while good-sized cod come close inshore to feed over the winter months.

CHRISTIAN

Wreck ★★★
Scenery ★
Depth 51 m
Reference N 55 05 923 W 001 17 108
5 miles E.S.E. of Blyth.

The *Christian* was an iron steamship of about 700 tons, registered in Germany and owned at the time of loss by Zerssen & Co. in Tonning, Germany. She was built in 1883 and had an iron-screw propeller, powered by a two-cylinder, compound-steam engine that used one boiler.

On 1 November 1895, the *Christian* was on a return voyage from Blyth to New Fairwater, under the command of Captain P. Plahn and carrying an unspecified cargo of coal, when she foundered and was lost, following a collision with the London-registered steamship *Albires*, five miles east-south-east of Blyth.

Wreck-site
The wreck, possibly that of the steamship *Christian*, lies within an area of the spoil-ground off Blyth. She is orientated in, more or less, a south-east to north-west direction in a general depth of 51m, the lowest astronomical depth. Little is known about the wreck-site, because she has not had a thorough investigation to-date, however her position is about correct. She is totally collapsed and well

broken up, with much of her buried under a heavy covering of fly-ash, dumped from the Blyth power-station. Unfortunately, fly-ash tends to set like cement once on the seabed. The highest section, which is around 2m high, is at the stern and the south-eastern end, where her boiler and engine are located. However, the wreck will still be definitely worth checking out by divers capable of diving to at least 51m, because most, if not all of the vessel's interesting bridge equipment will still be on site and is probably lying around loose somewhere. Visibility is reasonable during the summer months after a spell of dry settled weather, westerly winds and on a neap tide. The wreck is very difficult to locate using an echo sounder by itself and a magnatometer search would be much easier.

Tidal streams are fairly brisk, so this will be a low, slack water dive and a fair amount of pre-planning will be required. The site is in the main shipping lanes, so the boat cover will need to be on guard at all times and Lion's-mane jellyfish can also be a nuisance when diving between the months of July and Sepember.

MURISTAN

Wreck ★★★
Scenery ★
Depth 9m
Reference N 55 06 316 W 001 28 285
½ mile S. of Blyth, south pier.

The *Muristan* was a steel 2,886-ton British steamship, registered at the port of Swansea and had dimensions of 97.61m length, by 14.19m beam and a draught of 6.42m. She was built by W. Gray & Co. of West Hartlepool, in 1913 and was owned at the time of loss by the London & Paris Steamship Co. Ltd. Her single steel propeller was powered by a three-cylinder, triple-expansion engine that developed 288hp, using two boilers. Her machinery was built by Central Marine Engineering Works at West Hartlepool. She had one deck, five watertight bulkheads and a superstructure consisting of a 7.6m poop-deck, 29.8m bridge-deck and 10.3m forecastle.

On 19 November 1916, under the command of Captain G. Pritchard, the *Muristan* was on passage from the Tyne for Rouen in France with a cargo of coal and a crew of twenty-four when she encountered a severe easterly gale and heavy seas off Blyth. Her steering gear failed and she was driven into shallow water, just off the long stretch of sandy coastline. The vessel embedded herself firmly into the sand some 250m offshore, where huge waves crashed clean over her. Conditions were so bad, that at times only her funnel and the top of her masts were visible from the shore, then her Captain and one of the crew members went overboard and drowned, however three of the crew still managed to reach safety on shore. The rocket brigade arrived and tried repeatedly to fire lines over the stranded vessel, without success.

The pulling/sailing lifeboat stationed at Blyth was unable to launch, because of the prevailing conditions and eventually a message was sent to Tynemouth asking

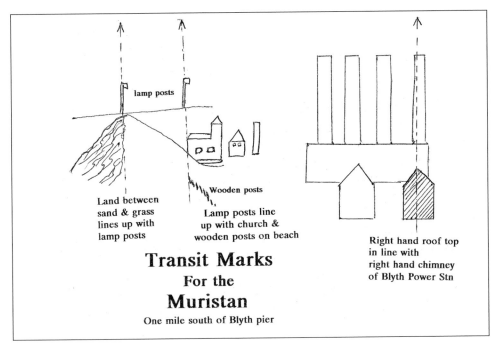

lamp posts

Land between
sand & grass
lines up with
lamp posts

Wooden posts

Lamp posts line
up with church &
wooden posts on beach

Right hand roof top
in line with
right hand chimney
of Blyth Power Stn

Transit Marks
For the
Muristan
One mile south of Blyth pier

Map of transit marks for the Muristan.

for help. At 7.30 a.m., Tynemouth's self-righting motorized lifeboat *Henry Vernon* slipped her moorings on 20 November, under the command of Coxswain Robert Smith (one of the heroes in the *Rohilla* rescue off Whitby). Unfortunately, the lifeboat had to wait inside the harbour until 9 a.m. for a lull in the storm, before they could make an attempt to get through the harbour entrance. When the lifeboat reached the scene late in the morning, conditions were so bad, all that the crew could see was the *Muristan's* bridge and chart-house; they were unable to render any assistance. Huge seas were still hurling over the wreck and vast quantities of wreckage were floating all around her.

There was no sign of life on board, so Coxswain Smith decided to make an attempt to return to their base at Tynemouth. However, after only half an hour, the lifeboat was hit by a massive wave, which flooded the boat and her engine failed. They dropped anchor until the sails could be set and tried desperately to restart the engine. Eventually they succeeded but it stopped soon after and Coxswain Smith decided to put into nearby Blyth using her auxiliary sails.

With help from the local naval authorities her engine was repaired during the night. At daybreak the following morning of 21 November, the *Henry Vernon* put back out to sea and in horrendous conditions rescued the remaining sixteen *Muristan* crew members, who were found huddled together in the remains of the chart-house. The men were taken to Blyth and the lifeboat arrived back at her station at 10.30 a.m. Altogether, five of the *Muristan's* crew were lost in the incident. The ship soon broke up and became a total wreck.

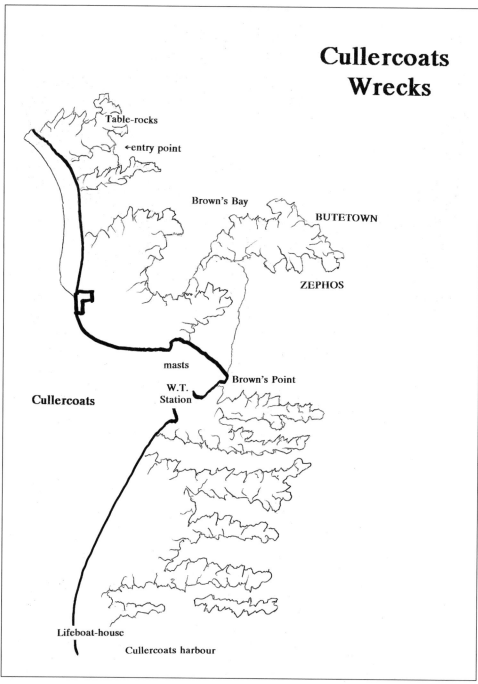

Map of Cullercoats Wrecks.

The Earl of Percy *(or* Pearcy*) was in a collision off Whitby on 15 September 1888. It is believed that this steamship was repaired and put back into service.* Courtesy of the Whitby Literary and Philosophical Society.

On 8 December 1916, Coxswain Robert Smith and Second Coxswain James Brownlee were both awarded silver medals by the R.N.L.I. for their part in the rescue. Coxswain Robert Smith was also awarded the R.N.L.I.'s gold medal for rescuing people from the wreck of the hospital-ship *Rohilla* off Whitby in October 1914.

Wreck-site
This is a very substantial wreck that lies close inshore, about 250m out from the beach and about one mile south of Blyth harbour. She has totally collapsed in on herself and is now one huge, jumbled pile of steel plates surrounding her two boilers. Very little nonferrous metal was visible when I visited her, however I have been informed that the winter storms usually dislodge the mass of steel plates, changing the wreck scene. Local divers collect a fair number of lobsters from under the wreckage, but many of them are difficult to extract from the deep, long holes and slots. Cod are also much in evidence, so a double-barbed spear often comes in handy. There are no real currents to worry about, so you can dive the wreck at any state of the tide. Visibility is often great during the summer months, however any swell soon spoils it. The surrounding seabed is all sand, and sometimes the winter storms stir the sand up so much, it covers much of the wreck. It is an excellent rummage dive and a good introductory novice dive, too.

KAMMA (ex-BLACK PRINCE, ex-XIA, ex-YORK MINSTER)

Wreck ★★★
Scenery ★★
Depth 15-16m
Reference N 55 06 588 W 001 27 665 (bows)
N 55 07 000 W 001 27 318 (stern)
1 mile S.E. of Blyth Harbour.

The *Kamma* was a steel 1,516-ton Swedish steamship, registered in the port of Helsingborg and had dimensions of 76.37m length, by 10.74m beam and a draught 5.25m. She was owned at the time of loss by Rederiaktieb Henckel N.P. and built as the *York Minster* by Palmers Co. Ltd, Newcastle in 1883. Her single iron propeller was powered by a two-cylinder, compound-steam engine that developed 150hp, using one boiler. She had one deck, four watertight bulkheads and a superstructure consisting of a 27.2m quarter deck, a 15.8m bridge-deck and forecastle of 9.1m.

On 22 January 1917, under the command of a Captain L.O. Norman, the *Kamma* was on passage from Gefle for Rouen, with an unspecified cargo of wood, when she foundered and was lost after striking a German mine, one mile south-east of Blyth harbour.

Wreck-site
The wreck lies on a well swept seabed of sand, rock, stone and very small reefs, in a general depth of 15-16m and broken up into two separate sections. Her stern-end, where the engine and boiler are situated, stand upright, more or less concreted together and carpeted in a myriad of Dead Man's Fingers, with a huge shoal of pout-whiting swarming all over and around them, which makes a fabulous and very picturesque sight.

The midships and bow section of the *Kamma* is well broken up and dispersed over an area of about 50 by 70m of seabed, lying inshore and 200m south-west of the stern section. Lost monofilament, cod trammel nets are inter-laced around this wreckage and often still ensnare unwary fish or even the occasional crustacean, (last time we dived on the *Kamma*, I removed three good sized lobsters from the nets). Copper and steel pipes lie dispersed and mixed up among the half buried steel frames, ribs, pipes and plates, where even the occasional porthole may still be found.

It is only about five years ago, that a colleague of mine discovered the *Kamma's* solid brass steam whistle in this area. It is possible to dive at most states of the tide, but it is difficult to stay in one place on the bottom during spring tides. Visibility is usually excellent during the summer months after a spell of dry, settled weather and westerly winds, however Lion's-mane jellyfish can be troublesome when diving, and even fishing, during the summer months.

6. Blyth to the Farne Islands

NIKE (ex-MARIO, ex-CALEDONIA)

Wreck ★★★★
Scenery ★
Depth 49m
Reference N 55 07 386 W 001 18 805
7 miles E. of Blyth Harbour.

The *Nike* was a steel 1,834-ton Swedish steamship, registered at of Gelfe and had dimensions of 82.39m length, by 11.58m beam and a draught of 5.63m. She was owned at the time of loss by Angf. Aktieb. of Nike and was built as the *Caledonia* by Oswald, Mordaunt & Co. at Southampton in 1883. Her single steel propeller was powered by a two-cylinder, compound-steam engine that developed 184hp, using two boilers. She had one deck, a well-deck, four water-tight bulkheads and a superstructure consisting of a 28.6m quarter-deck, 18.8m bridge-deck and 9.1m forecastle. She was also classed at Lloyds as 100 A1.

On 12 December 1917, the *Nike* was in convoy off Blyth, carrying a general cargo, including soft wood and deal, on a voyage from Malmo to London, under the command of a Captain Anderson, when she was attacked by German motor torpedo boats. Four of the high speed vessels, *V-100, G-101, G-103* and *G-104* attacked her with torpedoes one after the other and huge explosions rocked the *Nike* from stem to stern, sending her down to the bottom within minutes.

Wreck-site
This wreck has not been positively identified yet, but local fishermen call her the *Duen*, which is said to have been an old 'Clyde Puffer', powered by a two-cylinder, compound-steam engine. However, there is also the possibility that it may be the steamship *Nike*, because she sank close to this position. The wreck lies on a seabed of mud and sand in a general depth of 49m, the lowest astronomical depth. It has collapsed in on herself at midships and is rather decayed, but is still fairly substantial, standing around 5m high around her two boilers, condenser and engine, which are now exposed through a mound of steel debris, broken machinery and flattened copper pipes. Her bows and stern-end are said to be still fairly intact, where Dead Man's Fingers have established themselves on the upper-structures. The wreck has just recently been discovered and it is quite possible that much of her interesting bridge and navigational equipment will still be there to see.

The site is very dark and gloomy, so a good torch is essential. Everything is coated in hard white casings from marine worms, while the seabed is often carpeted with brittle-starfish. She is a long way from shore so a good look-out is required by the boat crew, because the location of the wreck is close to the main shipping lanes.

Tidal streams are very strong and visibility is usually poor, being only 1-2m. However, however during the summer months it is possible to see for up to 10m near to the seabed. The wreck has proved to be a good angling venue too, as local charter boats have begun visiting the wreck-site.

GUDBRAND

Wreck ★★★★
Scenery ★
Depth 50m
Reference N 55 12 098 W 001 23 160
Also: N 55 12 030 W 001 23 230
5 miles E. of Beacon Point, Newbiggen.

The *Gudbrand* was an iron 1,860-ton Norwegian steamship that had dimensions of 82.6m length, by 12.19m beam and a draught of 4.87m. She was built in 1860 by J. Priestman & Co. and her single iron-screw propeller was powered by a three-cylinder, triple-expansion steam engine that used two boilers.

On 16 March 1917, the *Gudbrand* was on passage from the Tyne for Christiania, with an unspecified cargo of coal, when she was torpedoed and sunk by the German submarine *UC-50*, seven miles north-east of Blyth.

Wreck-site

The wreck of the *Gudbrand* is lying on a seabed of sand and stone in a general depth of 50m. In 1967, she was swept clear to a least depth of 23.4m, with the least echo sounder depth of 42m. Her remains are still quite substantial, standing some 8m high, although her hull and superstructure has now collapsed in on itself. Her boilers and engine are visibly exposed and are surrounded by masses of iron plates, pipes, broken lifeboat davits, broken machinery and lots of debris at the ster-end, which is the highest point on the wreck. Large lengths of copper pipe can be seen through the plates and jumble of iron debris and probably most of her interesting brass navigational instruments could still be around.

The upper, most exposed, structures are impressive where soft corals have established themselves in a profusion of colour. At least one trawl net is also said to be entangled with the twisted, metal plates and with very strong, tidal streams, combined with usually poor, gloomy visibility, so diving the wreck needs some very careful planning.

BANGARTH

Wreck ★★★★
Scenery ★
Depth 47.4m
Reference N 55 13 733 W 001 19 123
Also: N 55 13 680 W 001 19 210
7 miles E.N.E. of Newbiggin

The *Bangarth* was steel 1,872-ton British steamship, registered in Liverpool and had dimensions of 83.82m length, by 12.19m beam and a draught of 6.4m. She was owned by the Rea Shipping Co. Ltd and built at Middlesbrough in 1872 by Sir Raylton Dixon & Co. Ltd. Her single steel-screw propeller was powered by a three-cylinder, triple-expansion steam engine that developed 217hp, using two boilers.

On 13 December 1917, the *Bangarth* was engaged as a Royal Navy Auxiliary collier and under the command of Captain J. Clarkson, on passage from Methil to Dunkirk, when she was torpedoed and sunk by the German submarine, *UB-34*, with loss of two of her crew.

Wreck-site
In 1967 the wreck was said to be almost completely intact, sitting upright on a seabed of dirty sand and stone, in a general depth of 47.4m, the lowest astronomical depth. Many years ago she was swept clear to 42m. Even though her superstructure and hull sides have crumpled up and collapsed in on themselves, she still stands 5m from the bottom. The wreck is very substantial and most, if not all, of her interesting navigational equipment is still somewhere among the jumbled wreckage. A number of large copper pipes, brass valves, winches, bollards, deck-rails, broken pieces of jibs or derricks and lots of unrecognisable broken machinery are visible in the mound of steel debris. Soft corals adorn the higher sections and at least one trawl net is tangled up and floating at her stern-end, so extreme caution is called for by anyone contemplating diving on this wreck.

A sizeable number of fish of varying species gather over the top of the wreck during the summer months and probably at other times of the year, so the wreck should make a good boat angling venue, when conditions allow. Her position at sea, means that there is an added danger from passing large ships, so a sharp watchful eye will be required by the boat crew when diving or fishing the site. Also, Lion's-mane jellyfish can be a problem during July and August.

RAGNHILD

Wreck ★★★★
Scenery ★
Depth 40m
Reference N 55 15 310 W 001 27 220
3½ miles N.E. by E. of Cresswell, near Blyth.

The *Ragnhild* was a steel 1,107-ton Norwegian steamship, registered at the port of Bergen and had dimensions of 69.8m length, by 10.66m beam and a draught of 4.57m. She was built in 1909 by Bergens M.V. at Bergen and owned at the time of loss by N.H. Hartmary & Co. Her single steel propeller was powered by a three-cylinder, triple-expansion steam engine that used one boiler.

On 27 April 1917, the *Ragnhild* was on a voyage from the Tyne to Skien, with a cargo of furnace fuel oil and coke, when she was torpedoed and sunk by the German submarine *UC-29*. (Lloyd's Confidential War Loss Records have recorded her as having detonated a German-laid mine, however the original Norwegian sources have her down as being torpedoed and name the U-boat, which is the most likely.)

Wreck-site
The wreck lies on a dirty seabed of mud and sand, in a general depth of around 40m. She stands about 4-5m high, is orientated in a north-west to south-east direction, is well broken up, fairly decayed and rather dispersed. The bow section is reported to be still intact, along with the boiler and engine, which are covered in soft corals at the highest and most exposed points and hard, white, marine worm casings cover the debris. The wreck appears to have been dispersed with explosives because there are lots of flattened and bent copper and steel pipes and piles of battered and broken machinery spread about the wreck-site.

Large pollack and a shoal of the pout-whiting, often referred to locally as 'blegs' or 'scotch haddocks', are usually swimming around and over the wreck, especially the higher points of it, so the wreck should make a decent boat-angling venue when conditions permit. Visibility is usually poor. The best time to visit the wreck is during the summer months on a neap tide and after a spell of dry, settled weather and westerly winds. Tidal streams are moderate, but very strong on a spring tide and Lion's-mane jellyfish can be a nuisance when fishing or diving between July and September.

INVERGYLE

Wreck ★★★★
Scenery ★
Depth 47m
Reference N 55 18 666 W 001 25 733

Also given: N 55 18 710 W 001 25 540
4 miles E.S.E. of Coquet Island

The *Invergyle* was a steel 1,794-ton British steamship, registered in Glasgow and owned at the time of loss by Stewart & Gray of Glasgow. She was built in 1907 and her single steel propeller was powered by a three-cylinder, triple-expansion steam engine that used two boilers.

On 12 March 1915, the *Invergyle* was in ballast, on passage from Scapa Flow for Hartlepool when she was torpedoed and sunk by the German submarine, *U-23*.

Wreck-site
The wreck lies on a well swept seabed of sand and small stone, in a general depth of 47m, the lowest astronomical depth. In the 1970s she was reported to be standing 9.5m high and intact with a massive gaping hole in her side where the torpedo had struck home. However, the latest information is that she has now collapsed onto the seabed, with her two boilers and engine exposed, surrounded by a huge jumbled heap of twisted, steel plates, wheels, cogs and broken machinery, with copper pipes protruding out of it all. Soft corals adorn the upper structures, especially around the bow and stern areas. Large ling and cod are to be seen and shoals of pout-whiting hover over the top of the wreck. This is a wreck worth considering taking your angling tackle and jiggers out to, to stock up the freezer.

Tidal streams are exceptionally strong and visibility is rather dark and eerie, however it can be very good at certain times during the summer months. A good torch is required when diving, so as not to miss out on the large lobsters. The wreck-site is a long way from shore, so very careful planning is required, as is a good watchful eye, because the site is close to the main shipping lanes.

HORNCHURCH

Wreck ★★★★
Scenery ★
Depth 40m
Reference N 55 21 800 W 001 28 166
Also: N 55 21 803 W 001 28 264
3½ miles N.E. of Coquet Island.

The *Hornchurch* was a steel 2,159-ton British steamship registered in London, and had dimensions of 85.34m length, by 12.31m beam and a draught of 5.61m. She was owned at the time of loss by J. Hudson & Co. Ltd and built by Osbourne, Graham Co. at Sunderland in 1916. Her single steel propeller was powered by a three-cylinder, triple-expansion steam engine that used two boilers.

On 3 August 1917, the *Hornchurch* was on passage from London for Methil, under the command of Captain J.W. Gagen and carrying an unspecified cargo of coal, when she foundered, with the loss of two of her crew, after detonating a German mine off Coquet Island.

Wreck-site
The wreck, believed to be the *Hornchurch*, is reported to be lying on a well swept seabed of sand, stone and shell in a general depth of 40m and surrounded by a $\frac{1}{2}$ m scour. It has totally collapsed, having fallen in on itself and is well broken up and decayed, but is still very substantial, with the highest section of some 4m, being around her engine, condenser and two boilers. Lots of large lengths of flattened copper-pipes, brass valves, iron and steel wheels and cogs, an anchor windlass, chain and two anchors are mixed up with the mound of broken machinery and twisted steel plates. The wreck has not seen too many divers, so it is feasible that there could still be some interesting articles to be found in the jumbled heap.

There are soft corals on the highest sections around her boilers and shoaling fish, mainly pout-whiting and pollack, are fairly common during the summer months, while some good cod of around 5kg have been observed in the wreck, so she should make an excellent boat angling venue. Tidal streams are very strong and the visibility is usually poor, but it significantly improves in the summer months, following a spell of dry, settled weather and westerly winds. The surrounding seabed is carpeted with millions of brittle-starfish. Schools of dolphins and porpoises and even the occasional whale, can sometimes be seen in this particular area during the late summer months.

OLYMPIA

Wreck ★★★
Scenery ★
Depth 44m
Reference N 55 22 110 W 001 28 450
$3\frac{1}{2}$ miles N.E. of Coquet Island

The *Olympia* was a steel 221-ton steam fishing trawler and had dimensions of 36.57m length, by 6.55m beam and a draught of 3.5m. She was built as trawler No.122687 in 1904-1905 by Cook, Welton & Gemmell in Yard 71 at Beverley. Then she was launched on 23 January 1905 and registered at the port of Grimsby as GY62 on 26 May by her new owners the Great Grimsby & East Coast Steam Fishing Co. Ltd, who were the owners at the time of loss. Her single steel propeller was powered by a three-cylinder, triple-expansion steam engine that developed 66hp, using one boiler giving her a recorded speed of 10.5 knots Her machinery was built by Amos & Smith.

On 3 August 1916 (though other sources say 8 April) the *Olympia* was in ballast on a fishing voyage from her home port of Grimsby when she was captured off Coquet Island by a German submarine. Her skipper, Captain A. Smith and his crew were ordered to abandon ship, then the Germans sunk the vessel with gunfire.

Wreck-site

The wreck of the *Olympia* lies on a seabed of hard sand and shell in a general depth of 44m, the lowest astronomical depth. It has totally collapsed in on itself, leaving the boiler and engine exposed to the strong tidal streams and is surrounded by a mound of decayed, twisted steel plates and broken machinery, but part of her bow section is still reasonably intact. Everything is coated with hard, white, marine-worm casings and soft corals, which make a very photogenic sight, when the visibility is at a premium during the summer months. The seabed is a carpet of brittle-starfish and numerous species of fish have adopted the wreck as a sanctuary, especially a large shoal of pout-whiting, so she will make a good one to visit on a boat angling trip.

Tidal streams are fairly strong and the best time to visit the site is on a neap tide after a spell of dry, settled weather and westerly winds.

HAZARD

Wreck ★★★
Scenery ★
Depth 33m
Reference N 55 25 090 W 001 30 360
2½ miles N.E. of Boulmer.

The *Hazard* was a wooden British steam tug, registered at Newport and owned at the time of loss by A. Bain of North Shields. She was built in 1873 and had a single four-bladed iron propeller, powered by a two-cylinder, compound-steam engine that used one boiler.

During wind conditions north-west force five, on 2 December 1892, the crew of the *Hazard* were out seeking towage work when there appears to have been an accident on board the vessel involving her machinery and main engine. The problem is thought to have caused a serious leak, which her pumps were unable to cope with and the vessel foundered two miles off Houghton Stile Reef, just north of Boulmer, soon after the incident.

Wreck-site

The wreck lies on a well-swept seabed of sand, shingle and broken shells in a general depth of 33m. It was said to have been first dived on in September 1989 and her wreckage was spread over an area of about 30 by 18m The boiler, standing about 4m high, an iron four-bladed propeller and a towing winch built by Clarke Chapman of Gateshead-on-Tyne were found. The wreck is well broken up, with broken machinery lying among the bent and twisted copper and lead pipes. Most of the wooden structure has been eaten away or dispersed by the sea and, although there has been no positive identification, its size, four-bladed propeller and named winch point to it being the steam tug *Hazard*.

Tidal streams are very strong, making this a low slack water dive and visibility is usually only moderate, however it vastly improves during the summer months after a spell of dry, settled weather and westerly winds. Lion's-mane jellyfish can also be a nuisance when diving or fishing during July and August.

HOOGHAMMEN

Wreck ★★
Scenery ★★★
Depth 5m
Reference N 55 29 20 W 001 35 30
200 metres S. of Dunstanborough Castle.

The *Hooghammen* was a Dutch iron-built steam trawler, (referred to in Holland as a *schuzte*), of around 200 tons that was registered in the port of Groningen and had dimensions of approximately 35m length and 6.5m beam. She was owned at the time of loss by Van der Wal of Groningen in Holland and had a single iron-screw propeller, powered by a two-cylinder, compound-steam engine that used one boiler.

Used as a cargo vessel, the steam trawler was on passage from London for Borrow-Stoness on 2 April 1907, when she stranded and was lost near Dunstanborough Castle, during wind conditions south-east force four. She was under the command of her owner, Captain Van der Wal, and carrying a cargo of scrap-iron and a crew of four.

Wreck-site
The remains of this vessel can be located about 50m out from the rocks, just to the south of the castle and almost in line with a deep 'V' shaped cut in the rocky shore-line. She lies on a kelp-covered rocky seabed, in a general depth of around 5m, about the lowest astronomical depth. The wreck is totally collapsed, broken up and well dispersed among the kelp-covered rocks. Only the iron ribs and a few twisted plates and girders remain, but it is not long since someone recovered a nice little intact porthole from the site, so she is still worth a rummage around. Crustaceans are quite common, including some fair sized lobsters, beneath the surrounding boulders and weed-covered reefs.

Tidal streams can be quite strong, especially on a spring tide, so extra care should be taken when diving from the shore.

NIDELVEN

Wreck ★★★★
Scenery ★
Depth 38m
Reference N 55 28 647 W 001 29 977
3 miles E. of Craster.

The *Nidelvin* was a steel 1,262-ton Norwegian steamship, owned at the time of loss by Nordenfjeldske Dampskibsselskab and registered in the port of Trondheim. She was built at Trondheim by Trondheims Mek Vaerks in 1908 and had dimensions of 70.43m length, by 10.13m beam and a draught of 4.11m. Her single iron propeller was powered by a three-cylinder, triple-expansion steam engine that developed 132hp, using one boiler.

Under the command of Captain F. Lugg, the *Nidelvin* was on passage from the Tyne for Svolvaer, with a cargo of coal, when she foundered on 27 April 1917, after detonating a mine laid by the German submarine, *UC-29*.

Wreck-site
This wreck was only discovered in the last couple of years, but since then, local divers have made numerous trips to her during the summer months. The wreck is very substantial, sitting upright in a general depth of 38m, the lowest astronomical depth. The ship's hull and outline is quite distinguishable all around and the hull is intact up to about half way, to just below her decks, where it has collapsed down along with the superstructure and decking. These have collapsed down onto the boiler and engine making access to anything rather difficult to get near, however portholes and other artefacts are still being recovered from time to time.

Tidal streams are very brisk, making this is a low, slack water dive, while underwater visibility is usually rather poor, being only a couple of metres or so, but it significantly improves during the summer months after a spell of dry, settled weather, neap tides and light westerly winds. With the likelihood of nets being caught up in the wreckage, extra care should be taken.

Cod and other species of fish can sometimes be observed around the wreck, making it an interesting boat-angling venue and Lion's-mane jellyfish can be an extra problem when ascending and descending during the late summer months.

BALLYCOTTON

Wreck ★
Scenery ★★★
Depth 8m
Reference N 55 31 15 W 001 36 05
Emblestone Rock, Newton point.

The *Ballycotton* was an iron 887-ton British steamship, registered in Glasgow and had dimensions of 68.58m length, by 9.22m beam and a draught of 4.74m. She was owned at the time of loss by T. MacGill of Glasgow and was built in 1880 by W. Simons & Co. at Refrew. Her single iron propeller was powered by a two-cylinder, compound-steam engine that developed 179hp, using one boiler. She had two decks, a well-deck and a superstructure consisting of a 38.7m poop-deck and 16.4m forecastle.

On 15 February 1900, the *Ballycotton* was on passage from Amsterdam for Grangemouth, under the command of Captain W.H. Barnetson and carrying a general mixed cargo, when she was driven inshore and struck the Emblestone Rock near Newton-by-the-Sea.

The North Sunderland lifeboat *Thomas Berwick* was launched on 15 February, after it was reported that the steamship *Ballycotton* was in great difficulties during extremely heavy seas and a full gale. However, as the lifeboat headed out, she was struck by a particularly heavy wave and Coxswain Robson was washed overboard. Fortunately, he was quickly picked up again by his colleagues. The lifeboat carried on, eventually returning to base, when, it was said, 'the steamer got out of trouble un-aided'. In fact, the *Ballycotton* was driven ashore and totally wrecked, with the loss of three of her crew.

The *Thomas Berwick* was a 10.3m by 2.4m, ten-oared, self-righting lifeboat. It first came into service on 5 September 1884, at a cost of £363, provided with a legacy from the late Miss Isabella Berwick, of Gateshead, in memory of her late father, the well known local artist and wood-carver.

Wreck-site

The wreck of this vessel is well smashed up, leaving only her upright boiler with a couple of bronze valves firmly attached to it, standing among the sand and boulders. A few lengths of copper-pipe also lie close to the boiler, but intermingled with pieces of very mangled iron girders which are partially buried in the sand. Numerous divers have attempted to dislodge what is left of the pipes and bronze valves, but they seem well encrusted and firmly concreted in. The seabed around the wreckage consists mostly of sand, so anything could turn up following a big storm. What remains of the wreck lies in about 8m and is located about 25m from the inside, and seaward end of the reef.

This area produces some good lobsters and crabs from time to time, but the visibility is often rather murky. The best time to dive the wreck and reefs is on a neap tide after a spell of dry, settled weather and westerly winds, during the summer months. It is possible to dive the site at any state of the tide, but it is best avoided if there is an easterly swell or spring tides. Some good hauls of mackerel and decent numbers of codling can be caught using strings of flies and jiggers from a boat just outside and away from the reefs during August and September. Many of the angling boats launching at Beadnell, come down to this area to fish during the summer months.

7. Farne Island Wrecks

SKODVAL

Wreck ★
Scenery ★★★★
Depth 12 metres
Reference N 55 37 620 W 001 35 450
Callers, Farnes Islands.

The *Skodval* was a steel 607-ton Norwegian steamship, registered in Oslo and had dimensions of 50.29m length, by 7.92m beam and a draught of 4.87m. Her single propeller was powered by a three-cylinder, triple-expansion engine that used one boiler.

On 27 January 1917 she was on passage from Middlesbrough for Skien with a cargo of salt, when she stranded on the Crumstone and Callers, the southerly-most rocks of the Farne Islands and became a total loss.

Wreck-site

The remains, of what are believed to be those of the *Skodval,* are totally collapsed, well broken up and decayed. They lie about 25m west from the Caller's reef wall, on the other side of a 15m deep, flat, well swept, stony valley/gully on a sloping bank of a submerged, boulder strewn reef. Although the wreckage is very old, decayed, scattered around and covered in hard, white, marine worm casings, it is still an interesting sight, especially to the underwater photographer. The upright boiler stands about 5m to the north of the engine frame/block, which has pieces of rope flowing up from it and looks very photogenic when the sun's rays shines through it. Very often crabs and lobsters can be found hiding among the pile of debris and surprisingly, there is still the glint of the odd piece of copper-pipe showing in the concreted pile. Close-by is an anchor and chain, iron prop, propeller shaft, lots of rusting ribs or frames and two big winches that lie close to the sloping bank.

Anemones and Dead Man's Fingers, which are attracted by the strong currents, carpet the side of the Caller's rock walls. This current runs around the inside of the Crumstone, then sweeps through the gullies between the Callers and is sometimes strong enough to purge your demand valve. Slack, low water is the best time to dive and the underwater visibility is usually in excess of 8m during neap tides in the summer months.

BRITANNIA

Wreck ★★
Scenery ★★★
Depth 6-30m
Reference N 55 37 200 W 001 36 100
W. side of Callers Reef, Farne Islands

The *Britannia* was a steel 726-ton British steamship, registered at the port of Leith and had dimensions of 64m length, by 8.22m beam and a draught of 4.57m. She was built in 1885 and owned at the time of loss by the Curry Steam Ship Co., (although another source says the Hull, Leith & Hamburg Steam Package Co.). Her single propeller was powered by a three-cylinder triple-expansion steam engine that used one boiler.

On 25 September 1915, *Britannia* was on passage from Newcastle-upon-Tyne for Leith, with a general cargo when she ran aground on the west side of the Caller's Reef in dense fog and became a total loss. The *Forster Fawsett* from Seahouses in north Sunderland, a self-righting 10.7m oared lifeboat was launched at 6.20 a.m. and rescued seven of her nineteen crew. However, two had already drowned while the other ten had succeeded in getting ashore in one of the ship's boats.

Incidentally, the *Britannia* ran aground off St Abb's Head in 1891, but was salvaged and put back into service. In total, there were about thirty-four ships around Britain called *Britannia* between 1753 and 1915, and practically all of them met the same watery fate. Four of those were wrecked off this part of the north-east coast.

Wreck-site
The remains of the *Britannia* can be found on the sloping bank off the south-west side of the third Caller's islet, lying just north-west of Crumstone. It is now well dispersed on the steep, sloping reef, in depths from around 6-30m. The ship's engine lies partly buried in sand on the bottom, close to the upright boiler and condenser, in a gully at 6-10m, while her iron propeller and shaft is in an adjacent gully. The winch is in 23m and her bows are some way out from the reef in 28-30m.

The wreck itself is not much of a dive, however the underwater scenery can be interesting. The tidal streams are very strong on both flood and ebb tides, but a little worse on the ebb, especially near the bow section. Visibility varies greatly, but can be exceptional at times, reaching 15m on neap tides during the summer months. The best time to dive this site is at low, slack water, ($1\frac{1}{2}$ to 1 $\frac{3}{4}$ of an hour after low water at Seahouses) and when the Callers are showing above water.

The 740 ton steamship Britannia, *taken on 4 June 1886, shortly after being built as a cable ship, owned by Telegraph Construction & Maintenance Co. Ltd. It was later owned by the Curry Steamship Co. and wrecked on the Caller's Reef in the outer Farne Islands, on 25 September 1915.* Courtesy of the National Maritime Museum, Greenwich, London.

FORFARSHIRE

Wreck ★
Drift Dive ★★★★
Scenery ★★
Depth 6-25m
Reference Piper Gut, Outer Farnes

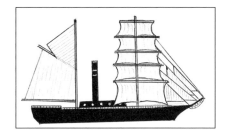

In her day the *Forfarshire* was a modern 400-ton wooden paddle steamer, being only four years old when she was wrecked on the Big Harcar in 1838, causing the deaths of forty-three people. She was built in Dundee in 1834 at a cost of £20,000 and was designed to carry both cargo and passengers between Dundee and Hull. She was equipped with two, two-cylinder, compound steam engines that developed 90hp using two boilers, supported by brigantine-rigged sails, with two masts and one funnel positioned in between the masts and had dimensions of 54.86m length and a 6.83m beam. She carried a crew of twenty-two and approximately forty-one passengers, but the true number of passengers would have only been known by the captain, who collected the fares during the journey. The *Forfarshire* could make about nine knots under her own power, without the use of the sails.

She left Hull for the journey to Dundee on the midnight tide on 6 September 1838 with a cargo of superfine cloths, hardware, soap, spinning gear and boiler plate. She'd had some problems with leaking boilers, which were repaired before she sailed from Hull, however by the time she was off the coast at Berwick, they had began to leak again, but much more seriously, rendering her engines useless. At 1 a.m., in the early hours of 7 September, she started losing ground and the chief engineer told the Captain, John Humble, that neither of the engines could be used. Soon the leaks got so bad that steaming hot water was filling the bilges. The only way the firemen could put out the fire, was by dousing the boilers. They realized the ship was in trouble, so the captain ordered her to be turned round to head for South Shields and at the same time he had the sails set fore and aft to keep the ship well off shore. At this moment she was not in any immediate danger, because she did not need to rely on her engines as she was a sailing ship in her own right. However, the weather was bad, with a northerly gale blowing and patches of thick fog making visibility extremely poor and it was to get worsed. The gale increased to storm force and the combination of wind, heavy rain and fog was seriously effecting the ship's headway.

The captain soon realized that, with the strong tidal streams, she was actually being driven backwards in the darkness of night. Captain Humble decided to run before the storm, in an attempt to find shelter behind the Farne Islands. He caught sight of a light that he presumed to be that of Farne Island on the Inner Farnes, but in fact was probably the Longstone light in the Outer Farnes. At 4 a.m. on 7 September, the *Forfarshire* drove into the western corner of Big Harcar, (now known as Forfar Rock).

Within fifteen minutes of grounding, one of her paddle axles broke off, leaving a massive hole in the hull, which allowed the sea to rush in, while at the same time, her stern section cracked in half and she settled on the bottom, drowning most of the people on board. Fortunately, nine people who had already left in one of the ship's boats, were rescued by a vessel from Montrose and were eventually landed at South Shields. Twelve people, although another report says thirteen, survived on the fore-section of the stranded vessel and as the tide fell away were able to scramble onto the Big Harcar rock, to await daylight and possible rescue.

Grace Darling
About half a mile away was the Longstone lighthouse, where the Keeper, William Darling, his wife Thomasin and their youngest daughter, 22-year-old Grace lived. Their son, William had gone across to Seahouses earlier, to help with the herring fleet. At first-light, at 7 a.m. on the following morning of 8 September, Grace spotted the wreck of the *Forfarshire* from her bedroom window and immediately told her father and mother. As the light grew stronger, they could just make out three or four people on the rocks and William Darling decided to try and rescue them. Helped by Grace, he launched his 21ft (6.1m) coble, by which time the tide had receded, and slowly, with great skill and tremendous courage, the two of them succeeded in making the perilous journey over to the wreck-site, via the south side of the Bluecaps and Harcar reefs, which dry at low tide. On arrival at the rock they found eight men and one woman clinging to life, but because of the size of their boat, could only take the woman and four men back to the lighthouse. Two

of the men bravely agreed to return with William Darling and between them they rescued the others.

Meanwhile William Robson, who was the Coxswain of North Sunderland lifeboat, had been informed of the tragedy and decided to launch a coble, instead of the lifeboat, because he believed that it would be better suited for getting right in among the rocks of the Farnes. With six other local men, James Robson, Michael Robson, Thomas Cuthbertson, William Swan, Robert Knox and William Darling, the son of the lighthouse-keeper, he set off in the coble and succeeded in reaching the Harcar rock, only to find that all of the survivors had been rescued, however they picked up three dead bodies, a man and two children, which they placed higher up on the island. The men then went on over to the Longstone, because a return journey was impossible in the terrible conditions. However, accommodation in the lighthouse was already full, so the men had to seek shelter in a derelict building on Longstone for the next two days.

At about the same time as the coble arrived with the coxswain and volunteers on board, a fishing smack also reached the wreck and its crew immediately began salvaging some of the cargo, including two boxes of soap. They carried it to the water's edge, but when they tried to load it, the fishing smack almost capsized and all they ended up with was two light, hair-filled mattresses. Part of the *Forfarshire* was so smashed up, that wood from her remains was actually being washed up as far as Beadnell. On 12 September, the loose and moveable objects from the wreck were transported to North Sunderland by a Mr Sinclair on behalf of Lloyds of London, then the wreck itself was sold for £70 to a shipwright, called Mr Adamson, from Dundee.

The bravery of William Darling and Grace was recognised by the R.N.L.I. who awarded them a Silver Medal each, while the Royal Humane Society awarded them both with a Gold Medallion. Grace also received Silver Medals from the Glasgow Humane Society and the Edinburgh and Leith Humane Society. Then when word about the rescue, spread around the country, public donations of £800 were raised for Grace, but only £270 was raised for her father. Grace became a national heroine. However, very soon the truth became distorted, with tales being told of how Grace rescued the people all by herself. Another story that was told was that after Grace saw the wreck and woke her father up, she had to, more or less, force him to help her to rescue the people. A Board of Inquiry was ordered by Trinity House to establish the truth. William Darling wrote this letter to the Secretary of Trinity House in reply:

> Dear Sir,
>
> In answer to your request of the 29th, I have to state that on the morning of the 7th September, it was blowing a gale, with rain from the north, my daughter and me, being both on the alert before high water, securing things out of doors, one quarter before five, my daughter observed a vessel on the Harcars Rock, but owing to the darkness and the spray going over her, could not observe any person

on the wreck, although the glass being incessantly applied until near seven o'clock, when, the tide being fallen, we observed 3 or 4 men upon the rock: we agreed that if we could get to them, some of them would be able to assist us back, without which we could not return: and having no idea of the possibility of a boat coming from North Sunderland, we immediately launched our boat and was enabled to gain the rock, where we found 8 men and one woman, which I judged rather too many for to take at once in the state of weather, therefore took the woman and four men to the Longstone. Two of them returned with me, and succeeded in bringing the remainder, in all 9 persons, to safety to the Longstone about nine o'clock. Afterwards a boat from North Sunderland arrived and found three lifeless bodies, viz, one man and two children, which they carried to the rock, and came to Longstone with great difficulty; and had to lodge in the barracks two days and nights, with scant provisions, no beds, nor clothes to change them with.

Your Obedient Servant
William Darling.

Even though officials knew the whole truth about the famous rescue and there is no doubt that Grace Darling performed a dangerous, brave and heroic feat with her father, the rumours and twisted tales prevailed throughout the country. People believed what they wanted to hear. Fan-mail for Grace poured in, with requests for her to sit for portraits and thousands of requests for locks of her hair. In fact she sent so many locks of hair, she was in danger of going bald. Busts of her were on sale everywhere, poems were written about her and she received many marriage proposals. Grace did not want any of the attention, she just wanted to be left in peace with her family on Longstone. Each time she made a visit to the mainland, it was like a royal occasion. Tragically, poor Grace only lived another four years after the famous rescue before she died of consumption (tuberculosis).

Wreck-site
The *Forfarshire* grounded on the northern side of the Big Harcar reef. It was reported later to have swung around in the strong currents of Piper-Gut and struck the two rocks of Roddam and Green on the western side of Piper-Gut. Then she was reputed to have broken her back and disintegrated in the mountainous seas. The heavy objects from ship's wreckage were strewn all over the seabed around Piper-Gut, on the south side of the Big Harcar, while wood from her was even washed up on the shore at Beadnell and Seahouses. Even now small and interesting objects are still being recovered from the seabed.

For many years, dozens of metres of brass hand rails could be seen in 20m on the south side of the Harcar, but obviously, with so many divers drift diving through Piper-Gut these days, they will almost certainly have been removed. The larger items remaining are things like large air-ducts, ladders and buckled metal framework which are all made of iron or steel. However, to the western side of Piper-Gut, there are a few rusting cannons, remnants from an earlier sunken vessel.

Depths range between 6-25m, but the tidal streams can run at ten knots on a spring tide. The trip boats and dozens of diving vessels also use Piper-Gut so S.M.Bs are an essential piece of equipment for anyone deciding to explore the Gut and look for her wreckage. The best time to dive the area is at low, slack water or on the neap, flood tide. Unless you want the journey of your life through Piper Gut, then a spring tide is the time to try it.

PEGGY

Wreck ?
Scenery ★★★
Depth 10-25m
Reference N 55 38 37 W 001 36 92
S. side of Little Harcar, Outer Farne Islands.

The *Peggy* was a large wooden sailing brig, owned by Charles Spalding of London.

On 3 December 1774, she was on passage from London for Leith under the command of Captain Thomas Boswell, when she unfortunately encountered the Great Storm of 1774. On that fateful day, the *Peggy* was carrying fifty passengers and crew, plus a valuable cargo, which included silver bullion belonging to the vessel's owner, Charles Spalding. The storm drove her foreward before the wind. Unable to control her direction the vessel ploughed into the Little Harcar, one of the barrier of islands in the Outer Farnes. With mountainous seas crashing over the island, howling winds of over 100mph and swirling currents all around, not a soul was spared in the horrendous conditions.

Soon after the *Peggy* struck the jagged reefs on the south side of Little Harcar, another three brigs came crashing into it. The *Liddle* went down with sixteen people on board; the fifteen passengers and crew went down with the *Success*. The *Industry*, owned by Drummond of London also on a voyage from London to Leith had an unknown number on board. The total number of people who perished on the rocks of Little Harcar that day is unknown but there were at least eighty-one people on these three vessels alone.

The force of the storm was so ferocious that it smashed off one of the huge black Whin Sill dolorite Pinnacles at the southern end of Staple Island and partially destroyed the old tower lighthouse on that island.

One report says that when the storm abated and news got out about the cargo of the *Peggy*, three enterprizing young men designed a kind of diving-bell from an upturned, open, weighted barrel. The air was replenished by sending down small barrels and the air in these was released into the larger barrel. They were fairly successful in salvaging much of the silver and became very rich from the proceeds.

After their success, the men were in great demand and moved south along the coast of England to work on other wrecks. However, they all died from diving-related problems within a year of salvaging the *Peggy*. Another report says that Charles Spalding, the owner and also a well-known diver, worked the wreck for himself and recovered a great quantity of his silver.

Wreck-site
The exact position of the *Peggy* or indeed the other three vessels that struck the island on that fateful day is not known for sure. The island itself is very small, being no more than about 100m across at the very most, so a proper search would not be very difficult, and to date it is thought that no one has seriously investigated the area. The wrecks would have struck the rocks and probably disintegrated in a very short time during such a storm. The heaviest parts would have slipped back down the steep sloping sides of the island into deeper water. The top of the reef is shallow (6-10m) with very large boulders all around, but the edge, about 10m out, is a steep sloping stone and rock bank down to around 20-25m.

Interestingly, a crushed bronze bell from a very old wreck was discovered in this area about four years ago, but, unfortunately, the name was unreadable.

Tidal streams are very moderate and you can dive the area at any state of the tide, however it is best avoided during strong south-south-easterly winds when there is a heavy chop on the surface and a back-wash from the islands.

Crustaceans can be found close in to the islands where there are lots of overhangs and crevices to poke around in. At high tide, especially during spring tides, when the islands to the east (seaward) of Little Harcar are covered by the sea, the water flows over and through the gap like an express train, so it should also be avoided then as well.

VAAGEN

Wreck ★
Scenery ★★
Depth 2-5m
Reference N 55 38 550 W 001 36 130
N.E. corner of Clove Car (behind Blue Caps) Outer Farnes Islands.

The *Vaagen* was an iron 201-ton Norwegian steamship, registered at the port of Stavanger and had dimensions of 32.79m length, by 6.52m beam and a draught of 2.97m. She was owned at the time of loss by M. Egeland of Stavanger and built by Akers Mek. Verkst in Christiania, Norway in 1872. Her single iron propeller was powered by a two-cylinder, compound-steam engine that developed 23hp, using one boiler and she had one deck.

On 27 January 1916, the *Vaagen* was on passage from Leith for Dunkirk, when she ran into Crayford's Gut and stranded on the Clove Car rocks in the Outer Farne Islands in dense fog. Her crew of nine, including the master, Captain

Fjogstad, managed to reach the safety of Longstone, some 50m to the east, but the vessel was holed and became a total loss.

Wreck-site
The wreck of this small vessel, always thought to have been a steam-trawler, is now well broken up and dispersed amongst the rocks and dense kelp forest, just behind the Blue Caps and Clove-Car rocks, to the west of Crayford's Gut. Her small and rather battered boiler is lying on its side and just breaks the surface on a low spring tide. The iron wreckage is well scattered about and sometimes makes a rewarding rummage dive in the kelp, when currents permit, because the tidal flow is ferociously strong, especially on the flood tide. Low water is usually too shallow to be able to swim around, so high water on a slack tide would make the best time to visit the site.

Visibility is usually very throughout the year, except maybe during a spring tide and after a storm. Trip-boats from Seahouses frequently pass by this area during the summer months, so extra care is needed by anyone wishing to visit the site.

ILLALA

Wreck ★★
Scenery ★★★★
Depth 18m
Reference N 55 38 450 W 001 35 900
Crawford's Gut, inside Longstone, Outer Farnes Islands.

The steamship *Illala* was the very first ship built at the W.B. Thompson shipyard on the river Tay in 1874. Mr Thompson, the owner of the yard, was born in 1837 and trained in Finland. When he came back to Britain, he built himself a foundry one mile from Dundee docks. His first four ships were actually hauled down to the river Tay on bogies driven by teams of horses, which was certainly not the most convenient way of launching ships. In 1874 he finally negotiated and acquired his very own riverside shipyard. The first ship he built at the new yard was the 178-ton SS *Illala*. Unfortunately, when it was completed, he did not have any ready customers for it, so being an enterprizing chap, he decided to trade with it himself. Then just fifteen months after the launching ceremony, on 23 January 1876, she was wrecked on the Farne Islands and became a total loss.

She had left Gainsborough for Gateshead-on-Tyne, but strong north-easterly gales forced her back to shelter in the mouth of the Humber near Hull. After leaving Hull roads, a strong, south-westerly gale sprang up, driving the *Illala* before it, past the mouth of the Tyne and right through the main mass of the Farne Islands, until she struck hard on the hidden Swadman Reef. The crew let go both anchors and lit the ship up to attract attention. Their signals were answered from the shore, but no lifeboat came to rescue them. They decided to cut the anchors and drifted out and onto the Longstone.

An account of the ship's loss was taken up with the *Dundee Courier* on 27 January 1876. The headlines read: 'The Loss of the *Illala* of Dundee, Strange Conduct of the Lifeboat Crew' and it went on to say:

> The crew then lowered their boat and four of them jumped into it, and made for the rocks. The boat was dashed forward towards the rock by the sea, and on nearing the rock one of the men sprang upon it from the boat. The boat was then carried away by the receding wave and upon again thrown towards the rock by the sea, two other men jumped out of it to the rock. The fourth man, however, was unable to get out before the boat was carried away, and feared that he would drown. Fortunately, however, a huge wave carried the boat above and close to the stern of the steamer, and at that moment the poor fellow sprang for his life.
>
> The steamer meanwhile was rapidly sinking and the four men still aboard were enabled with little difficulty to leap from the rail of the vessel to the rocks, and in this way saved their lives. About 20 minutes after all had safely landed on the rocks, the steamer swung round and tumbled to the side two or three times by the force of the tide and then went down in deep water. the crew remained on the rocks all night without food and exposed to the weather. At low water they made their way to the lighthouse.

The seamen went on to tell the reporter of their home town newspaper how a sinking smack had been ignored by the lighthouse keepers and they complained bitterly about Seahouses' lifeboat not coming to their rescue.

The account of the *Ilala* makes mention of her grounding on the hidden Swadman Reef, which I presume to mean the Swedman Rocks, some 500m west of the Megstone. The Swedman Rocks are about $2\frac{1}{2}$ miles north-north-west of Seahouses, so if the ship was lit up, it would have been clearly visible from the harbour. If it was the Swedman, then, after the crew cut the anchors away, the ship must have drifted almost three miles east and out to sea, missing the Megstone's surrounding reefs, Oxcar and North Wamses, before being swept through the very shallow water in Crayford's Gut before hitting the Longstone.

This seems incredible, with a strong south-westerly wind blowing. However, if the reef she struck was the Callers and not the Swedman, then, when the crew cut the anchors away they would have been driven in a south-westerly direction, directly onto the south corner of Longstone, at the southern end of Crayford's Gut where she now lies, which sounds much more feasible. However, they would have still been very visible from Seahouses harbour.

Wreck-site
The *Illala* is fairly easy to locate on the inside of Longstone, by positioning the tower on Staple over the channel between Bluecaps and Clove Car. The steep sides of the reef slope down to 18m to a stoney seabed which slopes away down into deeper water. At 18m you find the scattered remnants of Mr Thompson's once proud ship. Only an engine block, parts of her keel ribs, steel plates and framework lie strewn around. Little else is left to recognize her, or to get excited about. However, only recently, some visiting divers on Stan Hall's charter boat found a very large porthole, about 50m west of the wreck site, towards the Bluecaps, in 25m. It is possible to make a nice drift dive from this position on the mid water spring ebb tide, which takes you into Crayford's Gut and past the lighthouse.

Visibility is usually fairly good and it is not unusual to have 10-12m, especially during the summer months after neap tides, however the current can be very brisk. It runs south-east and around the Longstone end on the ebb tide and through Crayford's Gut on the flood. On spring ebb tides, the current runs at about five knots and overfalls with choppy waves developing, so it is wise not to anchor the boat anywhere in this area. It is also an area regularly visited by the trip boats as part of their route, so extra vigilance is required by both divers and boat cover. Also, it is important to use a S.M.B. Although this wreck site is only classed as a two star rating, it is an excellent dive all round, with smashing underwater scenery and plenty of crustaceans around for the pot.

CHRIS CHRISTENSON

Wreck ★★★
Scenery ★★★★
Depth 25-32m
Reference N 55 38 410 W 001 36 195
S. end of Longstone, Outer Farne Islands.

This vessel was a steel 1,491-ton Danish steamship, registered in Copenhagen and built in 1903. Her single iron propeller was powered by a three-cylinder, triple-expansion steam engine that used one boiler.

On 16 February 1915 the *Chris Christenson* was in ballast, on passage from Aarhus for Newcastle-upon-Tyne, when she stranded in very heavy seas on the southern end of the Longstone Reef. The North Sunderland self-righting, oared lifeboat *Forster Fawsett* was launched at 4.40 a.m. and rescued the nineteen crew, completing the rescue and returning to Seahouses by 6.30 p.m that evening. The stranding had torn a massive hole in the *Chrsitenson's* bottom plates and she eventually slipped back and sank in deep water.

Wreck-site
The wreck of the *Christenson* lies just off the south-west tip of Longstone in a depth between approximately 25-32m. She is totally collapsed, decayed and well broken

The Ben Corlic *was a 2,061 ton British steamship, registered at the port of North Shields and had dimensions of 83.33m length, 11.65m beam and 5.84m draught. She was owned by J. Morrison & Son of Newcastle and was built by J. Laing at Sunderland in 1889. Her single propeller was powered by a three-cylinder, triple-expansion steam engine that developed 170hp using two boilers and her machinery was built by G. Clark & Co. at Sunderland. She had one deck, a well-deck, four bulkheads and a superstructure consisting of a 31.3m bridge-deck, 33.8m quarter-deck and a 9.1m forecastle. On 30 May 1902 the vessel was enroute from North Sheilds to Guilianova in Italy, under the command of Captain G. Pearce, with an unspecified cargo of coal when in wind conditions north-east force four she stranded on Upgang Rock near Whitby and drove ashore. Two of her crew of twenty were lost in the incident and the vessel was written of as a total loss.* Courtesy of the Whitby Literary and Philosophical Society.

up, lying up against a small reef and until a few years ago her huge, iron steering wheel, with lots of urchins and starfish attached to it, stood vertically and proud of the wreck, which made a lovely picture. Unfortunately, three years ago some divers made a fruitless attempt to move it and it was left lying flat on the wreck. Selby Brown from the Lodge at Seahouses was one of the first people to discover the wreck. He was so impressed when he saw her steering wheel standing upright, complete with Dead Man's Fingers and urchins, that he had a friend take some photographs of him, standing holding the wheel, like a very determined Captain Ahab sailing after the great white whale Moby Dick.

This was no mean feat by anybody's standard, to stand on the seabed in 32m without his diving equipment on, especially in this particular area. There is now a set of those large coloured photographs of Selby holding the wheel, hanging on the wall of the Lodge at North Sunderland. Brian Shaw, ex-vice-chairman of the BSAC, (now sadly departed), even used one for the front cover of his book *Dive the North East*.

There is quite a variety of marine life around the *Christenson*, with shoals of small coley, wrasse, lobsters, crabs and usually dozens of seals. However, the current is very strong and at certain states of the tide, there is a pronounced downward flow, near the bottom, much like an underwater waterfall, which can be very alarming if you are not expecting it. Visibility can be excellent during the summer months and may be over 15m, on a good day. The cliff face on Longstone end, at this point is also a mass of anemones. One very important point to remember, is that trip boats visit this particular site in the summer months and they do not always acknowledge diver's 'A' flags or S.M.B.s, so extra vigilance should be maintained. Any problems from their skippers or dangerous situations should be reported to the Marine Police or DTI. Another thing to bear in mind, is that on big tides, very large curling waves form on the surface, combined with extremely strong currents, on the end and inside the Longstone end.

LOCH LEVEN

Wreck ★
Scenery ★★★★
Depth 7-12m
Reference N 55 38 850 W 001 36 330
N.W. corner of Northern Hares, (Longstone) Outer Farnes Islands.

The *Loch Leven* was an iron 851-ton British steamship, registered in Aberdeen and had dimensions of 64.11m length, by 8.71m beam and 4.69m draught. She was built by Gourlay Brothers in Dundee in 1878 and owned at the time of loss by J.&A. Davidson of Aberdeen. Her single iron propeller was powered by a two-cylinder, compound steam engine that developed 90hp, using one boiler. She had one deck, five watertight bulkheads and a superstructure consisting of a 20.1m quarter-deck, 15.2m bridge-deck and 7m forecastle. This vessel was also classed at Lloyds as A1.

On 15 April 1902, the *Loch Leven* was in ballast and carrying a crew of fourteen, under the command of Captain J.G. Smith on passage from Aberdeen for Sunderland, when she drove onto the shallow rocks of the Northern Hares, at the northern end of Longstone. As the tide flooded, she later drifted off and sank in deeper. However, another report says that she became stranded on the north side of Knivestone Reef, but later drifted back off the rocks and sank in the deeper water of Abraham's Bosom, just north-west, between the Knivestone and Longstone. Weather conditions at the time were reported to be a force two, with a light southerly wind, but thick fog.

Wreck-site
There is no concrete evidence that the remains of this vessel are those of the steamship *Loch Leven*, but over the years they have been accepted by most divers as such, however they may be of another ship.

The wreck is totally collapsed, decayed and well dispersed, lying in the gullies between the reefs, at the end and western side of the Northern Hares. There is nothing substantial to be found, except for a small box section of overhanging steel plates and frames. The wreckage is well scattered all over the seabed, but the plates, provide good shelter for crustaceans and various kinds of fish. The wreck in itself is hardly worth diving on, but the surrounding scenery and marine life more than makes up for it.

Tidal streams are severe during springs, but it is still possible to find shelter in the maze of gullies. However, great care should be taken when surfacing too far away from the cover boat when the tide is running. The best time to dive the area is on a low, neap tide at slack water. Visibility can be excellent during neaps in the summer months. It is also strongly recommended that S.M.B.s are used, if the tide is flowing, especially during flood tides.

QUEENSTOWN

Wreck ★
Scenery ★★★★
Depth 20-25m
Reference N.E. side of Knivestone, Outer Farnes Islands.

This vessel was a steel 161-ton steam trawler, registered at Grimsby and had dimensions of 31.75m length by 6.22m beam and 3.22m draught. She was built in 1897 by Mackie & Thompson at Glasgow for the Consolidated Steam Fishing & Ice Co. Her single steel propeller was powered by a three-cylinder, triple-expansion steam engine that developed 41hp, using one boiler. Her machinery was built by Muir & Houston of Glasgow and she had a superstructure that consisted of a 5.15m quarter deck and a 5.77m forecastle.

On 2 December 1916, the *Queenstown* was *en-route* to the fishing grounds from Grimsby under the command of Captain T. Hoult and carrying a crew of ten, when she stranded on the north-east side of the Knivestone Reef and became a total wreck.

Wreck-site
The *Queenstown* is literally now smashed to pieces, but what remains of her can be found on the east (seaward) side of the Knivestone rocks One source of information said that the vessel stranded, but was later refloated. However, two years ago some lucky diver searching among the scattered seabed debris at the base of the steep, sloping reef, on the eastern side, found the ship's bell lying half buried in the sand and stone. Very little remains of her now except for a few steel plates, ribs and frames. Nevertheless, it is still a fabulous dive, with plenty of marine life to be seen, as well as the chance of finding the odd souvenir, even if it comes from some other unfortunate vessel.

The currents are exceptionally strong both on the flood and ebb and it would be very easy to get swept away before being able to surface from the dive, so extra planning is required and a surface-marker buoy is essential. The best time to dive is at low, slack water on neap tides. Visibility can be exceptionally good, with 15m being quite common during the summer neap tides.

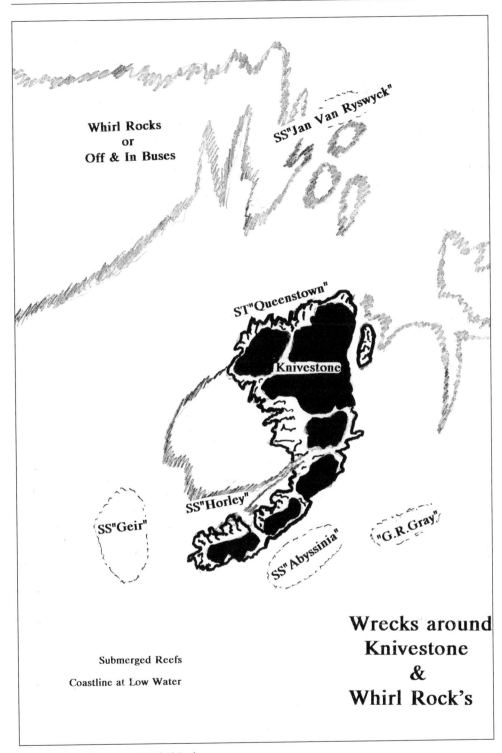

Whirl Rocks
or
Off & In Buses

SS"Jan Van Ryswyck"

ST"Queenstown"

Knivestone

SS"Horley"

SS"Geir"

SS"Abyssinia"

"G.R.Gray"

Submerged Reefs

Coastline at Low Water

Wrecks around
Knivestone
&
Whirl Rock's

Wrecks around Knivestone & Whirl Rocks.

GEIR

Wreck ★★★
Scenery ★★★★
Depth 6-10m
Reference N 55 39 02 W 001 36 08
N. side of Knivestone, Outer Farne Islands.

The *Geir* was an iron 848-ton Norwegian steamship, registered in the port of Bergen. She was owned by H. Kuhnle of Bergen and built in 1882, with dimensions of 61.26m length, by 9.75m beam and 4.57m draught. Her single iron propeller was powered by a three-cylinder, triple-expansion steam engine that used one boiler.

Early in the morning of 18 February 1908, the *Geir* was in ballast, steaming south, on passage from Bergen for Blyth, under the command of a Captain J. Blue, when she ran aground on the Knivestone Rock during a force eight north-north-easterly gale and heavy seas. The north Sunderland (Seahouses) self-righting lifeboat *Forster Fawsett* was launched in pitch darkness at 7 a.m. and went to her aid. However, it proved impossible for the lifeboat to get along side the stricken steamer, because of the powerful swirling white water and the number of large rocks in the area. After carefully considering the situation, the boat's 28-years-old Coxswain, James Robson, took the lifeboat to a small rock nearby where he landed with a lifebuoy and ropes, then the lifeboat moved off to a safer distance. With the use of lines and the lifebuoy, Mr Robson brought the fourteen crew members off the *Geir* onto the Knivestone where they were hauled one by one over to the lifeboat. With everyone safely on board, the *Forster Fawsett* returned to North Sunderland Harbour at 11a.m. that morning to be greeted by a large crowd of cheering people who had gathered on the harbour pier.

Later, the *Geir* gradually slipped back off the Knivestone and sank in 10m of water, where she quickly broke up and became a total loss.

For his outstanding gallantry, Coxswain James Robson was awarded the Silver Medal by the R.N.L.I. At a public meeting on 12 March 1908, he was presented with his medal by the Chairman of North Sunderland Lifeboat Station, Lt. Col. Marshal on behalf of the R.N.L.I. James' father, a former coxswain, was also presented with a framed certificate to mark his years of dedication to the service. The King of Norway presented James Robson with a silver medal for his noble deeds in rescuing the crew of the *Geir*.

Wreck-site
Some thirty metres out from the north of the Knivestone, at the western side and opposite the gully where the remains of the *Horley* lie, is the wreck of the steamship *Geir*. The ship's boiler lies on its side next to an iron propeller, along with masses of steel plates, framework, ribs, steel pipes of all sizes and broken hollow masts. The wreckage is spread all over the seabed, in depths between 15-

18m, but owing maybe to the wreck lying a bit offshore from the island it is rather exposed and the current is very noticeable, especially on the flood. This is a good rummage dive and there are often a few crustaceans and large cod hiding under the steel plates and framework or in the boiler.

Underwater visibility sometimes appears a bit dismal compared to what it is closer in to the island, while depths just north of the wreck, drop away to over 25m, where the seabed is very stony and currents are very strong. The best time to visit the site is during a neap, ebb tide at low water, but is also possible to dive on the early part of the flood.

ST ANDRE

Wreck ★★
Scenery ★★★
Depth 17-23m
Reference N 55 37 797 W 001 37 287
S. side of Staple Island, Outer Farne Islands.

The *St Andre* was a steel 1,121-ton French-registered steamship and had dimensions of 70.1m length, by 9.88m beam and a draught of 4.19m. She was owned at the time of loss by F. Bonnet and built in 1903 at Stockton by Craig, Taylor & Co. Her single steel propeller was powered by a three-cylinder, triple-expansion steam engine that developed 900hp, using two Scotch type boilers with a working pressure of 180p.s.i. and her machinery was built by the North Eastern Marine Engineering Co. Ltd at Sunderland.

On 28 October 1908, when on passage from Caen for Grangemouth with a crew of sixteen and a cargo of iron ore, the *St Andre* stranded on Crumstone in dense fog. The vessel stood there for several days before being washed off and then she drifted across to Staple Island and sank against the cliff face.

Just off the southern end of Staple Island and close to the *St Andre*, stand the three huge Whin Sill pillars of the Pinnacles, which are home to hundreds of nesting guillemots.

Wreck-site
The wreck lies at the base of the cliff-face, half way along the southern end of Staple Island, orientated in an east to west direction in depths between 17-23m. She is totally collapsed, well broken up and rather decayed, with just ribs, steel plates, framework and her boilers and broken engine remaining. There is very little to find in the way of souvenirs, however this is still a nice and very popular dive-site, during the summer months. The wreck was positively identified by the builder's name plate in 1974, which confirmed that she was the *St Andre*, ship number 1502.

The wreck is sheltered from the main currents and you can dive the site at most states of the tide, however, the area is prone to a lot of backwash from the island during

The Dimitry *and another unknown sailing vessel, ashore at Whitby in 1885. This wooden barque of around 250 tons was made famous in the film* Dracula *when the Count's coffin was found in the abandoned ship, after being washed ashore in a gale. His body is supposed to now lie in a hallowed marked grave on the cliff tops, just outside of the Abbey grounds, however this is only a tourist attraction. Both vessels were believed to have been refloated later.* Courtesy of the Whitby Literary and Philosophical Society.

strong south and south-easterly winds. Also a little more care should be taken when diving close to the north-east corner of Staple Island on the flood towards high tide, due to the strong current running between Brownsman and Staple Islands. Visibility is often in the over 15m during the summer months after a spell of westerly winds.

SNOWDONIA

Wreck ★
Scenery ★★★
Depth 6-8 metres
Reference N 55 38 03 W 001 37 55
S.W. corner of Brownsman, Outer Farne Islands.

The *Snowdonia* was a 419-ton wooden sailing barque, registered in the port of London and had dimensions of 42.11m length, by 8.76m beam and a draught of 5.23m She was built in 1875 and owned at the time of loss by E. Griffiths of Carnarvonshire. She was a well built ship with a copper-sheathed bottom and carried a crew of eleven.

Under the command of a Captain J. Roberts, the *Snowdonia* was on passage from the Coosaw river, Carolina for Berwick-on-Tweed with a cargo of Phosphate rock, when she encountered a force ten north-north-east storm off the Farne Islands and was driven onto the western side of Brownman Island in the Outer Farnes, where she quickly broke up and was lost with her crew of eleven. Apparently, she was driven into the rock face so violently, that reputedly the ship left a groove in the hard dolorite rock-face.

Wreck-site
What remains of the *Snowdonia* lies on sand and stone at the base of the cliff face at the extreme south-west corner of Brownsman, in 6-8m of water. A number of nice little trinkets have been recovered in recent years on this site. One diver found a complete sextant while another picked up the compass. However, in May 1999, a friend of mine found two brass ship's chronometers and one of them was in beautiful condition. It has a brass face of Roman numerals with two intact pointers and even the maker's name and date etched into it.

Usually after a storm, parts of the ship's copper bottom it can sometimes be seen protruding out of the sand. There are still a few remnants of the wreck left, including the anchor, chain, keel and a few spars, frames and some concretion. However, it is not a lot to write home about, but it is always worth a rummage around. The nearby boulders by Brownsman and between the two islands of Brownsman and Staple often produce a few lobsters as well.

ARMED DUTCH VESSEL

Wreck ★★
Scenery ★★★★
Depth 7-10m
Reference N 55 37 81 W 001 37 67
S. end of Gun Rocks, Outer Farne Islands.

The remains of this vessel lie on the south side of what is known as Gun Rocks, in the Outer Farnes group. These two rocks can be located at low tide, about 150m out from and half way along Staple Island, on the western side. They are dry to 3.6m at low tide and they are connected to the sland at the southern end by a shallow underwater sand and stone bank, which is visible on the bottom of a spring tide. The water here is too shallow to navigate even in a small RIB. The name of Gun Rocks came from the pile of cannon guns discovered there in the 1700s. One of the cannons was taken away and used in Bamburgh Castle during the 1700 and 1800s, to alert the villagers when a ship had been wrecked.

The wreck was at first thought to have been an Armada ship wrecked when the Spanish fleet was driven up the North Sea coast, however after her cannons were dated, it was later discovered that she was an armed, Dutch merchant vessel wrecked between 1650 and 1715.

On 17 August 1939, the steam trawler *Excell* ran aground on Gun Rocks, but was successfully refloated later.

Wreck-site
There were as many as twenty-six cannons lying scattered around. However, over the years, some divers have had their own peculiar motives for removing many of them which has spoilt the site for everyone else. The wreck has never been a protected site because it was not deemed to be of historical importance, yet there have been lots of encrusted artefacts like sword hilts, cannon balls, bar-shot, musket balls and at least two brass swivel guns found. A few years ago, a group of university divers recovered a small tin box with an inscribed lid. There has been an enormous amount of digging into the concretion, with holes left over a metre deep and literally piles of cannon balls and bar-shot have been taken in the last twenty-five years.

The wreck site is on the south side of Gun Rocks, in 7-10m, but you really have to look hard to find the rusting concretion under the thick covering of kelp. Even the remaining cannons are not as obvious as you might expect either, because they lie half buried and partially concreted into the surrounding rocks. The first time I visited the site in the early 1970s, I swam right over them, even though the guns were all over the place, at the time. The area is fairly sheltered on the bottom half of the flood tide, but the current is exceptionally strong when you move away from the rocks into the Sound. The western edge of Gun Rocks is a cliff wall covered in an array of different coloured anemones, which makes a splendid extension to the dive.

SPICA

Wreck !
Scenery ★★★
Depth 0-3m
Reference N 55 38 25 W 001 37 60
South Wamses, Outer Farne Islands.

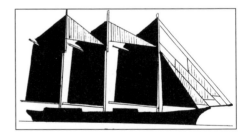

The *Spica* was a 265-ton wooden schooner, registered in Russia and built in 1902. On 1 January 1916 the *Spica* was on passage from Christiania for West Hartlepool with a cargo of pit-props and a crew of six when she encountered a full westerly gale and heavy seas off the north Northumberland coast. After developing an uncontrollable leak and being in danger of sinking, she was reported as having been abandoned and left to sink. The power of the wind and massive rolling seas drove her onto the shallow reefs on the western side of South Wamses in the Outer Farne Islands, where she broke up and became a total loss.

Another tale about the *Spica* and the most unlikely one that I have ever heard of, suggests that she was an old Norwegian sailing vessel called *Spica*. In 1915 she was on passage for Hartlepool with a cargo of pit-props when she encountered a storm and, being in danger of sinking, the crew abandoned her. The vessel was never heard of again, until 6 February 1953, when she was reportedly seen by local fishermen off the mouth of the river Tyne. They said they had seen a 'tall sailing ship with rotting timbers and bare ribs, slipping in and out of the fog banks'. Then on 16 February, just ten days later, she was discovered aground on Brownsman Island in the channel known as Brownsman Haven, between Brownsman and South Wamses. This sounds like a real *Marie Celeste* story and as tall as the ship itself. It is difficult to believe that any type of vessel could just float around aimlessly for thirty-eight years, especially in the North Sea, through two world wars, hundreds of storms and even hurricanes, without either being driven ashore or sinking, which would be the most likely.

Jeff Morris of Coventry says in his book *The History of the Seahouses Lifeboats* 'After escorting five local cobles to safety on November 16th, 1915, the *Forster Fawsett* was launched at 1.35 a.m. in the morning of January 2nd, 1916, to the aid of the schooner *Spica* of Riga, which had run aground and been wrecked on the Farne Islands, in heavy seas and a full westerly gale, the lifeboat rescuing the whole crew of six men.'

Remnants of the vessel are reported to be still lying on the top of Wamses Island even today, although her valuable oak timbers were salvaged by local Seahouses people many years ago. It is possible that her anchors and some of the brass instruments still lie in the kelp on the western side of the island.

PEARLE

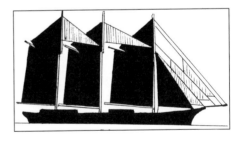

Wreck ★
Scenery ★★★
Depth 4-8m
Reference N 55 38 30-40 W 001 37 38
W. side of North Wamses, Outer Farne Islands.

The *Pearle*, built in 1717, was a large, wooden British registered sailing vessel, probably that of a schooner, brig, snow or barquentine of around 200-250 tons. She was built during the same period in time when the infamous pirate and hell-raiser Black Beard sailed the seven seas.

On 10 February 1740, the *Pearle* was in ballast on passage from London for Newcastle-upon-Tyne, under the command of Captain Emmett and carrying a crew of six, when she encountered south-westerly storm force winds. She was driven before the wind and past her destination, until she encountered the barrier of islands in the Outer Farne Islands, where she struck the shallow reefs on the western side of North Wamses Rock and was lost, with her crew of six. The official report from Lloyds quotes: 'From London to Newcastle, is lost to the Northward of Newcastle, and six men drowned'.

Wreck-site

The wreck is all but gone now, except for a few isolated remnants lying in the thick kelp forest in depths between 4-8m. Her anchor lies in a gully near to the top of the reef plateau about 20m away from the island in around 5m, or at least we presumed it is from the *Pearle*. Lots of large copper pins and two huge brass rudder pintles have been recovered from the small gullies, 15m from the northern end of North Wamses and close to the large deep 'V' shaped cut on the western side of the island. On the seabed close to the 'V', there are pieces of iron concretion in the seabed rocks, in 6-7m of water.

I discovered the ship's bell in February 1987, engraved THE PEARLE 1717. It was sitting upright in a patch of sand surrounded by some kelp strands, on the south side of the rock plateau and some 25m away from the island, in 7m. The bell definitely came from a fairly large vessel, because it was about 31.5cm. (12in) high and 35.6cm. (14in) across the base. There was no clapper fitted inside, so it must have been struck from the outside with some kind of hammer.

This whole area is reasonably good ground for finding crustaceans, because there are lots of gullies and small reefs, however it is subject to very strong tidal streams, especially on the flood tide, making it almost impossible to stay in one place long enough to catch them. During the spring and summer months, the boat crew will also be subjected to the horrible stench emitted from the nesting colonies of seabirds, which include puffins, shags, eider-ducks, kittiwakes, cormorants and 800 pairs of guillemots.

8. Farne Islands to Berwick

PEGASUS

Wreck ★★
Scenery ★★★★
Depth 15-18m
Reference N 55 40 21 W 001 43 39
S.W. side of North Goldstone

The *Pegasus* was an early, wooden, two-masted. passenger paddle steamer powered by a two-cylinder, compound-steam engine that used one boiler.

On Wednesday 19 July 1843, the steamer left Leith on her regular return passage to Hull, with fifty-four passengers and crew on board. At approximately 12.20 p.m. on a calm, clear night she struck the Goldstone Rock, which lies about one and three quarter miles east of Holy Island, off north Northumberland. At first many of the passengers were still in their beds and totally unaware of the situation, but then panic broke out. Some of the passengers and crew scrambled into a lifeboat without clearing both of the securing ropes. Unfortunately, it was just at that moment that the captain ordered her great paddle wheels put into reverse, in an attempt to pull the ship back off the rock. Sadly, the lifeboat overturned and was swamped by the paddles before the engines could be stopped. Most of the people in the boat were killed or drowned. As the *Pegasus* began to fill up with water, several people knelt in prayer on the quarter-deck, with a Reverend McKenzie. The mate managed to burn two distress rockets and a blue light, but to no avail. Within half an hour of striking the rock, she foundered, sucking many of the passengers down with her.

Only 2.4m of her mast was left showing above the surface. Screaming people and the bodies of the dead and dying filled the sea. One seaman, who was a passenger at the time, was attending to an invalid gentleman and by almost superhuman exertions, managed to save himself. He gave the following account:

> I have been a seaman for about eighteen years but was recently in attendance upon Mr Torry, who was one of the passengers on the *Pegasus* when she went down. I think it was about twenty minutes past twelve when the vessel struck. I was down in the cabin lying on a sofa and when I found that the vessel had struck, I ran on deck and having seen the state of matters there I went down to the cabin for Mr Torry. I told the passengers below that I believed the ship had struck, but they did not seem to comprehend what I meant. Some of the passengers, chiefly the ladies, were in bed. When I reached the deck with Mr Torry, I saw the crew in the act of lowering the lifeboats. I put Mr Torry in the starboard quarter-boat, when it was in the act of being

lowered; and when it reached the water I jumped in myself.

There were about nine of us in the boat. A lady, I remember was sitting in the bow. When we were in the boat there was a cry from the quarter-deck to 'stick to the ship'. At that moment the engines were set in motion and the boat, being hooked to the ship's stern, but unhooked at the bow, the back-water raised by the paddles filled the boat and upset her, throwing the passengers into the sea. I got hold of the ship's rudder chain and the Chief-Mate having thrown a rope to me, I got into the ship again.

Seeing the danger increasing, I undressed myself to prepare for my life and laid my clothes upon the companion. By this time the engine had stopped and the ship was fast settling by the head. Looking around me, I saw the Re. Mr Mckenzie on the quarter-deck praying with several of the passengers on their knees around him. Mr Mackenzie seemed calm and collected. All the passengers around him were praying also, but Mr Mackenzie's voice was distinctly heard above them all. I heard the Captain say that we must do our best we could for our selves. I saw a lady with two children, close beside me on the companion, calmly resign herself to the Almighty: the children seemed unconscious of the danger, for they were talking about some trifling matter.

When I found the vessel fast filling, I leaped overboard: and the Engineer and I were the first drawn into the sea by the suction occasioned by the vessel sinking. I soon got up again, however, and got hold of a plank and the steps which led to the quarter-deck. The Stewardess attempted to get hold of me, but I extricated myself from her to save my own life.

By this time the scene was a most dismal one; the surface of the water was covered in the dead and the dying, the screeching was fearful. One of the Firemen also tried to get hold of the plank which I had, but I swam away from him. I remained floating about till half past six, when I was picked up by a boat from the *Martello*.

I was then about a mile from the wreck and people in the *Martello* for some time did not observe me, till I attracted their attention, by waving a stick. One little boy kept himself afloat for about three hours on part of the skylight covering and made great exertions to save himself, but he sunk at last. His body was still warm when he was picked up. I was once wrecked before about twenty years ago, off the coast of St Domingo, when I was three days and nights on a reef. It was the experience I learnt then which gave me the idea of taking off my clothes before leaping into the sea.

The Rev. Mr Mackenzie mentioned above, was a devoted Christian. He was the Pastor of the Independent Church in Nile Street, Glasgow and afterwards became Tutor of the Theological Seminary in the city.

At dawn, the *Pegasus's* sister ship *Martello*, on passage in the opposite direction, arrived at the scene. However, only six people were still alive; the mate, the engineer, the ship's carpenter, one seaman and two passengers. It appears that the passengers and crew were responsible for their own misfortune when they panicked, upsetting and swamping the lifeboats, which were their only means of escape. Herring fishermen, returning to Holy Island after a night's fishing assisted in the rescue and, the *Martello*, after picking up everybody they could find, both dead and alive, continued on her voyage to Leith.

The disaster brought national interest and was reported in the *Illustrated London News* on 19 August 1843.

> As proof of the morbid feelings of the British public, it may be mentioned that the Holy Island, scene of the disastrous wreck of the *Pegasus*, is daily visited by throngs of fashionably dressed persons, who were attracted thither by the most idle and most unveiling curiosity. One day last week two open carriages, filled with ladies and gentlemen, and drivers in bright red livery forming most dashing and distinguishing equipages, visited the Island. They were said to be a party of bathers from Spittal. They had a large bugle or French horn with them, by means of which they awoke the echoes of the dreary sands in their progress and astonished the inhabitants on the shore. It is said that the party formed a deputation from the Royal Humane Society, but the rumour has not been authenticated.

The *Illustrated London News* goes on to say 'Divers employed on the *Pegasus* steamer at Holy Island have succeeded in picking up an additional number of dead bodies'. On 11 November 1843, another quote from the same paper read, 'A Relic of the *Pegasus*'. The 'Journal des Debats' states that a few days since, a bottle was found on the coast of Holland, containing a slip of paper, on which was written *Pegasus* steamer, to Fern Islands, night of Wednesday, July 1843. In great distress: struck upon the rocks. On board 55 persons, vessel must go down, and no Grace Darling'. Was this a hoax?

Wreck-site
The Goldstone Rock, which is located some one and three quarter miles east of Holy Island and approximately 150m west and inside of the actual rock, is marked by a green conical buoy with the word 'Goldstone' written on it. The top of the Goldstone is mostly bare rock with a few strands of stringy tangleweed clinging to it, while the seaward and eastern part is a high, gradually sloping reef, covered in kelp and tangleweed. The western side of the rock is a sheer face to 10m, which is absolutely covered in bunches of beautiful large Plumose anemones that light up the reef wall. The seabed slopes steeply down to the west and south, levelling out at about 15-18m. The *Pegasus* lies on the south side among the massive scrap yard of wreckage, where ships which had met the same fate over the last two centuries have just piled on top of each other.

STUCK IN THE MUD 39 FMS.

The Danube *ashore beneath the cliffs at Upgang, near Whitby, on 9 December 1874. It is believed that the vessel was later refloated. Note the horse and cart near to the ship's bows.* Courtesy of the Whitby Literary and Philosophical Society.

The wreck-site does not see very many divers and is well worth a visit, because anything could turn up in the dispersed pile of mixed wreckage, although most of what can be seen is either iron or steel. The brass steam whistle from the *Pegasus* now hangs in the Old Ship Inn at Seahouses and was presented to the inn's owner, Alan Glen, by Brian Pouting some twenty years ago. Sadly, Brian, one of the 'old school' of divers, passed away a few years ago.

Tidal streams are very strong on the western end and over the top of the reef, but there is adequate shelter on the north and south sides of the Goldstone, depending on which way the tide is running. The site is best dived at low, slack water on neap tides when the rock is showing above the surface. On springs there is very little slack water time and it is best avoided due to the ferocity of the tidal run. During the summer months, Lion's-mane jellyfish can be a real nuisance too, as they hurtle passed in the current. The site is very exposed, with very little passing traffic. It is a long haul from either Beadnell or Seahouses, so extra care should be taken.

ARBUTUS

Wreck ★★
Scenery ★★★★
Depth 15-18m
Reference N 55 40 20 W 001 43 39
S.W. side of North Goldstone.

The *Arbutus* was an iron 356-ton British steamship, registered in Dundee and owned at the time of loss by R. Taylor of Dundee. She had dimensions of 54.86m length, by 7.01m beam and a draught of 3.65m. Her single iron propeller was powered by a two-cylinder, compound-steam engine that used one boiler.

On 17 January 1890, under the command of a Captain A. Herd, the *Arbutus* was in ballast on passage from Dundee for Seaham, with a crew of twelve and four passengers when she stranded on the Goldstone Rock during a force five southerly wind. The crew and passengers were eventually rescued, but the ship was holed and became a total loss.

The wreckage of the steamer lies mixed up with that of the paddle steamer *Pegasus* and a host of other vessels, which have come to grief on the infamous Goldstone Rock, most of which have probably long since gone, including:

The wooden brig *Augusta* on 2 February 1823, lost with all hands.
The wooden steamship *Northern Yacht*, which hit the rock on 11 October 1840 with the loss of all of her twenty-two passengers and crew.
On the 9 January 1851 the wooden schooner *Lady Panmure* was wrecked and four of her crew were drowned.
The wooden schooner *Cheviot* was wrecked in October 1853.
In December 1856 the wooden schooner *Jean & Jesse* was lost.
5 June 1860 the wooden schooner *Peace & Plenty* went down after colliding with the rock.
On 20 December 1863 the wooden schooner *Maid of Aln* was lost.

SCOTTISH PRINCE

This vessel was a steel 131-ton British steam trawler, registered at the port of North Shields, which was in ballast from the fishing grounds to North Shields, when she stranded on the rock on 3 May 1913 and became a total loss. She was built in 1899 and had a single steel-screw propeller, powered by three-cylinder, triple-expansion engine that used one boiler. None of her crew of nine were lost when she stranded.

The Flag of Distress.

Wreck-site
The site is the same as that of the *Pegasus* and the seabed is like the proverbial scrap-yard, with steel frames, pipes, girders and steel plate spread out as far as you can see. Although most of it is iron and steel, there must be ship's bells lying there for the taking, but it is probably almost buried in the piles of steel rubble and concretion, but well worth a good forage, because this wreck site is seldom dived.

OTTO M'COMBIE

Wreck ★
Scenery ★★★
Depth 11m
Reference N 55 40 18 W 001 45 30
Plough Seat Reef, east of Holy Island.

The *Otto M'Combie* was a small iron 341-ton British steamship, registered in Glasgow and had dimensions of 45.72m length, by 6.7m beam and a draught of 3.96 metres. She was owned at the time of loss by J. Service of London and built in 1879. The single iron propeller was powered by a two-cylinder, compound-steam engine that used one boiler.

On 9 January 1895, the vessel was taking a cargo of coal from Amble to Dundee, under the command of Captain A. Johnson and carrying a crew of ten, when she struck the Plough Seat Reef off the east side of Holy Island and became a total wreck.

Wreck-site
The wreck of *Otto M'Combie* is well broken up and concreting into the surrounding sand and rocks, although it is impossible to say which wreck is which, as the *Thistle* lies next to her. Her boiler is there, along with the battered remains of her machinery, sheet iron plates, a few pieces of copper pipe and the anchor, with lengths of rusting iron chain leading away into the seabed. The surrounding seabed of rock and sand, and the ship's wreckage is all covered in billions of minute mussels.

Tidal streams can be very strong, especially on a spring tide, but there is shelter on the south side of the big reef, which runs out west to east. Most of the seabed around Holy Island is fairly shallow and there is quite a lot of sediment lying on the rocks and seabed, so visibility tends to be very poor when there is any swell on the sea. However, during the summer months, on a neap tide and after a spell of dry, settled weather and westerly winds, visibility can reach 10-15m. The area half to one mile south-east of the Plough Reef, is an excellent boat angling ground for cod.

THISTLE

Wreck ★
Scenery ★★★
Depth 11m
Reference N 55 40 200 W 001 45 500
Plough Seat Reef, east of Holy Island

The *Thistle* was an iron 401-ton British steamship, registered in Dundee and had dimensions of 46.22m length, by 7.03m beam and a draught of 3.58m. She was owned at the time of loss by R. Taylor of Dundee and built in 1883 by Pearce at Dundee. Her single iron propeller was powered by a two-cylinder, compound-steam engine that developed 60hp using one boiler. She had one deck, four watertight bulkheads and was classed as 100 A1 at Lloyds

On 22 November 1883, the *Thistle* was transporting a cargo of coal from Sunderland to Montrose, under the command of Captain J. Potter, when she encountered storm force nine westerly winds off the north Northumberland coast. To ease the terrible sea conditions, her skipper brought the vessel closer inshore and stranded on the long Plough Seat Reef, off the east side of Holy Island. Of her eleven crew and one passenger, only one crewman was drowned. However, the *Thisltle* was so seriously damaged, that she soon became a total wreck (surprisingly, no mention is made of the Holy Island lifeboat *Grace Darling*, being called out to attend to either the *Thistle* or the *Otto M'Combie*, when they stranded and were wrecked on the Plough Seat Reef).

Wreck-site

The wreck of the *Thistle* is very close to that of the *Otto M'Combie* wrecked twelve years later, in 1895. It is impossible say which wreck is which. The boiler and the remains of her engine are still there lying on the mussel encrusted seabed in 11m, surrounded by lots of rusting sheet iron plates, lead pipes and bent and flattened copper piping, which are all gradually concreting into the sand and rocks. Her propeller can be seen along with an anchor and piles of rusty chain, with billions of baby mussels thickly coating them all. The area is subjected to some very strong currents on a spring tide, but it is possible to get shelter behind the Plough Seat Reef on a flood tide.

Visibility is very poor when there is just the slightest of swell on the sea, but is excellent after a spell of dry, settled weather and westerly winds, especially during neap tides. Numerous large plaice, flounders and dabs can be seen, feeding on the little mussels all around the surrounding rocks and wreck sites.

CYDONIA

Wreck ★★
Scenery ★★★★
Depth 5-8m
Reference N 55 41 650 W 001 47 200
N. side of Castlehead Rocks, Holy Island

The *Cydonia* was a steel 3,085-ton British steamship, registered at the port of North Shields and owned at the time of loss by the Stag Line Ltd. She was built in 1910 by W. Dobson & Co. Ltd at Newcastle-upon-Tyne and had dimensions of 101.01 metres length, by 14.63m beam and a draught of 6.75m. Her single steel propeller was powered by a three-cylinder, triple-expansion steam engine that developed 249hp using two boilers and her machinery was built by North East Marine Engineering Co. Ltd at Newcastle-upon-Tyne. She had one deck and a superstructure consisting of an 8.8m poop-deck, 28.3m bridge-deck and 10m forecastle.

The *Cydonia* was employed by the Admiralty as a collier and on 28 September 1916, under the command of Captain W. Gill, she was on passage from Burntisland for Brest, with a crew of twenty-nine and an unspecified cargo of coal when, in heavy weather and mountainous seas she stranded on the north (seaward) side of Castlehead Rocks at Holy Island. The self-righting lifeboat, *Lizzie Porter*, from Holy Island was launched and rescued all of her crew members and returned to render further assistance the following day. However, the *Cydonia* soon started to break up and became a total loss.

Holy Island is probably the oldest lifeboat station in the United Kingdom. Records that record the history of the island mention a lifeboat on the island as far back as 1786 and there was definitely one there in 1802. However, the first official launching of a lifeboat on the island was not recorded until 1829. It was at that time that a second boat was subsequently stationed at the Snook Point, making Holy Island unique, in that it was probably the only place in the country to have two lifeboats at the same time. During the late 1800s and early 1900s, the R.N.L.I lifeboats were all of similar design to the *Lizzie Porter* pulling sailing lifeboat, which now has pride of place in the Grace Darling Museum at Bamburgh. This famous lifeboat, that was donated to the R.N.L.I. by a Miss Elizabeth Porter of Halifax, was rescued from a farmer field in a dilapidated state and donated to the museum by a Mr Rowbotham, of Nottingham. The one in question is the *Lizzie Porter* number ON597 Self Righting boat. She was built at Thames Iron Works in 1909 at a cost of £823, is 10.7m long, with a beam of 2.5m and weighs 4 tons. The boat is built of diagonal planking on rock elm frames, had ten oars, two masts, setting lugger sail and a jib.

In 1904 the Admiralty awarded £1000 to the crew of the lifeboat who rescued the 5,000-ton *Harcula*, in mountainous seas off Holy Island.

In 1907 the island had one inshore lifeboat and a heavier vessel, which was used around the Farne Islands. The *Lizzie Porter* was used regularly until 1925 when she was replaced by a motorized lifeboat and she was sent to North Sunderland, where she worked until her retirement in 1936. She was launched thirty-five times and rescued seventy-seven people.

On 15-16 January 1922, the *Lizzie Porter* went to the rescue of the crew of the steam-trawler *James B. Graham* of Hartlepool, when in a south-easterly gale, horrendous seas and freezing conditions she ran aground off False Emmanuel Head, at the north side of the island. It was 8 p.m., dark and snowing, but the whole village of sixty people, both men and women helped, wading out waist deep in the freezing water to launch the lifeboat. The *Lizzie Porter's* crew managed to weave between the shallow reefs in extremely difficult conditions and found the trawler lying close to the iron remnants of an older wreck. It took three attempts to reach the *James B. Graham*, but eventually they rescued the nine crew on board and returned to station at 2 a.m.

For splendid seamanship and great courage the lifeboat Coxswain George Cromarty was awarded the R.N.L.I.'s silver medal and bronze medals were awarded to the three second coxswains, while the rest of the crew received extra monetary awards for their bravery. Unfortunately, in 1968, the R.N.L.I. withdrew the last of its lifeboats from Holy Island.

Wreck-site
The remains of the *Cydonia* are well dispersed across a wide area among the rocks and boulders some 200m out, on the north side of Castlehead Rocks. Her two boilers are still there, standing upright among twisted steel framework, steel plates and masses of iron pipes. However, much of it is hidden from view under the thick carpet of kelp that covers this huge, long reef. It makes an excellent rummage dive, especially at low, slack water, because, although the site is fairly shallow, the tidal streams are very strong.

Visibility is very hit and miss. The best time to dive it would be after a dry spell, with neap tides and westerly winds when it may reach 15m or more. As a result of the shallow water off Holy Island, any surface swell at Seahouses or Beadnell, will be multiplied ten-fold at Holy Island. Also, great care should be taken when approaching the dive-site, because many of the reefs are close to the surface at low tide and reach far out to sea.

The water around Castlehead Rocks and the nearby reefs abound with marine life. Numerous species can be found, including various crustaceans, cod, wrasse, wolffish, conger, pollack, 'and lots of juicy mussels, if you find the right place.

Castlehead Rocks are just an extension of False Emmanuel Head. It is actually the same reef where the *James B. Graham* came ashore in 1922, close to an older iron wreck. So with a bit of searching, there is the possibility of finding other remains too.

RING

Wreck ★★★
Scenery ★
Depth 50m
Reference N 55 47 332 W 001 50 596
4 miles E x N of Berwick

The *Ring* was a steel 998-ton Norwegian-registered steamship that had dimensions of 69.8m length, by 10.05m beam and a draught of 5.18m. She was owned at the time of loss by A. Jacobsen in Norway and built in 1897 by Nylands Vaerkstad in Christiania who also built her machinery. Her single steel propeller was powered by a three-cylinder, triple-expansion steam engine that used one boiler.

On 3 March 1917, the *Ring* was on passage from Skien to Charente via Tonnay, when she was torpedoed and sunk by the German submarine *UC-41*.

Wreck-site
The wreck of the *Ring* is reported to be lying orientated in a north-west to south-west direction on a seabed of sand, gravel and stone in a general depth of 50m, the lowest astronomical depth. She is fairly substantial, but has collapsed in on herself, with the boiler, condenser and engine visibly exposed and surrounded by a mound of broken steel and machinery. However, the bow section is standing proud of the seabed and covered in an array of soft corals, with the anchor lying close by.

The wreck is not dived very much and there are still quite a lot of copper pipes and brass valves to be seen. Many of her interesting artefacts may also still be around, including a number of large portholes. Soft corals cover the highest parts of wreck and some decent sized lobsters have been seen under the plates. Shoals of fish are attracted to the wreck during the summer months, mostly pout-whiting, cod and the occasional large ling, making this wreck worthy of investigation for a day's boat angling, when conditions are right.

Tidal streams are very strong and a lot of careful planning is called for by anyone considering diving on the wreck. The best time would be at low, slack water on a neap tide. However, it is a deep wreck and should only be done by people with the knowledge and expertise, probably using mixed gasses.

VENUS (ex-FRI, ex-SIF, ex-SERANTIS)

Wreck ★★★★
Scenery ★
Depth 56m
Reference N 55 47 150 W 001 50 300
5 miles E. of Berwick-on-Tweed.

The *Venus* was a steel 715-ton Norwegian steamship, registered in Porsgrund and had dimensions of 63.72m length, by 8.68m beam and a draught of 4.11m. She was owned at the time of loss by Dmpsk. Akties. of Venus and built as the *Serantis* in 1872 by A. Simey & Co. at Sunderland. Her single iron propeller was powered by a two-cylinder, compound-steam engine that developed 111hp using one boiler and her machinery was built by J. Stewart in London. She had one deck and one watertight bulkhead.

On 14 April 1917, the *Venus* was carrying an unspecified cargo of coal on a voyage from Blyth to Drammen, under the command of Captain P. Valdussen, when she foundered and was lost after detonating a mine laid by the German submarine *UC-50*, five miles east of Berwick-on-Tweed.

Wreck-site
The wreck of the *Venus* lies on a well swept seabed of sand and stone in a general depth of 56m, the lowest astronomical depth. She has totally collapsed on top of herself, exposing her boiler, condenser and engine which are surrounded by mass of bent steel plate, pipes, broken machinery, a windlass and some broken hollow mast pieces. The bow section is reported to be still intact and is home to a huge shoal of striped pout-whiting. Lots of other species of fish congregate in the shelter of the wreckage, including some large cod. At least one fair sized conger has been observed there in a large pipe or section of broken mast.

Tidal streams are very strong, making this a slack water dive, however only the most experienced divers should ever attempt to dive on wrecks at this sort of depth. Visibility is usually reasonable and can reach as much as 15-20m during the summer months after a spell of settled, dry weather on a neap tide.

A-Z of Shipwrecks